TWO HUNDRED POEMS

TWO HUNDRED POEMS

Edited with an Introduction by

RICARDO QUINTANA

LONGMANS, GREEN AND CO.

NEW YORK · LONDON · TORONTO

1947

LONGMANS, GREEN AND CO., INC.
55 FIFTH AVENUE, NEW YORK 3

LONGMANS, GREEN AND CO. LTD.
OF PATERNOSTER ROW
43 ALBERT DRIVE, LONDON, S.W. 19
NICOL ROAD, BOMBAY 1
17 CHITTARANJAN AVENUE, CALCUTTA 13
36A MOUNT ROAD, MADRAS 2

LONGMANS, GREEN AND CO.
215 VICTORIA STREET, TORONTO 1

TWO HUNDRED POEMS

PUBLISHED SIMULTANEOUSLY IN THE DOMINION OF CANADA
BY LONGMANS, GREEN AND CO., TORONTO

FIRST EDITION

Printed in the United States of America
Vail-Ballou Press, Inc., Binghamton, N.Y.

I am not under the impression that there is anything particularly significant about the number 200, nor do I believe that this book of selections contains the two hundred "best" poems in the English language. As an editor I have worked with the everyday reader in mind, and there seemed some point — for reasons that are suggested in the Introduction — in trying to put together a volume of this sort composed of a limited number of fairly representative poems. It is only in regard to the selections from the twentieth century that any explanation seems really necessary. The poets who are represented in the last section are now known to everyone. It seemed better to confine the selections to them, and in each case to give as many of their poems as practicable, rather than to present — of necessity inadequately — the work of a greater number of present-day writers. My chief regret is that the basic plan of this book — which I have seen no reason to abandon — makes it impossible to do anything like justice to the poetry now being written, which should be of as much concern to us as the poetry of the past.

The order in which the selections are arranged is conventional, roughly chronological, and in most cases self-explanatory. Gerard Manley Hopkins, it will be noted, is included in the twentieth century : though he died in 1889, his poems were generally unknown until the present century, and in manner and influence he seems entirely of our age rather than of the latter Victorian period.

I take this opportunity to make the following acknowledgments :

To Harcourt, Brace and Company, for permission to print five poems by T. S. Eliot ("Portrait of a Lady," "Sweeney Among the Nightingales," "The Hollow Men," Part I of "Ash Wednesday," "Journey of the Magi") appearing in Eliot's *COLLECTED POEMS*, 1909–1935. Likewise to Harcourt, Brace and Company, for permission to print "Burnt Norton" from T. S. Eliot's *FOUR QUARTETS*.

To Harper and Brothers, for permission to use Swinburne's "The Garden of Proserpine," included in *SWINBURNE'S COLLECTED POETICAL WORKS*.

To Henry Holt and Company, for permission to print four poems by Robert Frost ("The Death of the Hired Man," "Noth-

ing Gold Can Stay," "Tree at My Window," "To a Thinker")
appearing in COLLECTED POEMS OF ROBERT FROST.
Also to Henry Holt and Company, for permission to use three
poems by A. E. Housman from *A SHROPSHIRE LAD*.

To Houghton Mifflin Company, for permission to print nine
poems by Archibald MacLeish ("The Seafarer," "The Too-Late
Born," "The Night Dream," "Not Marble Nor the Gilded Monu-
ments," "You, Andrew Marvell," "The End of the World," "Ars
Poetica," "Memorial Rain," and "Background with Revolution-
aries," from "Frescoes for Mr. Rockefeller's City . . .") appearing
in MacLeish's *POEMS, 1924–1933*.

To The Macmillan Company, for permission to print three
poems by Thomas Hardy ("The Darkling Thrush," "Beeny Cliff,
and the Oxen") appearing in Hardy's *COLLECTED POEMS*.

Likewise to The Macmillan Company, for permission to print
nine poems by Yeats ("The Magi," "The Dolls," "The Wild
Swans at Coole," "The Second Coming," "Sailing to Byzantium,"
"Leda and the Swan," "Among School Children," "Byzantium,"
"Blood and the Moon") appearing in *THE COLLECTED
POEMS* of W. B. Yeats; and for the poem "The Man the Echo,"
from Yeats's *LAST POEMS AND PLAYS*.

To the Oxford University Press, and to the family of Gerard
Manley Hopkins, for permission to print four poems by Hopkins
("The Windhover," "Pied Beauty," "Spring and Fall," "I Wake
and Feel the Fell of Dark"), from *POEMS OF GERARD MAN-
LEY HOPKINS*.

To Random House, for permission to print nine poems by
W. H. Auden ("Musée Des Beaux Arts," "In War Time," "The
Cultural Presupposition," "In Memory of W. B. Yeats," "Septem-
ber 1, 1939," "Petition," "Happy Ending," "Pur," and "Sing,
Ariel, Sing," from "The Sea and the Mirror") appearing in *THE
COLLECTED POETRY OF W. H. AUDEN*.

Likewise to Random House, for permission to print, from
POEMS BY STEPHEN SPENDER, the poem "I Think Continu-
ally of Those Who Were Truly Great," and three poems by
Spender ("The Fates," "In a Garden" and "Into Life") from
RUINS AND VISIONS : POEMS BY STEPHEN SPENDER.

Also to Random House, for permission to print three poems by
Louis MacNeice ("Eclogue for Christmas," "The Sunlight on the
Garden," "Refugees") appearing in *POEMS, 1925–1940. BY
LOUIS MACNEICE.*

CONTENTS

Introduction : Poetry and the Everyday Reader . . . xvii

EARLY ENGLISH LYRICS

"I Have Twelve Oxen" 3
"As I Me Walk'd in One Morning" 3
"This Endurs Night" 4

BALLADS

Edward 9
The Wife of Usher's Well 11
Lord Randal 13

THE SIXTEENTH CENTURY :
Skelton to Ben Jonson

JOHN SKELTON : FROM The Tunnyng of Elynour
Rummyng 17
SIR THOMAS WYATT : "My galley, chargèd with for-
getfulness" 20
HENRY HOWARD, EARL OF SURREY : "From
Tuscan came my lady's worthy race" 21
EDMUND SPENSER
FROM Amoretti : Sonnets
III. "The sovereign beauty which I do admire" . 22
IX. "Long while I sought to what I might compare" 23
XVIII. "The rolling wheel, that runneth often
round" 23

XXXIV. "Like as a ship, that through the ocean wide" 24

LXVII. "Like as a huntsman after weary chace" . 25

Prothalamion 25

SIR PHILIP SIDNEY

FROM Astrophel and Stella : Sonnets

I. "Loving in truth, and fain in verse my love to show" 31

V. "It is most true that eyes are form'd to serve" . 32

XIV. "Alas, have I not pain enough, my friend?" . 33

XXXI. "With how sad steps, O Moon, thou climb'st the skies !" 33

XXXIX. "Come, Sleep ! O Sleep, the certain knot of peace" 34

SAMUEL DANIEL

FROM Delia

To Delia 35

MICHAEL DRAYTON

FROM Sonnets, To Delia

LXI. "Since there's no help, come, let us kiss and part" 36

Ode to the Cambro-Britons and Their Harp, His Ballad of Agincourt 36

CHRISTOPHER MARLOWE : The Passionate Shepherd to His Love 41

WILLIAM SHAKESPEARE

SEVEN SONGS FROM THE PLAYS

FROM THE CLOSE OF Love's Labour's Lost . . . 42

FROM Twelfth Night

"O Mistress mine, where are you roaming?" . 44

"Come away, come away, death" 45

FROM Cymbeline

"Fear no more the heat o' the sun" 46

FROM The Tempest
"Come unto these yellow sands" 47
"Full fathom five thy father lies" 47
FROM Sonnets
XVIII. "Shall I compare thee to a summer's day?" 48
XXIX. "When in disgrace with fortune and men's eyes" 48
XXX. "When to the sessions of sweet silent thought" 49
XXXIII. "Full many a glorious morning have I seen" 50
LV. "Not marble nor the gilded monuments" . . 50
LX. "Like as the waves make towards the pebbled shore" 51
LXIV. "When I have seen by Time's fell hand defac'd" 52
LXXIII. "That time of year thou mayst in me behold" 52
CVI. "When in the chronicle of wasted time" . . 53

JOHN DONNE
Song 54
The Sun Rising 55
The Good Morrow 56
The Funeral 57
FROM Holy Sonnets
VII. "At the round earth's imagin'd corners" . . 58
X. "Death, be not proud" 58
A Hymn to God the Father 59
BEN JONSON
FROM Cynthia's Revels
Hymn 60
Two Songs to Celia
"Come, my Celia, let us prove" 61

"Drink to me only with thine eyes" 61
FROM The Masque of Queens
    Witches' Charms 62
FROM A Celebration of Charis
    IV. Her Triumph 64
To the Memory of My Beloved Mr. William Shake-
    speare and What He Hath Left Us 65
An Epitaph. On Salathiel Pavy, A Child of Queen
    Elizabeth's Chapel 68

THE SEVENTEENTH CENTURY :
Herrick to Dryden

ROBERT HERRICK
    An Ode for [Ben Jonson] 71
    To Daffodils 72
    To the Virgins, To Make Much of Time . . . 72
    Delight in Disorder 73
    Upon Julia's Clothes 74
    The Night-Piece : To Julia 74
    To Anthea Who May Command Him Any Thing . 75
    Another Grace for a Child 76
GEORGE HERBERT
    "Immortal Love, author of this great frame" . . . 76
    The Collar 77
    The Pulley 78
    Virtue 79
THOMAS CAREW : Song 80
JOHN MILTON
    On the Morning of Christ's Nativity 81
    "How soon hath Time, the subtle thief of youth" . 91
    Lycidas 91
    On the Late Massacre in Piemont 97

"When I consider how my light is spent" 98
"Methought I saw my late espoused Saint" . . . 98
CLOSING PASSAGES FROM Samson Agonistes 99
SIR JOHN SUCKLING
Song 102
"Out upon it ! I have loved" 103
RICHARD CRASHAW
FROM The Flaming Heart 104
A Song 105
RICHARD LOVELACE
To Althea, from Prison 106
To Lucasta. Going to the Wars 107
ANDREW MARVELL
Bermudas 108
The Garden 109
To His Coy Mistress 112
HENRY VAUGHAN
The Retreat 113
The Water Fall 114
The World 116
"They are all gone" 118
THOMAS TRAHERNE : Wonder 120
JOHN DRYDEN : Mac Flecknoe 122

THE EIGHTEENTH CENTURY :
Pope to Blake

ALEXANDER POPE: The Rape of the Lock . . . 133
THOMAS GRAY
Ode on a Distant Prospect of Eton College . . . 158
Elegy Written in a Country Church-yard . . . 161
WILLIAM COLLINS : Ode to Evening 166

WILLIAM COWPER
  The Shrubbery, Written in a Time of Affliction . . . 168
  The Castaway 169
WILLIAM BLAKE
  To the Evening Star 172
  The Lamb 172
  The Tiger 173
  The Sick Rose 174
  London 174

THE NINETEENTH CENTURY :
Wordsworth to Housman

WILLIAM WORDSWORTH
  Lines Composed a Few Miles above Tintern Abbey . 179
  "She dwelt among the untrodden ways" 184
  "A slumber did my spirit seal" 185
  "My heart leaps up when I behold" 185
  London, 1802 185
  Composed upon Westminster Bridge, Sept. 3, 1802 . 186
  "It is a beauteous evening, calm and free" 187
  The Solitary Reaper 187
  To the Cuckoo 188
  "I wandered lonely as a cloud" 190
  "The World is too much with us ; late and soon" . . 191
  Ode : Intimations of Immortality from Recollections
    of Early Childhood 191
  Thought of a Briton on the Subjugation of Switzer-
    land 199
SAMUEL TAYLOR COLERIDGE
  Kubla Khan 199
  FROM Zapolya
    Song, by Glycine 201

PERCY BYSSHE SHELLEY
   Ode to the West Wind 202
   To a Skylark 205
JOHN KEATS
   On First Looking into Chapman's Homer 209
   On Seeing the Elgin Marbles for the First Time . . 210
   On the Sea 210
   "When I have fears that I may cease to be" . . . 211
   Hyperion : A Fragment 212
   The Eve of St. Agnes 239
   "Bright star ! would I were steadfast as thou art" . . 254
   La Belle Dame sans Merci 254
   Ode to Psyche 257
   Ode on Indolence 259
   Ode to a Nightingale 261
   Ode on a Grecian Urn 265
   Ode on Melancholy 267
   To Autumn 268
ALFRED, LORD TENNYSON
   Mariana 269
   The Lotos-Eaters 272
   Ulysses 279
   "Break, break, break" 281
   "Tears, idle tears, I know not what they mean" . . 282
   FROM In Memoriam
      VII. "Dark house, by which once more I stand" . 283
   Crossing the Bar 283
ROBERT BROWNING
   My Last Duchess 284
   Porphyria's Lover 286
MATTHEW ARNOLD
   Memorial Verses 288
   Dover Beach 291

DANTE GABRIEL ROSSETTI
  FROM The House of Life
    SONNET XIX.   Silent Noon 292
  Sudden Light 293
ALGERNON CHARLES SWINBURNE : The Garden
of Proserpine 294
THOMAS HARDY
  The Darkling Thrush 297
  Beeny Cliff 298
  The Oxen 300
A. E. HOUSMAN
  FROM A Shropshire Lad
    II.   "Loveliest of trees, the cherry now" . . . 301
    XXXVI.   "White in the moon the long road lies" . 302
    LII.   "Far in a western brookland" 302

THE TWENTIETH CENTURY :
Hopkins to Spender

GERARD MANLEY HOPKINS
  The Windhover 307
  Pied Beauty 307
  Spring and Fall 308
  "I wake and feel the fell of dark, not day" . . . 309
WILLIAM BUTLER YEATS
  The Magi 309
  The Dolls 310
  The Wild Swans at Coole 311
  The Second Coming 312
  Sailing to Byzantium 313
  Leda and the Swan 314
  Among School Children 315
  Blood and the Moon 317

Byzantium 320
The Man and the Echo 321
T. S. ELIOT
Portrait of a Lady 323
Sweeney Among the Nightingales 328
The Hollow Men 330
FROM Ash-Wednesday : 1 334
Journey of the Magi 335
FROM Four Quartets
Burnt Norton 337
ROBERT FROST
The Death of the Hired Man 343
Nothing Gold Can Stay 350
Tree at My Window 350
To a Thinker 351
ARCHIBALD MACLEISH
The Seafarer 352
The Too-Late Born 352
The Night Dream 353
"Not Marble nor the Gilded Monuments" . . . 354
You, Andrew Marvell 356
The End of the World 357
Ars Poetica 358
Memorial Rain 359
FROM Frescoes for Mr. Rockefeller's City . . .
6. Background with Revolutionaries 361
W. H. AUDEN
Musée des Beaux Arts 363
In War Time 364
The Cultural Presupposition 366
In Memory of W. B. Yeats 367
September 1, 1939 370
Petition 373

Happy Ending 373
Pur 374
FROM The Sea and the Mirror
  "Sing, Ariel, sing" 375
LOUIS MACNEICE
An Eclogue for Christmas 376
The Sunlight on the Garden 382
Refugees 383
STEPHEN SPENDER
"I think continually of those who were truly great" . 385
The Fates 386
In a Garden 391
Into Life 392

INTRODUCTION: POETRY AND THE
EVERYDAY READER

1

The character of modern civilization makes it increasingly difficult for everyday readers to take poetry for granted. Though poetry is one of the natural forms of human expression, we no longer instinctively think of it as such. We have come to regard it, instead, as a strange way of speaking, often a difficult and obscure way, and frequently we are at a loss to understand what purposes it serves. In contrast with poetry, there are certain kinds of writing which all modern readers accept without question. Unless we are specialists we may not be able to follow a technological treatise, but we understand perfectly the nature and purpose of technological writing. It is practical, utilitarian. It has a well-defined place in our scheme of things. So, too, does the vast and steadily growing literature of amusement, for such literature (which ranges all the way from the stories in the pulps to the most skillfully written detective novels) is equally practical though in a different fashion, affording us relaxation after the day's serious work. But what purpose does poetry serve? Obviously it is not written to convey scientific information. Nor, we recognize, is its intent merely to divert us. Poetry, in our modern world, has become an anomaly.

This does not mean that poetry is no longer enjoyed. There is a widespread feeling, however, shared both by modern readers and modern critics, that before our enjoyment can be entirely valid and complete it must be accounted for : poetry must be shown to have significant purpose, it must be placed within our scheme of things. And so we proceed to explore this modern mystery, the nature of poetry, using all the approaches given us by modern knowledge. As critics in search of the meaning of poetry we become in turn philosophers, psychologists, sociologists, and anthropologists. What — we are determined to find out — is the function of poetry in civilization ? What are its peculiar values and its proper uses ? What is the nature of the creative experience ? What happens to us while we are reading a poem ?

If we are genuinely interested in poetry, if we take it seriously, it is quite right that we should concern ourselves, sooner or later, with such inquiries. Many of us, however, take up these theoretical matters before we fully realize their implications, and before we can benefit much from such answers as may be forthcoming. For our characteristic questions do have wide implications. Observe how, while we are asking these questions, we are at the same time giving a definite pattern to our problem. On the one hand, we agree, there is the poet ; on the other, the reader of the poem. In reference to the poet, we identify poetry with the creative experience, in reference to the reader with the experiences of reaction, response, appreciation. And in addition we understand by poetry something more than either creation or appreciation, something that involves both and goes beyond them : that is, the over-all significance of poetry in civilization.

What such an approach as this too frequently leaves out of account is the poem itself — the thing fashioned by the poet ; the very tangible thing, in ink, on paper, to which the reader responds ; the thing from which all our generalizations about poetry arise — or ought to. Perhaps the most helpful advice that can be given to anyone interested in poetry is this. Dismiss, at least for the time being, these theoretical questions. Instead, go to actual poems. Read them. Stay with them over extended periods of time. Learn what coming to understand them means. Until one has had first-hand experience with poems, it is difficult to see how one can profit from any sort of inquiry into the general nature of poetry.

2

To imply that the skillful reading of a poem is a matter of the right technique, and that something in the nature of a correct procedure can be set forth in a series of directives, would be absurd. A poem is a work of art, not a machine, a mechanism ; and no two poems are quite alike. Short of sending the reader to detailed analyses of individual poems — which are of more value than anything else — one can only suggest an attitude, a manner of approach. Perhaps this can be done by way of three assertions : a poem has been *made* ; a poem is rhythmic ; a poem discloses a situation.

It is difficult if not impossible to make assertions of this kind without smuggling in by the back door certain of those general concepts about the nature of poetry which we have been at pains to exclude. We may point out, however, that all three assertions have strict reference to a poem as a concrete object. Here is an approach which, temporarily at least, demands that we forgo any consideration of the creative experience, of the psychology of response and appreciation, and of the significance of poetry in social history. We are asked to concentrate on the poem.

Saying that a poem has been made is a way of reminding ourselves, first, that a poet is among other things and all the time a maker, a kind of craftsman, one who fashions ; and second, that the poem so fashioned is an art object quite as real and tangible as, for instance, a piece of sculpture, a painting, a cathedral. Now, there are those who seem to hold that one's response to any sort of art object is valid only when it is immediate ; if the response is not immediate, either the work of art is inferior or the observer is lacking in aesthetic education and sensibility. To confine the matter to poetry, do we, ought we to have something approaching a full and immediate response to a certain poem that we are taking up for the first time ? (If we have previously read the poem, our response cannot be called immediate.) There are, indeed, lyrics that *seem* to be so simple as to disclose themselves instantly, directly, fully. There are other poems that at first reading leave us frustrated and bewildered. Is the simple lyric, by virtue of its ready communication, the better poem ? The experienced reader might well insist that first impressions are not always reliable. The "simple" lyric, we may in time discover, is not so simple as it seemed at first, nor the "difficult" poem as cryptic as we once imagined. In any event, we ought to be thinking in terms of the poem as an objective reality rather than of our reactions to it. What is its precise nature ? Until we have made an effort to find out, until we are assured that we have begun to comprehend the object before us, any reactions and responses we may have are really trivial, unless we regard poetry merely as an occasion which allows us to indulge our wayward moods.

A poet is a maker, a subtle craftsman. He is not, however, a mere artisan or journeyman, turning out a finished product in accordance with a standardized pattern and by means of a predetermined technique. A fashioned poem is an infinitely complex configuration, wherein the details are functional to the whole. The true appreciation of a poem is something that takes shape and grows as one comes to understand this configuration ; it is our total experience with the poem — a sequence of experiences, really, ending only when we dismiss the poem once and for all. We read the poem, we put it down and turn to other matters, we come back to it the next day or the next year. No good poem, no good work of art of any sort, gives itself away — becomes flat, obvious, unnecessary — through prolonged acquaintance. It increases in depth, in integrity, as our knowledge of it becomes more precise and refined.

From the point of view here advanced, appreciation cannot be other than a form of analysis. Analysis does not mean pedantic dissection, a stereotyped technique ; nor the study of the words, allusions, and rhyme schemes without reference to their assigned rôle in the poem as a whole. It means the discovery of that whole and of the functioning of the details within the informing pattern. In the case of a symphonic score, most of us would probably agree that some form of exploratory analysis is necessary. The symphony is there in musical notation, but even an accomplished conductor must work his way into it before a first rehearsal with the orchestra. Those who have heard the same symphony played at different times by the same conductor might likewise agree that analysis does not necessarily end with preliminary exploration.

If we would only think of a poem as something very like a musical score we would be better readers. We would take it for granted, that is, that a poem is an object, a construct, outside ourselves. Instinctively we would know that reading and appreciating a poem mean coming to understand it through careful and extended study.

3

A poem is rhythmic. The way in which we take this fact into account has much to do with our skill and enjoyment as readers. The rhythmic character of poetry we all acknowledge, being aware of the striking difference in this respect between verse and prose. But our actual response to poetic rhythm is determined by more specific considerations. There are undoubtedly a few people who believe that rhythm is merely an encumbrance and that anything said in the manner of poetry can therefore be said more effectively in prose. At the other extreme are those for whom poetry is so much a kind of music that rhythm together with word sound is of exclusive importance. Naturally, no one who regards rhythm as an encumbrance is going to read poetry for pleasure. Those who read it for the sheer music may find keen delight, but their response is so limited as to make the nonmusical aspects of a poem of little consequence.

Because a poem is an integrated whole, its rhythmic qualities are not to be thought of as standing forth independently. A poem is, and means, many things ; but though complex it is a unity. We may — we should — recognize the rhythmic pattern of a poem explicitly, but we ought to be aware that in doing so we are coming to know something of the informing nature of the whole organism. Experienced readers might agree that the most effective way to take up a new poem is to read it aloud until the rhythmic pattern has disclosed itself ; but they would point out that by that time a great deal more than the rhythmic pattern has been unfolded.

To imply that this is the *right* way to begin to read a poem would be unfortunate. All that is meant is that such an approach, with our attention directed in the beginning more to the rhythmic pattern than anything else, is a better way than certain others. For one thing, it diverts us from too great an initial concern with what we often refer to mistakenly as a poem's "prose meaning." A poem has no such meaning ; and if we try to convince ourselves that it has by making a "translation" into prose, we are only further deluding ourselves and pushing the poem itself still farther into the background. Of course a poem makes statements — but not in the manner of prose. What it says it says rhythmically, and though its rhythm may not be the master key to its sense, at least it is not a key that opens the wrong doors.

In one respect, however, rhythm comes very close to being a right key. Because not all poetry is "rhetorical," we sometimes forget that a poem is a form of rhetoric : it may not be bombastic ; it may not employ the devices of the orator for securing certain effects ; but someone is speaking to some purpose or other, and his speech is subtly and exactly modulated. Until we have heard these modulations, we have really neither read nor understood the poem. For not only does intonation sometimes disclose the actual sense of a phrase, a line, a passage; it reveals, since it has been determined by, the poet's controlling attitude toward himself, his subject, his audience. The quality of a poem is first sensed through its tone as spoken language ; and this tone, though not identical with the poem's rhythmic pattern, is closely engaged in it.

To anyone who is willing to approach a poem in this way but who is still at a loss how to proceed, this may be said. Read the poem aloud ; let yourself go ; let the words and the rhythm lead you. Some knowledge of metrics will probably help, but it is not essential — and most handbooks on metrics are misleading unless one happens to know more about the subject than do the authors. Ordinarily, the rhythmic pattern of the poem as a whole — a pattern first sensed through the arrangement of the lines and stanzas in print — will indicate the number of stressed beats to a given line. If we can feel the beats as we read, we may forget the metrical "laws." (We do not find Mother Goose rhymes difficult to read, yet the dipodic measure in which many of them are written can be explained only in complicated metrical terms involving pauses and primary and secondary stresses.)

4

The rhythmic nature of a poem is perfectly apparent. How the reader deals with rhythmic pattern is the important thing — that there is a rhythmic pattern to deal with goes without question. But what is meant by saying that a poem discloses a situation ? Though the experienced reader may feel that this too is quite obvious, some explanation is in order.

When we read a play instead of seeing it performed we still understand it in dramatic terms : it is not the author who is speaking but his characters ; and the characters speak and act within and by virtue of the situations which develop on the stage. However, when we turn to a lyric poem we sometimes assume that because drama and lyric poetry differ in such striking ways, they are for this reason different in all respects. Actually, even the simplest lyric, for all its unpremeditated air, is likely to be more "dramatic" than we realize. Neither the "I" nor the anonymous person who may be speaking is necessarily the poet himself ; often he is a person, a character, who, much as in a play, lives only in so far as he is involved in a dramatic situation. We have been speaking of "simple lyric poetry." There is of course much poetry that is frankly dramatic in one way or another : one of Shakespeare's sonnets, arising out of the complex situation created by the whole cycle of one hundred and fifty-four sonnets ; a dramatic monologue by Browning ; the early English poem "This Endurs Night," in which Mary, Joseph, and the Christ child speak in turn. Again, there is a kind of poetry — used extensively by modern writers — which is dramatic in construction without appearing so outwardly : a character or characters are speaking, there is a scenic background, but in the absence of anything in the nature of stage directions the reader has to discover all this for himself.

Many poems — far more than we sometimes realize — are dramatic in this specific sense, but the situation which every poem discloses is not always to be accounted for by means of this analogy with play-writing. Whether or not there is anything resembling dramatic technique, there is always a situation. A poem makes statements, but not at random : there is exclusion, concentration, with a resulting intensity of apprehension. A situation, a context, grows, is established. Here is a world quite to itself, isolated, with its own regulating principles and laws. Feelings and perceptions are made articulate by being given a pattern within which to develop and organize. As readers we are not required to project ourselves into the poet's mind in an effort to explain in psychological terms what is taking place there as he creates this situation. For us, the situation *is* the poem. It is there in the form and language of the poem, and our full response to this form and language is acknowledgment that we too have found our way into the unique situation.

5

Here, then, are three considerations that indicate a certain kind of approach to poems. They are not directives, for there can be no certain and invariable precepts insuring appreciation of the arts. The individual poem is always a new and special problem. One can only suggest a point of departure, the sort of expectations the reader can properly have, and the general direction of the course lying before him.

Before we turn to other matters, something may be said by way of summary and amplification concerning the approach we have been discussing. The fundamental point is that the enjoyment of poetry is a disciplined enjoyment, requiring complete immersion in the particular poem. If it is difficult nowadays to establish this convincingly, it is not because the ways of poetry are mysterious but because we are rapidly forgetting that enjoyment and discipline can ever go together. Discipline is associated with technology and technique, and when these are involved we submit to discipline as no other age ever has. But when we turn to the arts, we are frequently looking for a holiday — for amusement without effort. Poetry does, of course, refresh ; often it amuses ; it speaks in natural terms to normal people. The demands it makes are not excessive, but acknowledge them we must.

Another point, implicit in the preceding sections but not fully developed there, has to do with "meaning" in poetry. What does a poem mean ? It is doubtful whether this question can be answered in a way that will be understood by the incorrigibly literal-minded. To say to them that a poem means what it is will scarcely prove enlightening. There are many readers, however, whose failure to sense the genuine meaning of a poem is merely the result of a wrong approach. They assume that poetic statement is essentially the same as factual statement in prose — that a poem says no more than what can be translated into a prose summary. Indeed, it is to be feared that a good many teachers of literature, misled themselves or desirous of introducing discipline into literary studies, hit upon translation into prose, or something close to it, as a method. When we have begun to understand a poem we know that any such translation is futile. There is nothing to translate. We may take certain of its words, certain allusions, an extended statement, or the "overall theme" ; these we may comment on. But in the poem these are all functional to the whole ; the meaning they bear has been bestowed on them by the configuration, the situation, which is the poem itself.

Like all men of intelligence, the poet has interests, beliefs, theoretical views, deep concerns. It is inevitable that these should be reflected in his poems. Poetry is not trivial in import, neutral and impotent before the great issues that stir us. But it engages these issues in its own way ; and that is not the way of the treatise, the essay, the pamphlet, the fighting speech.

6

There are many approaches to poetry. The one along which we have thus far been proceeding — how can a reader best come to know a poem ? — affords certain clear advantages in that it enables us to short-circuit many problems — or what, by other approaches, become problems. Nevertheless, it has its limitations since there is much that needs to be said about poetry which can be better said in an unsystematic way. The poet's creative experience, the rôle of the reader, the significance of poetry in civilization are three topics touching in one way or another upon many aspects of poetry which all people interested in literature regard as important. In discussing each of these topics briefly, we will not find it necessary to commit ourselves to any theoretical approach. Much modern criticism has in fact concerned itself with precisely these topics in an effort to establish the nature of poetry, and has frequently arrived at comprehensive theories of literature and art. We are not searching for any theory ; what follows is by way of running commentary.

As for the poet. The way in which we regard the creative experience and try to explain it depends largely upon what age we happen to be conditioned by. Living in the Seventeenth or Eighteenth Century, we would probably interpret the creative experience according to the doctrines of Imitation ; in the Romantic Era — the earlier decades of the Nineteenth Century — we would naturally identify it with Imagination.

Today we customarily speak of Expression. Such terms and the concepts they carry with them cannot be taken up here ; nor is there any need to do so.* The point is merely this : the theories that are evolved from time to time by critics and aestheticians reflect the changing views and opinions of our civilization. This is not to say that as theories they are therefore basically unsound. Each of the three theories mentioned is, in its own fashion, a valid explanation — but an explanation grounded in certain assumptions characteristic of a particular era. There are, in short, more ways than one of interpreting the creative experience. An admirable statement, from a modern point of view, will be found in R. G. Collingwood's *The Principles of Art*. Mr. Stephen C. Pepper's recent study, *The Basis of Criticism in the Arts*, proceeds in a different fashion, but is an excellent introduction to certain of the outstanding aesthetic theories of western culture.

It should be remembered, too, that the poets themselves sometimes come to our assistance by commenting both in their poems and in factual prose essays on the meaning of poetry or their own experience as artists. The poets, however, are sometimes less helpful than we expect, despite what would seem to be their absolute authority here. They can be positively misleading when, for instance, they seek to interpret poetry and art by means of certain aesthetic theories which they have embraced ; for as aestheticians, supposed to be dealing in a systematic fashion with the theoretical aspects of literature, they are often inferior to the professional philosopher-critics. They are most enlightening when they refuse to be drawn deeply into any theoretical discussion, and are content to give us direct insight into their own creative experiences. Mr. Eliot's *The Uses of Poetry* and Mr. Spender's "The Making of a

* Mr. De Witt H. Parker's article, "Aesthetics," in *Twentieth Century Philosophy*, will be found an extremely helpful guide by anyone who wants to go into these matters.

Poem" are two modern commentaries that ought to be read by everyone.

A somewhat different matter, but still apropos of the poet. Poets once claimed for themselves the gift of prophetic vision. No one today believes a poet to be divinely or otherwise inspired. He is, we say, a man of talent, of genius, but not radically different from the rest of mankind. And the poets themselves now encourage us to take this view. Nevertheless, it is right to regard a poet as a kind of prophet — by virtue of his sensitiveness, his sharpened perceptions, and his moral realism. This, it should be pointed out, is *not* a theory of poetry : a poet shares these qualities with many of his contemporaries who are not poets. It is characteristic of great literature, however, that the facts, past, present, and emergent, should be shown as they are, stripped of all the easy illusions. Death, sex, terror, joy, and for some decades now the agony of a civilization in decay — these the poet knows because he has looked with clear eyes.

7

If our inquiries center on the reader instead of the poet, it is the appreciative experience rather than the creative which assumes major importance. As a matter of fact, the theory of poetry most popular today makes appreciation almost as vital a part of the poetic process as creation by giving to the reader a function only less important than the artist's. Poetry, according to this view, is communication between poet and reader ; what is communicated, what is shared by the reader, is an emotion, a mood.* It is significant that such a theory, by taking

* We are speaking, it should be understood, of a popular view given at a rather low critical level. Some of the most brilliant critical investigations of our time have been directed at poetry as communication, as symbolic language. We are not referring to these.

poetry as a charming kind of conversation, and appreciation as a matter of ready sympathy, succeeds in making the reader's part as easy as it is important. One obvious weakness here is the assumption that any sort of responsive feeling on the part of the reader means that a mood has been shared. What mood, whose mood ? If two readers get two quite different impressions from the same poem, are both impressions right ? Another weakness, more serious, lies in the inevitable trivialization of all literary art which this theory leads to : poetry ceases to have deep, significant meaning ; it becomes pleasant emotion to be prescribed in cases of mild debility.

Concerning the effect of poetry upon the reader, much can be said. If poetry is thought of as shared emotion, its effect is usually described as one of healthy stimulation. Those who emphasize the moral and educational values of poetry point out how it extends our experience and refines our sensibilities. But there are many who would prefer to speak merely of the enjoyment of poetry, giving to that term all possible flexibility. They have found that the enjoyment of a poem, without ever ceasing to be enjoyment in manifold ways, increases in depth and scope until it seems to engage much of their significant experience.

8

What is the significance of poetry in civilization ? Each age has managed to find its own answers. It was not until the nineteenth century, however, that the question became a crucial one, for it was then that science finally established itself as absolute knowledge. If everything that is understood by knowledge is embodied in scientific law and in scientific law alone, what significance has poetry ? One answer — explicit or implied in much nineteenth-century criticism — is that science gives us the facts, literature the human interpretation of these facts. A more recent answer is that poetry is a form of make-believe, biologically essential to the human race : as science destroys the myths we must cherish deep in ourselves if we are to go on living, we can re-establish these myths in poetry, where they can continue to function, disinherited though they are by reason. The dignity of poetry is thus reasserted, its high office reaffirmed, but at the cost of a curiously ironic paradox. In a universe whose sole reality is scientific law there is surely no place for mysticism. Yet the theory we have been speaking of confers on poetry a far greater mystical character than would ordinarily have been claimed for it by those of pre-scientific eras.

In any event, there are unmistakable signs that this dualism of science and poetry, so long dominant in criticism, is no longer sensed as the fundamental issue. Criticism is turning to other matters, and science is claiming less for itself. Perhaps we are coming to the conclusion that both science and poetry are ways of looking at things, ways of making statements.

9

The mature reader is not only on good terms with the poetry of the past, he is also receptive to contemporary poetry. As for the poetry of the past, we have now pretty well succeeded in forgetting or at least discounting heavily both the touch-stone theory advanced by Matthew Arnold — who remains a great critic — and those distinctions between Classic and Romantic art which Irving Babbitt — likewise a great critic — was insisting upon not so long ago. Neither high seriousness nor classic restraint means much to us any longer. It is enough — and a good deal — to be able to detect the fraudulent, the shoddy, the pretentious on the one hand, and competence and artistic logic on the other. The modes and the periods of art differ, each from all others, and the differences are crucial both in respect of art and the human experiences reflected in it.

Standards of taste, principles of criticism — these are acquired readily enough. Unfortunately, those of us who are everyday readers often seem to acquire them long before we are ready for them. In this event they can scarcely serve us as valid standards and principles — by extending and at the same time organizing our perceptions — but only as conditioned responses. Contemporary art always suffers from such predetermined responses. Mr. T. S. Eliot, for instance, is now accepted everywhere as a modern classic, but some of us remember how difficult it once was for many people of taste and wide experience in poetry to see anything but the wildest disorganization and nonsense in *The Waste Land*. If the contemporary poet is one of any artistic validity, he will, in so far as he is addressing anyone, be addressing his contemporaries, and it is they who can best understand him if they choose to listen. The willingness to listen, to receive the full impact of contemporary statement — this is more important than any presuppositions regarding the nature of poetry or of poetic techniques, standards, and values. The essential thing is to read the poem first, making quite certain that our formulated critical judgments concern specific works of art with which we have had first-hand and prolonged experience.

EARLY ENGLISH LYRICS

"I HAVE TWELVE OXEN"

I have twelve oxen that be fair and brown,
And they go a grasing down by the town.
   With hey ! With ho ! With hey !
Sawest thou not mine oxen, you little pretty boy ?

I have twelve oxen, and they be fair and white,
And they go a grasing down by the dike.
   With hey ! With ho ! With hey !
Sawest thou not mine oxen, you little pretty boy ?

I have twelve oxen, and they be fair and black,
And they go a grasing down by the lak.
   With hey ! With ho ! With hey !
Sawest thou not mine oxen, you little pretty boy ?

I have twelve oxen, and they be fair and rede,
And they go a grasing down by the mede.
   With hey ! With ho ! With hey !
Sawest thou not mine oxen, you little pretty boy ?

"AS I ME WALK'D IN ONE MORNING"

As I me walk'd in one morning,
I heard a bird both wepe and sing,
This was the tenor of her talking :
   Timor mortis conturbat me.

I askèd this bird what he meant.
He said, "I am a musket gent ;
For dread of death I am nigh shent —
   Timor mortis conturbat me."

Jesu Christ, when he should die,
To his Father loud gan he cry :
"Father," he said, "in Trinity,
   Timor mortis conturbat me."

When I shall die know I no day ;
In what place or country can I not say.
Therefore this songe sing I may :
   Timor mortis conturbat me.

"THIS ENDURS NIGHT"

This endurs night
I saw a sight
All in my sleep :
Mary, that may,
She sang, "Lullay,"
And sore did weep.
To keep she sought
Full fast about
Her son from cold.
Joseph said, "Wife,
My joy, my life,
Say what ye wold."
"Nothing, my spouse,

musket, sparrow-hawk
gent, of gentle breeding
nigh shent, almost beside myself

endurs night, a night not long past
may, maid

Is in this house
Unto my pay ;
My son, a King,
That made all thing
Lieth in hay."

"My mother dear,
Amend your cheer,
And now be still.
Thus for to lie
It is soothly
My Father's will.
Derision,
Great passion,
Infinitely,
As it is found,
Many a wound
Suffer shall I.
On Calvary
That is so high
There shall I be,
Man to restore,
Nailèd ful sore
Upon a tree."

pay, liking

BALLADS

of Unknown Authorship and Date

EDWARD

"Why dois your brand sae drap wi bluid,
            Edward, Edward ?
Why dois your brand sae drap wi bluid,
    And why sae sad gang yee, O ?"
"O I hae killed my hauke sae guid,
            Mither, mither,
O I hae killed my hauke sae guid,
    And I had nae mair bot hee, O."

"Your haukis bluid, was nevir sae reid,
            Edward, Edward,
Your haukis bluid was nevir sae reid,
    My deir son, I tell thee, O."
"O I hae killed my reid-roan steid,
            Mither, mither.
O I hae killed my reid-roan steid.
    That erst was sae fair and frie, O."

"Your steid was auld, and ye hae gat mair,
            Edward, Edward,
Your steid was auld, and ye hae gat mair ;
    Sum other dule ye drie, O."
"O I hae killed my fadir deir,
            Mither, mither.
O I hae killed my fadir deir,
    Alas, and wae is mee, O !"

"And whatten penance wul ye drie for that,
                    Edward, Edward ?
And whatten penance wul ye drie for that,
    My deir son, now tell me, O ?"
"Ile set my feit in yonder boat,
                    Mither, mither,
Ile set my feit in yonder boat,
    And Ile fare ovir the sea, O."

"And what wul ye doe wi your towirs and your ha,
                    Edward, Edward ?
And what wul ye doe wi your towirs and your ha,
    That were sae fair to see, O ?"
"Ile let thame stand tul they doun fa,
                    Mither, mither,
Ile let thame stand tul they doun fa,
    For here nevir mair maun I bee, O."

"And what wul ye leive to your bairns and your wife,
                    Edward, Edward ?
And what wul ye leive to your bairns and your wife,
    Whan ye gang ovir the sea, O ?"
"The warldis room, late them beg thrae life,
                    Mither, mither,
The warldis room, late them beg thrae life,
    For thame nevir mair wul I see, O."

"And what wul ye leive to your ain mither deir,
                    Edward, Edward ?
And what wul ye leive to your ain mither deir,
    My deir son, now tell me, O ?"
"The curse of hell frae me sall ye beir,
                    Mither, mither,

The curse of hell frae me sall ye beir.
　　Sic counseils ye gave to me, O."

THE WIFE OF USHER'S WELL

There lived a wife at Usher's Well,
　　And a wealthy wife was she ;
She had three stout and stalwart sons,
　　And sent them oer the sea.

They hadna been a week from her,
　　A week but barely ane,
Whan word came to the carline wife
　　That her three sons were gane.

They hadna been a week from her,
　　A week but barely three,
Whan word came to the carline wife
　　That her sons she 'd never see.

"I wish the wind may never cease,
　　Nor fashes in the flood,
Till my three sons come hame to me,
　　In earthly flesh and blood !"

It fell about the Martinmas,
　　When nights are lang and mirk,
The carline wife's three sons came hame,
　　And their hats were o' the birk.

carline, old woman　　　　*fashes*, troubles　　　　*birk*, birch

It neither grew in sike nor ditch,
  Nor yet in ony sheugh,
But at the gates o' Paradise,
  That birk grew fair eneugh.

"Blow up the fire, my maidens,
  Bring water from the well !
For a' my house shall feast this night,
  Since my three sons are well."

And she has made to them a bed,
  She 's made it large and wide,
And she 's taen her mantle her about,
  Sat down at the bed side.

Up then crew the red, red cock,
  And up and crew the gray ;
The eldest to the youngest said,
  " 'Tis time we were away."

The cock he hadna crawd but once,
  And clappd his wings at a',
When the youngest to the eldest said,
  "Brother, we must awa'.

"The cock doth craw, the day doth daw,
  The channerin' worm doth chide ;
Gin we be mist out o' our place,
  A sair pain we maun bide.

"Fare ye weel, my mother dear,
  Fareweel to barn and byre !

sike, streamlet   sheugh, ditch   channerin', fretting

And fare ye weel, the bonny lass
    That kindles my mother's fire !"

LORD RANDAL

"O where hae ye been, Lord Randal, my son ?
O where hae ye been, my handsome young man ?"
"I hae been to the wild wood ; mother, make my bed soon,
For I 'm weary wi hunting, and fain wald lie down."

"Where gat ye your dinner, Lord Randal, my son ?
Where gat ye your dinner, my handsome young man ?"
"I dined wi my true-love ; mother, make my bed soon,
For I 'm weary wi hunting, and fain wald lie down."

"What gat ye to your dinner, Lord Randal, my son ?
What gat ye to your dinner, my handsome young man ?"
"I gat eels boild in broo ; mother, make my bed soon,
For I 'm weary wi hunting, and fain wald lie down."

"What became of your bloodhounds, Lord Randal, my son ?
What became of your bloodhounds, my handsome young
    man ?"
"O they swelld and they died ; mother, make my bed soon,
For I 'm weary wi hunting, and fain wald lie down."

"O I fear ye are poisond, Lord Randal, my son !
O I fear ye are poisond, my handsome young man !"
"O yes ! I am poisond ; mother, make my bed soon,
For I 'm sick at the heart, and I fain wald lie down."

THE SIXTEENTH CENTURY

Skelton to Ben Jonson

JOHN SKELTON

(c. 1460–1529)

from
THE TUNNYNG OF ELYNOUR RUMMYNG

Tell you I chyll
If that ye wyll
A whyle be styll
Of a comely gyll
That dwelt on a hyll.
   But she is not gryll !
For she is somewhat sage
And well worne in age
For her vysage
It would aswage
A mannes courage.
Her lothely lere
Is nothynge clere
But ugly of chere
Droupy and drowsy
Scurvy and lowsy
Her face all bowsy
Comely crynkled
Woundersly wrynkled
Lyke a rost pygges eare

chyll, will
gyll, wench
gryll, horrible

lere, complexion
chere, look

17

Brystled wyth here.
Her lewde lyppes twayne
They slaver (men sayne)
Lyke a ropy rayne
A gummy glayre.
She is ugly fayre
Her nose somdele hoked
And camously croked
Never stoppynge
But ever droppynge,
Her skynne lose and slacke
Grained lyke a sacke,
With a croked backe.
Her eyen gowndy
Are full unsoundy
For they are blered
And she grey hered
Jawed lyke a jetty.
A man would have pytty
To se how she is gumbed
Fyngered and thumbed
Gently joyntd
Gresed and annoynted
Up to the knockles,
The bones of her huckles
Lyke as they were with buckels
Togyther made fast.
Her youth is farre past.
Foted lyke a plane
Legged lyke a crane

ropy, sticky
glayre, slime
camously, like a camus nose

gowndy, bleared
unsoundy, unhealthy
huckles, hips

And yet she wyll jet
Lyke a jolyvet
In her furred flocket
And gray russet rocket
With symper the cocket.
Her huke of Lyncolne grene
It had been hers (I wene)
More then fourty yere
And so doth it apere
For the grene bare thredes
Loke lyke sere wedes
Wyddered lyke hay
The woll worne away,
And yet I dare saye
She thynketh herselfe gaye
Upon the holy daye
Whan she doth her aray
And gyrdeth in her gytes
Styched and pranked with pletes,
Her kyrtel Brystow red,
With clothes upon her hed
That wey a some of led
Wrythen in wonder wyse
After the Sarasyns gyse
With a whym wham
Knyt with a trym tram
Upon her brayne pan
Lyke an Egyptian

jet, strut
jolyvet, gay little creature
flocket, loose, long-sleeved gown
rocket, outer mantle
symper the cocket, a coquettish air

huke, cloak or cape
sere, dry
gytes, gown
wrythen, wound

Capped about.
When she goeth out
Herselfe for to shewe
She dryveth downe the dewe
Wyth a payre of heles
As brode as two wheles,
She hobles as a gose
With her blanket hose
Over the falowe,
Her shone smered wyth talowe
Gresed upon dyrt
That baudeth her skyrt.

SIR THOMAS WYATT

(*c.* 1503–1542)

"MY GALLEY, CHARGÈD WITH FORGETFULNESS"

My galley, chargèd with forgetfulness,
  Thorough sharp seas in winter nights doth pass
  'Tween rock and rock ; and eke mine enemy, alas,
  That is my lord, steereth with cruelness.
And every hour a thought in readiness,
  As though that death were light in such a case.
  An endless wind doth tear the sail apace,
  Of forcèd sighs and trusty fearfulness.
A rain of tears, a cloud of dark disdain,
  Hath done the wearied cords great hinderance,
  Wreathèd with error and with ignorance.

blanket hose, woolen hose   *baudeth,* soils

The stars be hid that led me to this pain ;
   Drown'd is reason that should be my comfort,
   And I remain despairing of the port.

HENRY HOWARD, EARL OF SURREY

(1517 ?–1547)

"FROM TUSCAN CAME MY LADY'S WORTHY RACE"

From Tuscan came my lady's worthy race ;
Fair Florence was sometime her ancient seat ;
The western isle whose pleasant shore doth face
Wild Chambar's cliffs did give her lively heat ;
Foster'd she was with milk of Irish breast ;
Her sire an earl, her dame of princes' blood ;
From tender years in Britain she doth rest
With a king's child, where she tastes costly food.
Hunsdon did first present her to mine eyne ;
Bright is her hue, and Geraldine she hight ;
Hampton me taught to wish her first for mine ;
And Windsor, alas ! doth chase me from her sight.
Her beauty, of kind ; her virtues, from above,
Happy is he that may obtain her love.

EDMUND SPENSER

(1552 ?–1599)

from
AMORETTI: SONNETS

III

"THE SOVEREIGN BEAUTY
WHICH I DO ADMIRE"

The sovereign beauty which I do admire,
Witness the world how worthy to be prais'd,
The light whereof hath kindled heavenly fire
In my frail spirit, by her from baseness rais'd,
That being now with her huge brightness daz'd,
Base thing I can no more endure to view,
But looking still on her, I stand amaz'd
At wondrous sight of so celestial hue.
So when my tongue would speak her praises due,
It stoppèd is with thought's astonishment ;
And when my pen would write her titles true,
It ravish'd is with fancy's wonderment.
   Yet in my heart I then both speak and write
   The wonder that my wit cannot indite.

IX

"LONG WHILE I SOUGHT TO WHAT I MIGHT COMPARE"

Long while I sought to what I might compare
Those powerful eyes which lighten my dark spright,
Yet find I naught on earth to which I dare
Resemble th' image of their goodly light.
Not to the sun, for they do shine by night ;
Nor to the moon, for they are changèd never ;
Nor to the stars, for they have purer sight ;
Nor to the fire, for they consume not ever ;
Nor to the lightning, for they still persever ;
Nor to the diamond, for they are more tender ;
Nor unto crystal, for naught may them sever,
Nor unto glass, such baseness mought offend her :
    Then to the Maker self they likest be,
    Whose light doth lighten all that here we see.

XVIII

"THE ROLLING WHEEL, THAT RUNNETH OFTEN ROUND"

The rolling wheel, that runneth often round,
The hardest steel in tract of time doth tear ;
And drizzling drops, that often do redound,
The firmest flint doth in continuance wear.
Yet cannot I, with many a dropping tear,
And long entreaty, soften her hard heart,

That she will once vouchsafe my plaint to hear,
Or look with pity on my painful smart :
But when I plead, she bids me play my part ;
And when I weep, she says tears are but water ;
And when I sigh, she says I know the art ;
And when I wail, she turns herself to laughter.
  So do I weep and wail and plead in vain,
  Whiles she as steel and flint doth still remain.

XXXIV

"LIKE AS A SHIP, THAT THROUGH THE OCEAN WIDE"

Like as a ship, that through the ocean wide,
By conduct of some star, doth make her way,
Whenas a storm hath dimm'd her trusty guide,
Out of her course doth wander far astray ;
So I, whose star, that wont with her bright ray
Me to direct, with clouds is overcast,
Do wander now in darkness and dismay,
Through hidden perils round about me plac'd ;
Yet hope I well that when this storm is past
My Helicè, the loadstar of my life,
Will shine again, and look on me at last
With lovely light, to clear my cloudy grief.
  Till then I wander careful, comfortless,
  In secret sorrow and sad pensiveness.

LXVII

"LIKE AS A HUNTSMAN AFTER WEARY CHACE"

Like as a huntsman after weary chace,
Seeing the game from him escape away,
Sits down to rest him in some shady place,
With panting hounds beguilèd of their prey ;
So after long pursuit and vain assay,
When I all weary had the chace forsook,
The gentle deer return'd the self-same way,
Thinking to quench her thirst at the next brook ;
There she beholding me with milder look,
Sought not to fly, but fearless still did bide,
Till I in hand her yet half trembling took,
And with her own goodwill her firmly tied.
    Strange thing, me seem'd, to see a beast so wild
    So goodly wone, with her own will beguil'd.

PROTHALAMION

Calm was the day, and through the trembling air
Sweet breathing Zephyrus did softly play,
A gentle spirit, that lightly did delay
Hot Titan's beams, which then did glister fair,
When I, whom sullen care,
Through discontent of my long fruitless stay
In princes' court, and expectation vain
Of idle hopes, which still do fly away,
Like empty shadows, did afflict my brain,

Walkt forth to ease my pain
Along the shore of silver streaming Thames,
Whose rutty bank, the which his river hems,
Was painted all with variable flowers,
And all the meads adorn'd with dainty gems,
Fit to deck maidens' bowers,
And crown their paramours,
Against the bridal-day, which is not long.
   Sweet Thames ! run softly till I end my song.

There in a meadow by the river's side,
A flock of nymphs I chancèd to espy,
All lovely daughters of the flood thereby,
With goodly greenish locks all loose untied,
As each had been a bride ;
And each one had a little wicker basket,
Made of fine twigs entrailèd curiously,
In which they gather'd flowers to fill their flasket,
And with fine fingers cropt full feateously
The tender stalks on high.
Of every sort which in that meadow grew
They gather'd some ; the violet, pallid blue,
The little dazie, that at evening closes,
The virgin lillie, and the primrose true,
With store of vermeil roses,
To deck their bridegroom's posies
Against the bridal-day, which was not long.
   Sweet Thames ! run softly till I end my song.

With that I saw two swans of goodly hue
Come softly swimming down along the Lee ;
Two fairer birds I yet did never see ;
The snow which doth the top of Pindus strew

Did never whiter shew,
Nor Jove himself, when he a swan would be
For love of Leda, whiter did appear ;
Yet Leda was (they say) as white as he,
Yet not so white as these, nor nothing near ;
So purely white they were,
That even the gentle stream, the which them bare,
Seem'd foul to them, and bade his billows spare
To wet their silken feathers, lest they might
Soil their fair plumes with water not so fair,
And mar their beauties bright,
That shone as heaven's light.
Against their bridal-day, which was not long.
   Sweet Thames ! run softly till I end my song.

Eftsoons the nymphs, which now had flowers their fill,
Ran all in haste to see that silver brood,
As they came floating on the crystal flood ;
Whom when they saw, they stood amazèd still,
Their wondering eyes to fill ;
Them seem'd they never saw a sight so fair,
Of fowls so lovely, that they sure did deem
Them heavenly born, or to be that same pair
Which through the sky draw Venus' silver team ;
For sure they did not seem
To be begot of any earthly seed,
But rather angels, or of angels' breed ;
Yet were they bred of summer's heat, they say,
In sweetest season, when each flower and weed
The earth did fresh array ;
So fresh they seem'd as day,
Even as their bridal-day, which was not long.
   Sweet Thames ! run softly till I end my song.

Then forth they all out of their baskets drew
Great store of flowers, the honor of the field,
That to the sense did fragrant odors yield,
All which upon those goodly birds they threw,
And all the waves did strew,
That like old Peneus' waters they did seem,
When down along by pleasant Tempe's shore,
Scattrèd with flowers, through Thessaly they stream,
That they appear, through lillies' plenteous store,
Like a bride's chamber floor.
Two of those nymphs, meanwhile, two garlands bound
Of freshest flowers which in that mead they found,
The which presenting all in trim array,
Their snowy foreheads therewithal they crown'd,
Whilst one did sing this lay,
Prepar'd against that day,
Against their bridal-day, which was not long :
    Sweet Thames ! run softly till I end my song.

"Ye gentle birds, the world's fair ornament,
And heaven's glory, whom this happy hour
Doth lead unto your lovers' blissful bower,
Joy may you have, and gentle hearts' content
Of your love's couplement ;
And let fair Venus, that is queen of love,
With her heart-quelling son, upon you smile,
Whose smile, they say, hath virtue to remove
All love's dislike, and friendship's faulty guile
For ever to assoil.
Let endless peace your steadfast hearts accord,
And blessèd plenty wait upon your board ;
And let your bed with pleasures chaste abound,
That fruitful issue may to you afford,

Which may your foes confound,
And make your joys redound
Upon your bridal-day, which is not long."
    Sweet Thames ! run softly till I end my song.

So ended she, and all the rest around
To her redoubled that her undersong,
Which said their bridal-day should not be long ;
And gentle Echo from the neighbor ground
Their accents did resound.
So forth those joyous birds did pass along,
Adown the Lee, that to them murmur'd low,
As he would speak, but that he lackt a tongue,
Yet did by signs his glad affection show,
Making his stream run slow.
And all the fowl which in his flood did dwell
'Gan flock about these twain, that did excel
The rest so far as Cynthia doth shend
The lesser stars. So they, enrangèd well,
Did on those two attend,
And their best service lend,
Against their wedding-day, which was not long.
    Sweet Thames ! run softly till I end my song.

At length they all to merry London came,
To merry London, my most kindly nurse,
That to me gave this life's first native source,
Though from another place I take my name,
An house of ancient fame.
There when they came, whereas those bricky towers
The which on Thames' broad agèd back do ride,
Where now the studious lawyers have their bowers,
There whilom wont the Templar Knights to bide,

Till they decay'd through pride ;
Next whereunto there stands a stately place,
Where oft I gainèd gifts and goodly grace
Of that great lord which therein wont to dwell,
Whose want too well now feels my friendless case ;
But ah ! here fits not well
Old woes, but joys, to tell,
Against the bridal-day, which is not long.
    Sweet Thames ! run softly till I end my song.

Yet therein now doth lodge a noble peer,
Great England's glory, and the world's wide wonder,
Whose dreadful name late through all Spain did thunder,
And Hercules' two pillars standing near
Did make to quake and fear —
Fair branch of honor, flower of chivalry,
That fillest England with thy triumph's fame,
Joy have thou of thy noble victory,
And endless happiness of thine own name,
That promiseth the same ;
That through thy prowess and victorious arms
Thy country may be freed from foreign harms,
And great Eliza's glorious name may ring
Through all the world, fill'd with thy wide alarms,
Which some brave Muse may sing
To ages following,
Upon the bridal-day, which is not long.
    Sweet Thames ! run softly till I end my song.

From those high towers this noble lord issuing,
Like radiant Hesper, when his golden hair
In the ocean billows he hath bathèd fair,
Descended to the river's open viewing,

With a great train ensuing.
Above the rest were goodly to be seen
Two gentle knights of lovely face and feature,
Beseeming well the bower of any queen,
With gifts of wit and ornaments of nature,
Fit for so goodly stature,
That like the Twins of Jove they seem'd in sight,
Which deck the bauldrick of the heavens bright.
They two, forth pacing to the river's side,
Receiv'd those two fair brides, their love's delight ;
Which at the appointed tide
Each one did make his bride,
Against their bridal-day, which is not long.
Sweet Thames ! run softly till I end my song.

SIR PHILIP SIDNEY

(1554–1586)

from
ASTROPHEL AND STELLA :
SONNETS

I

"LOVING IN TRUTH, AND FAIN IN VERSE
MY LOVE TO SHOW"

Loving in truth, and fain in verse my love to show,
That she, dear she, might take some pleasure of my pain,
Pleasure might cause her read, reading might make her know,
Knowledge might pity win, and pity grace obtain,
I sought fit words to paint the blackest face of woe,

Studying inventions fine, her wits to entertain,
Oft turning others' leaves, to see if thence would flow
Some fresh and fruitful showers upon my sunburnt brain.
But words came halting forth, wanting Invention's stay ;
Invention, Nature's child, fled step-dame Study's blows ;
And others' feet still seem'd but strangers in my way.
Thus, great with child to speak, and helpless in my throes,
Biting my truant pen, beating myself for spite,
"Fool," said my Muse to me, "look in thy heart, and write !"

V

"IT IS MOST TRUE THAT EYES ARE FORM'D TO SERVE"

It is most true that eyes are form'd to serve
The inward light, and that the heavenly part
Ought to be king, from whose rules who do swerve,
Rebels to Nature, strive for their own smart.
It is most true, what we call Cupid's dart
An image is, which for ourselves we carve,
And, fools, adore in temple of our heart,
Till that good god make church and churchmen starve.
True, that true beauty virtue is indeed,
Whereof this beauty can be but a shade,
Which elements with mortal mixture breed.
True, that on earth we are but pilgrims made,
And should in soul up to our country move :
True, and yet true — that I must Stella love.

XIV

"ALAS, HAVE I NOT PAIN ENOUGH, MY FRIEND?"

Alas, have I not pain enough, my friend,
Upon whose breast a fiercer gripe doth tire
Than did on him who first stole down the fire,
While Love on me doth all his quiver spend, —
But with your rubarb words ye must contend,
To grieve me worse, in saying that Desire
Doth plunge my well-form'd soul even in the mire
Of sinful thoughts, which do in ruin end?
If that be sin which doth the manners frame,
Well stay'd with truth in word and faith of deed,
Ready of wit, and fearing naught but shame;
If that be sin which in fix'd hearts doth breed
A loathing of all loose unchastity,
Than love is sin, and let me sinful be.

Sonnet - coming
to life
(probably silly)

XXXI

"WITH HOW SAD STEPS, O MOON, THOU CLIMB'ST THE SKIES!"

With how sad steps, O Moon, thou climb'st the skies!
How silently, and with how wan a face!
What, may it be that even in heavenly place
That busy archer his sharp arrows tries?
Sure, if that long-with-love-acquainted eyes
Can judge of love, thou feel'st a lover's case;

An the moon women
are as cruel as their
are here on earth

I read it in thy looks ; thy languish'd grace,
To me, that feel the like, thy state descries.
Then, even of fellowship, O Moon, tell me,
Is constant love deem'd there but want of wit ?
Are beauties there as proud as here they be ?
Do they above love to be lov'd, and yet
Those lovers scorn whom that love doth possess ?
Do they call virtue there ungratefulness ?

XXXIX

"COME, SLEEP ! O SLEEP, THE CERTAIN KNOT OF PEACE"

Come, Sleep ! O Sleep, the certain knot of peace,
The baiting-place of wit, the balm of woe,
The poor man's wealth, the prisoner's release,
The indifferent judge between the high and low ;
With shield of proof shield me from out the press
Of those fierce darts despair at me doth throw ;
Oh make in me those civil wars to cease ;
I will good tribute pay if thou do so.
Take thou of me smooth pillows, sweetest bed,
A chamber deaf to noise and blind to light,
A rosy garland and a weary head :
And if these things, as being thine by right,
Move not thy heavy grace, thou shalt in me,
Livelier than elsewhere, Stella's image see.

SAMUEL DANIEL

(*c.* 1562–1619)

from
DELIA

TO DELIA

Fair is my love, and cruel as she 's fair —
Her brow shades frowns, although her eyes are sunny ;
Her smiles are lightning, though her pride despair ;
And her disdains are gall, her favors honey.
A modest maid, deck'd with a blush of honor,
Whose feet do tread green paths of youth and love ;
The wonder of all eyes that look upon her,
Sacred on earth, design'd a saint above.
Chastity and beauty, which were deadly foes,
Live reconcilèd friends within her brow ;
And had she pity to conjoin with those,
Then who had heard the plaints I utter now ?
For had she not been fair, and thus unkind,
My muse had slept, and none had known my mind.

MICHAEL DRAYTON

(1563–1631)

from
SONNETS, TO DELIA

LXI

"SINCE THERE'S NO HELP, COME, LET US KISS AND PART"

Since there's no help, come, let us kiss and part.
Nay, I have done, you get no more of me.
And I am glad, yea, glad with all my heart,
That thus so cleanly I myself can free ;
Shake hands for ever, cancel all our vows,
And when we meet at any time again,
Be it not seen in either of our brows
That we one jot of former love retain.
Now at the last gasp of Love's latest breath,
When, his pulse failing, Passion speechless lies,
When Faith is kneeling by his bed of death,
And Innocence is closing up his eyes —
　　Now, if thou wouldst, when all have given him over,
　　From death to life thou might'st him yet recover.

ODE

TO THE CAMBRO-BRITONS AND THEIR HARP,
HIS BALLAD OF AGINCOURT

Fair stood the wind for France,
When we our sails advance,

Nor now to prove our chance
  Longer will tarry ;
But putting to the main,
At Caux, the mouth of Seine,
With all his martial train,
  Landed King Harry.

And taking many a fort,
Furnish'd in warlike sort,
Marcheth towards Agincourt,
  In happy hour ;
Skirmishing day by day
With those that stopped his way,
Where the French general lay
  With all his power.

Which in his height of pride,
King Henry to deride,
His ransom to provide
  To the king sending ;
Which he neglects the while,
As from a nation vile,
Yet with an angry smile,
  Their fall portending.

And turning to his men,
Quoth our brave Henry then,
"Though they to one be ten,
  Be not amazèd.
Yet have we well begun —
Battles so bravely won
Have ever to the sun
  By fame been raisèd.

"And, for myself," quoth he,
"This my full rest shall be ;
England ne'er mourn for me,
     Nor more esteem me.
Victor I will remain,
Or on this earth lie slain ;
Never shall she sustain
     Loss to redeem me.

"Poitiers and Cressy tell,
When most their pride did swell,
Under our swords they fell ;
     No less our skill is
Than when our grandsire great,
Claiming the regal seat,
By many a warlike feat
     Lop'd the French lilies."

The Duke of York so dread
The eager vaward led ;
With the main Henry sped,
     Amongst his henchmen.
Exeter had the rear,
A braver man not there.
O Lord, how hot they were
     On the false Frenchmen !

They now to fight are gone,
Armor on armor shone,
Drum now to drum did groan ;
     To hear, was wonder ;
That with the cries they make

The very earth did shake,
Trumpet to trumpet spake,
　Thunder to thunder.

Well it thine age became,
O noble Erpingham,
Which didst the signal aim
　To our hid forces ;
When from a meadow by,
Like a storm suddenly,
The English archery
　Struck the French horses.

With Spanish yew so strong,
Arrows a cloth-yard long,
That like to serpents stung,
　Piercing the weather ;
None from his fellow starts,
But playing manly parts,
And like true English hearts,
　Stuck close together.

When down their bows they threw
And forth their bilbos drew,
And on the French they flew,
　Not one was tardy ;
Arms were from shoulders sent,
Scalps to the teeth were rent,
Down the French peasants went —
　Our men were hardy.

This while our noble king,
His broad sword brandishing,

Down the French host did ding,
  As to o'erwhelm it ;
And many a deep wound lent,
His arms with blood besprent,
And many a cruel dent
  Bruisèd his helmet.

Gloucester, that duke so good,
Next of the royal blood,
For famous England stood,
  With his brave brother,
Clarence, in steel so bright,
Though but a maiden knight,
Yet in that furious fight
  Scarce such another.

Warwick in blood did wade,
Oxford the foe invade,
And cruel slaughter made,
  Still as they ran up ;
Suffolk his axe did ply,
Beaumont and Willoughby
Bare them right doughtily,
  Ferrers and Fanhope.

Upon Saint Crispin's day
Fought was the noble fray,
Which fame did not delay
  To England to carry.
Oh, when shall English men
With such acts fill a pen,
Or England breed again
  Such a King Harry ?

CHRISTOPHER MARLOWE

(1564–1593)

THE PASSIONATE SHEPHERD TO HIS LOVE

Come live with me and be my love,
And we will all the pleasures prove
That valleys, groves, hills, and fields,
Woods, or steepy mountains yields.

And we will sit upon the rocks,
Seeing the shepherds feed their flocks,
By shallow rivers, to whose falls
Melodious birds sing madrigals.

And I will make thee beds of roses
And a thousand fragrant posies,
A cap of flowers, and a kirtle
Embroider'd all with leaves of myrtle ;

A gown made of the finest wool,
Which from our pretty lambs we pull ;
Fair linèd slippers for the cold,
With buckles of the purest gold ;

A belt of straw and ivy-buds
With coral clasps and amber studs —
And if these pleasures may thee move,
Come live with me and be my love.

The shepherd swains shall dance and sing
For thy delight each May morning —
If these delights thy mind may move,
Then live with me and be my love.

WILLIAM SHAKESPEARE

(1564–1616)

SEVEN SONGS FROM THE PLAYS

from the close of
LOVE'S LABOUR'S LOST

Enter Armado.

Armado. Sweet majesty, vouchsafe me —
Prince. Was not that Hector ?
Dumain. The worthy knight of Troy.
Armado. I will kiss thy royal finger, and take leave. I am a
votary. I have vowed to Jaquenetta to hold the plough for her
sweet love three year. But, most esteemed greatness, will you
hear the dialogue that the two learned men have compiled in
praise of the owl and the cuckoo ? It should have followed in
the end of our show.
King. Call them forth quickly. We will do so.
Armado. Holla ! approach !

Enter all.

This side is Hiems, Winter ; this Ver, the Spring ; the one
maintained by the owl, the other by the cuckoo. Ver, begin.

THE SONG

Spring. When daisies pied and violets blue,
   And lady-smocks all silver-white,
And cuckoo-buds of yellow hue
   Do paint the meadows with delight —
The cuckoo then on every tree
Mocks married men, for thus sings he :
             "Cuckoo,
Cuckoo, cuckoo."
O word of fear,
Unpleasing to the married ear !

When shepherds pipe on oaten straws,
   And merry larks are ploughmen's clocks,
When turtles tread, and rooks, and daws,
   And maidens bleach their summer smocks —
The cuckoo then on every tree
Mocks married men ; for thus sings he :
             "Cuckoo ;
Cuckoo, cuckoo."
O word of fear,
Unpleasing to a married ear !

Winter. When icicles hang by the wall,
   And Dick the shepherd blows his nail,
And Tom bears logs into the hall,
   And milk comes frozen home in pail ;
When blood is nipp'd and ways be foul,
Then nightly sings the staring owl,
             "Tu-whit, tu-who !"
A merry note,
While greasy Joan doth keel the pot.

When all aloud the wind doth blow,
　　And coughing drowns the parson's saw,
And birds sit brooding in the snow,
　　And Marian's nose looks red and raw ;
When roasted crabs hiss in the bowl,
Then nightly sings the staring owl,
　　　　　　　　"Tu-whit, tu-who !"
A merry note,
While greasy Joan doth keel the pot.

Armado. The words of Mercury are harsh after the songs of
Apollo. You that way : we this way.

　　　　　　　　　　　　　　　Exeunt.

from
TWELFTH NIGHT

"O MISTRESS MINE,
WHERE ARE YOU ROAMING ?"

O mistress mine, where are you roaming ?
O, stay and hear ; your true love 's coming,
　　That can sing both high and low.
Trip no further, pretty sweeting,
Journeys end in lovers meeting —
　　Every wise man's son doth know.

What is love ? 'tis not hereafter.
Present mirth hath present laughter ;
　　What 's to come is still unsure.
In delay there lies no plenty ;
Then come kiss me, sweet and twenty —
　　Youth 's a stuff will not endure.

"COME AWAY, COME AWAY, DEATH"

Come away, come away, death,
   And in sad cypress let me be laid ;
Fly away, fly away, breath ;
   I am slain by a fair cruel maid.
My shroud of white, stuck all with yew,
      O, prepare it !
My part of death, no one so true
      Did share it.

Not a flower, not a flower sweet,
   On my black coffin let there be strown ;
Not a friend, not a friend greet
   My poor corpse, where my bones shall be thrown.
A thousand thousand sighs to save,
      Lay me, O, where
Sad true lover never find my grave,
      To weep there !

from
CYMBELINE

"FEAR NO MORE THE HEAT O' THE SUN"

Fear no more the heat o' the sun,
  Nor the furious winter's rages ;
Thou thy worldly task hast done,
  Home art gone and ta'en thy wages.
Golden lads and girls all must,
As chimney-sweepers, come to dust.

Fear no more the frown o' the great ;
  Thou art past the tyrant's stroke ;
Care no more to clothe and eat ;
  To thee the reed is as the oak.
The sceptre, learning, physic, must
All follow this, and come to dust.

Fear no more the lightning-flash,
  Nor the all-dreaded thunder-stone ;
Fear not slander, censure rash ;
  Thou hast finish'd joy and moan.
All lovers young, all lovers must
Consign to thee, and come to dust.

No exorciser harm thee !
Nor no witchcraft charm thee !
Ghost unlaid forbear thee !
Nothing ill come near thee !
Quiet consummation have,
And renownèd be thy grave !

from
THE TEMPEST

"COME UNTO THESE YELLOW SANDS"

Come unto these yellow sands,
  And then take hands.
Curtsied when you have, and kiss'd, —
  The wild waves whist, —
Foot it featly here and there ;
And, sweet sprites, the burden bear.
      Hark, hark !
          Bow-wow,
The watch-dogs bark;
          Bow-wow.
Hark, hark! I hear
The strain of strutting chanticleer
Cry, "Cock-a-diddle-dow !"

"FULL FATHOM FIVE THY FATHER LIES"

Full fathom five thy father lies ;
  Of his bones are coral made ;
Those are pearls that were his eyes.
  Nothing of him that doth fade
But doth suffer a sea-change
Into something rich and strange.
Sea-nymphs hourly ring his knell.
              Ding-dong.
Hark ! now I hear them — Ding-dong, bell !

from
SONNETS

XVIII

"SHALL I COMPARE THEE TO A SUMMER'S DAY?"

Shall I compare thee to a summer's day?
Thou art more lovely and more temperate.
Rough winds do shake the darling buds of May,
And summer's lease hath all too short a date ;
Sometime too hot the eye of heaven shines,
And often is his gold complexion dimm'd ;
And every fair from fair sometimes declines,
By chance, or nature's changing course, untrimm'd.
But thy eternal summer shall not fade,
Nor lose possession of that fair thou ow'st
Nor shall death brag thou wander'st in his shade,
When in eternal lines to time thou grow'st.
　So long as men can breathe, or eyes can see,
　So long lives this, and this gives life to thee.

XXIX

"WHEN IN DISGRACE WITH FORTUNE AND MEN'S EYES"

When in disgrace with fortune and men's eyes
I all alone beweep my outcast state,
And trouble deaf heaven with my bootless cries,

And look upon myself, and curse my fate,
Wishing me like to one more rich in hope,
Featur'd like him, like him with friends possess'd,
Desiring this man's art, and that man's scope,
With what I most enjoy contented least ;
Yet in these thoughts myself almost despising, *Turning pt.*
Haply I think on thee — and then my state,
Like to the lark at break of day arising
From sullen earth, sings hymns at heaven's gate ; *effective simile*
    For thy sweet love remember'd such wealth brings
    That then I scorn to change my state with kings.

XXX

Tricky one

"WHEN TO THE SESSIONS OF SWEET SILENT THOUGHT"

When to the sessions of sweet silent thought   *Court of law – witnesses are being called*
I summon up remembrance of things past,   *regretting things of the past – that he desired*
I sigh the lack of many a thing I sought,
And with old woes new wail my dear time's waste. *life was wasted*
Then can I drown an eye, unus'd to flow,
For precious friends hid in death's dateless night,
And weep afresh love's long since cancell'd woe,
And moan the expense of many a vanish'd sight.
Then can I grieve at grievances foregone,
And heavily from woe to woe tell o'er
The sad account of fore-bemoanèd moan,
Which I new pay as if not paid before.
    But if the while I think on thee, dear friend,
    All losses are restor'd and sorrows end.

first 12 lines
1 metaphor

XXXIII

"FULL MANY A GLORIOUS MORNING HAVE I SEEN"

Full many a glorious morning have I seen
Flatter the mountain-tops with sovereign eye,
Kissing with golden face the meadows green,
Gilding pale streams with heavenly alchemy ;
Anon permit the basest clouds to ride
With ugly rack on his celestial face,
And from the forlorn world his visage hide,
Stealing unseen to west with this disgrace.
Even so my sun one early morn did shine
With all-triumphant splendour on my brow ;
But out, alack ! he was but one hour mine ;
The region cloud hath mask'd him from me now.
    Yet him for this my love no whit disdaineth ;
    Suns of the world may stain when heaven's sun staineth.

LV

"NOT MARBLE NOR THE GILDED MONUMENTS"

Not marble nor the gilded monuments
Of princes shall outlive this powerful rime ;
But you shall shine more bright in these contents
Than unswept stone, besmear'd with sluttish time.
When wasteful war shall statues overturn,
And broils root out the work of masonry,

Nor Mars his sword nor war's quick fire shall burn
The living record of your memory.
'Gainst death and all-oblivious enmity
Shall you pace forth ; your praise shall still find room
Even in the eyes of all posterity
That wear this world out to the ending doom.
   So, till the judgment that yourself arise,
   You live in this, and dwell in lovers' eyes.

LX

"LIKE AS THE WAVES MAKE TOWARDS THE PEBBLED SHORE"

Like as the waves make towards the pebbled shore,
So do our minutes hasten to their end ;
Each changing place with that which goes before,
In sequent toil all forwards do contend.
Nativity, once in the main of light,
Crawls to maturity, wherewith being crown'd,
Crooked eclipses 'gainst his glory fight,
And Time that gave doth now his gift confound.
Time doth transfix the flourish set on youth
And delves the parallels in beauty's brow,
Feeds on the rarities of nature's truth,
And nothing stands but for his scythe to mow.
   And yet to times in hope my verse shall stand,
   Praising thy worth, despite his cruel hand.

LXIV

"WHEN I HAVE SEEN BY TIME'S FELL HAND DEFAC'D"

When I have seen by Time's fell hand defac'd
The rich-proud cost of outworn buried age ;
When sometime lofty towers I see down-raz'd,
And brass eternal slave to mortal rage ;
When I have seen the hungry ocean gain
Advantage on the kingdom of the shore,
And the firm soil win of the watery main,
Increasing store with loss, and loss with store ;
When I have seen such interchange of state,
Or state itself confounded to decay ;
Ruin hath taught me thus to ruminate —
That Time will come and take my love away.
  This thought is as a death which cannot choose
  But weep to have that which it fears to lose.

English sonnet

LXXIII

"THAT TIME OF YEAR THOU MAYST IN ME BEHOLD"

That time of year thou mayst in me behold *a*
When yellow leaves, or none, or few, do hang *b*
Upon those boughs which shake against the cold — *a* } 4
Bare ruin'd choirs where late the sweet birds sang. *b*
In me thou see'st the twilight of such day *c*
As after sunset fadeth in the west, *d* } 4

Which by and by black night doth take away, ε
Death's second self, that seals up all in rest. d
In me thou see'st the glowing of such fire ε
That on the ashes of his youth doth lie, f
As the death-bed whereon it must expire, ε
Consum'd with that which it was nourish'd by. f

This thou perceiv'st, which makes thy love more strong, g
To love that well which thou must leave ere long. g

CVI

"WHEN IN THE CHRONICLE OF WASTED TIME"

When in the chronicle of wasted time
I see descriptions of the fairest wights,
And beauty making beautiful old rime
In praise of ladies dead and lovely knights ;
Then, in the blazon of sweet beauty's best, *celebration*
Of hand, of foot, of lip, of eye, of brow,
I see their antique pen would have express'd
Even such a beauty as you master now.
So all their praises are but prophecies
Of this our time, all you prefiguring ;
And, for they look'd but with divining eyes,
They had not still enough your worth to sing ;

For we, which now behold these present days,
Have eyes to wonder, but lack tongues to praise.

JOHN DONNE

(1572–1631)

SONG

Go, and catch a falling star,
  Get with child a mandrake root,
Tell me, where all past years are,
  Or who cleft the devil's foot ;
Teach me to hear mermaids singing,
Or to keep off envy's stinging,
      And find
      What wind
Serves to advance an honest mind.

If thou beest born to strange sights,
  Things invisible to see,
Ride ten thousand days and nights,
  Till age snow white hairs on thee.
Thou, when thou return'st, wilt tell me
All strange wonders that befell thee,
      And swear
      No where
Lives a woman true and fair.

If thou find'st one, let me know ;
  Such a pilgrimage were sweet.
Yet do not, — I would not go,
  Though at next door we might meet.
Though she were true when you met her,

And last, till you write your letter,
      Yet she
      Will be
False, ere I come, to two, or three.

THE SUN RISING

      Busy old fool, unruly Sun,
      Why dost thou thus
Through windows, and through curtains call on us ?
Must to thy motions lovers' seasons run ?
      Saucy pedantic wretch, go chide
      Late schoolboys and sour prentices,
    Go tell court huntsmen that the king will ride,
    Call country ants to harvest offices ;
Love, all alike, no season knows, nor clime,
Nor hours, days, months, which are the rags of time.

      Thy beams, so reverend and strong,
      Why shouldst thou think ?
I could eclipse and cloud them with a wink,
But that I would not lose her sight so long.
      If her eyes have not blinded thine,
      Look, and to-morrow late, tell me,
    Whether both the Indias of spice and mine
    Be where thou left'st them, or lie here with me.
Ask for those kings whom thou saw'st yesterday,
And thou shalt hear, "All here in one bed lay."

      She is all States, and all Princes, I ;
      Nothing else is.
Princes do but play us ; compared to this,

All honor 's mimic, all wealth alchemy.
Thou, Sun, art half as happy as we,
In that the world 's contracted thus :
Thine age asks ease, and since thy duties be
To warm the world, that 's done in warming us.
Shine here to us, and thou art everywhere ;
This bed thy center is ; these walls, thy sphere.

THE GOOD MORROW

I wonder by my troth, what thou and I
Did, till we lov'd ? Were we not wean'd till then,
But suck'd on country pleasures, childishly ?
Or snorted we in the Seven Sleepers' den ?
'Twas so. But this, all pleasures fancies be.
If ever any beauty I did see,
Which I desir'd and got, 'twas but a dream of thee.

And now good morrow to our waking souls,
Which watch not one another out of fear ;
For love all love of other sights controls,
And makes one little room an everywhere.
Let sea-discoverers to new worlds have gone,
Let maps to other, worlds on worlds have shown,
Let us possess one world ; each hath one, and is one.

My face in thine eye, thine in mine appears,
And true plain hearts do in the faces rest ;
Where can we find two better hemispheres
Without sharp north, without declining west ?
What ever dies, was not mixt equally ;
If our two loves be one, or thou and I
Love so alike, that none do slacken, none can die.

THE FUNERAL

Who ever comes to shroud me, do not harm,
    Nor question much
That subtle wreath of hair, which crowns my arm ;
The mystery, the sign you must not touch,
    For 'tis my outward Soul,
Viceroy to that, which then to heaven being gone,
    Will leave this to control,
And keep these limbs, her provinces, from dissolution.

For if the sinewy thread my brain lets fall
    Through every part,
Can tie those parts, and make me one of all,
These hairs, which upward grew, and strength and art
    Have from a better brain,
Can better do it. Except she meant that I
    By this should know my pain,
As prisoners then are manacled, when they'are condemn'd
            to die.

What ere she meant by it, bury it with me,
    For since I am
Love's martyr, it might breed idolatry
If into others' hands these reliques came.
    As 'twas humility
To afford to it all that a Soul can do,
    So, 'tis some bravery,
That, since you would save none of me, I bury some of you.

was against women
later - wrote religious poetry

from
HOLY SONNETS

Appeals to all
1. Checks your
imagination
2. Covers so much

VII

"AT THE ROUND EARTH'S IMAGIN'D CORNERS"

Everyone will die

At the round earth's imagin'd corners, blow
Your trumpets, Angels, and arise, arise
From death, you numberless infinities
Of souls, and to your scattered bodies go ;
All whom the flood did, and fire shall, o'erthrow,
All whom war, dearth, age, agues, tyrannies,
Despair, law, chance hath slain, and you whose eyes
Shall behold God, and never taste death's woe.— *people on earth when*
But let them sleep, Lord, and me mourn a space, *Judgment day*
For, if above all these, my sins abound, *comes*
'Tis late to ask abundance of Thy grace,
When we are there. Here on this lowly ground,
Teach me how to repent ; for that 's as good
As if Thou hadst seal'd my pardon with Thy blood.

He thought he was a sinner

X

"DEATH, BE NOT PROUD"

Death, be not proud, though some have callèd thee
Mighty and dreadful, for thou art not so ;
For, those whom thou think'st thou dost overthrow,
Die not, poor Death, nor yet canst thou kill me.

From rest and sleep, which but thy pictures be,
Much pleasure ; then from thee, much more must flow,
And soonest our best men with thee do go,
Rest of their bones, and soul's delivery.
Thou art slave to fate, chance, kings, and desperate men,
And dost with poison, war, and sickness dwell,
And poppy, or charms can make us sleep as well,
And better than thy stroke ; why swell'st thou then ?
One short sleep past, we wake eternally,
And Death shall be no more ; Death, thou shalt die.

A HYMN TO GOD THE FATHER

Wilt thou forgive that sin where I begun,
  Which was my sin, though it were done before ?
Wilt thou forgive those sinnes through which I run,
  And do run still ; though still I do deplore ?
    When thou hast done, thou hast not done,
      For I have more.

Wilt thou forgive that sin which I have won
  Others to sin, and made my sin their door ?
Wilt thou forgive that sin which I did shun
  A year or two ; but wallowed in a score ?
    When thou hast done, thou hast not done,
      For I have more.

I have a sin of fear, that, when I have spun
  My last thread, I shall perish on the shore ;
Swear by thyself that at my death thy son
  Shall shine as he shines now, and heretofore ;
    And, having done that, thou hast done,
      I fear no more.

BEN JONSON
(1572–1637)

from
CYNTHIA'S REVELS

HYMN

Queen and huntress, chaste and fair,
Now the sun is laid to sleep,
Seated in thy silver chair,
State in wonted manner keep.
   Hesperus entreats thy light,
   Goddess, excellently bright.

Earth, let not thy envious shade
Dare itself to interpose ;
Cynthia's shining orb was made
Heaven to clear, when day did close.
   Bless us, then, with wishèd sight,
   Goddess, excellently bright.

Lay thy bow of pearl apart,
And thy crystal-shining quiver ;
Give unto the flying hart
Space to breathe, how short soever.
   Thou that mak'st a day of night,
   Goddess, excellently bright.

TWO SONGS TO CELIA

"COME, MY CELIA, LET US PROVE"

Come, my Celia, let us prove,
While we may, the sports of love.
Time will not be ours for ever ;
He, at length, our good will sever.
Spend not, then, his gifts in vain ;
Suns, that set, may rise again :
But, if once, we lose this light,
'Tis with us perpetual night.
Why should we defer our joys ?
Fame, and rumor are but toys.
Cannot we delude the eyes
Of a few poor household spies ?
Or his easier ears beguile,
So removèd by our wile ?
'Tis no sin, love's fruit to steal,
But the sweet theft to reveal :
To be taken, to be seen,
These have crimes accounted been.

"DRINK TO ME ONLY WITH THINE EYES"

Drink to me only with thine eyes,
  And I will pledge with mine ;
Or leave a kiss but in the cup,
  And I 'll not look for wine.

The thirst, that from the soul doth rise,
   Doth ask a drink divine.
But might I of Jove's nectar sup,
   I would not change for thine.

I sent thee, late, a rosy wreath,
   Not so much honoring thee,
As giving it a hope, that there
   It could not wither'd be.
But thou thereon did'st only breathe,
   And sent'st it back to me.
Since when, it grows, and smells, I swear,
   Not of itself, but thee.

from
THE MASQUE OF QUEENS

WITCHES' CHARMS

Sisters, stay ; we want our Dame.
Call upon her by her name,
And the charm we use to say,
That she quickly anoint, and come away.

I. CHARM

Dame, Dame, the watch is set.
Quickly come, we all are met.
From the lakes, and from the fens,
From the rocks, and from the dens,
From the woods, and from the caves,
From the churchyards, from the graves,

From the dungeon, from the tree
That they die on, here are we.

Come she not, yet ?
Strike another heat !

II. CHARM

The weather is fair, the wind is good ;
Up, Dame, o' your horse of wood.
Or else tuck up your grey frock,
And saddle your goat, or your green cock,
And make his bridle a bottom of thrid,
To roll up how many miles you have rid.
Quickly, come away ;
For we all stay.

Nor yet ? Nay, then,
We'll try her again !

III. CHARM

The owl is abroad, the bat, and the toad,
    And so is the cat-à-mountaine.
The ant, and the mole sit both in a hole,
    And frog peeps out o' the fountayne ;
The dogs they do bay, and the timbrels play ;
    The spindle is now a turning ;
The moon it is red, and the stars are fled,
    But all the sky is a burning.
The ditch is made, and our nails the spade,
With pictures full, of wax and of wool ;
Their livers I stick, with needles quick.

There lacks but the blood, to make up the flood.
  Quickly, Dame, then ; bring your part in ;
  Spur, spur upon little Martin ;
  Merrily, merrily, make him sail,
  A worm in his mouth, and a thorn in 's tail ;
  Fire above, and fire below,
  With a whip i' your hand to make him go.

  O, now, she 's come ;
  Let all be dumb !

from
A CELEBRATION OF CHARIS

IV. HER TRIUMPH

See the chariot at hand here of Love,
  Wherein my lady rideth !
Each that draws is a swan, or a dove,
  And well the car Love guideth.
As she goes, all hearts do duty
    Unto her beauty ;
And, enamor'd, do wish, so they might
    But enjoy such a sight,
That they still were to run by her side,
Through swords, through seas, whither she would ride.

  Do but look on her eyes, they do light
    All that Love's world compriseth !
  Do but look on her hair, it is bright
    As Love's star when it riseth !
  Do but mark, her forehead 's smoother
    Than words that soothe her !

And from her arch'd brows, such a grace
    Sheds itself through the face,
As alone there triumphs to the life,
All the gain, all the good, of the elements' strife.

Have you seen but a bright lily grow,
    Before rude hands have touch'd it ?
Ha' you mark'd but the fall o' the snow,
    Before the soil hath smutch'd it ?
Ha' you felt the wool of beaver ?
    Or swan's down ever ?
Or have smelt o' the bud o' the brier ?
    Or the nard in the fire ?
Or have tasted the bag of the bee ?
O so white ! O so soft ! O so sweet, is she !

TO THE MEMORY OF MY BELOVED
MR. WILLIAM SHAKESPEARE
AND WHAT HE HATH LEFT US

To draw no envy, Shakespeare, on thy name,
Am I thus ample to thy book and fame :
While I confess thy writings to be such,
As neither man nor Muse can praise too much.
'Tis true, and all men's suffrage. But these ways
Were not the paths I meant unto thy praise,
For seeliest ignorance on these may light,
Which, when it sounds at best, but echoes right ;
Or blind affection, which doth ne'er advance
The truth, but gropes, and urgeth all by chance ;
Or crafty malice might pretend this praise,
And think to ruin where it seemed to raise.

These are, as some infamous bawd or whore
Should praise a matron. What could hurt her more ?
But thou art proof against them, and, indeed,
Above the ill fortune of them, or the need.
I therefore will begin. Soul of the age,
The applause, delight, the wonder of our stage !
My Shakespeare, rise ! I will not lodge thee by
Chaucer, or Spenser, or bid Beaumont lie
A little further to make thee a room.
Thou art a monument without a tomb,
And art alive still, while thy book doth live,
And we have wits to read, and praise to give.
That I not mix thee so, my brain excuses —
I mean with great, but disproportioned Muses :
For, if I thought my judgment were of years,
I should commit thee surely with thy peers,
And tell how far thou didst our Lyly outshine,
Or sporting Kyd, or Marlowe's mighty line.
And though thou hadst small Latin and less Greek,
From thence to honor thee, I would not seek
For names ; but call forth thundering Aeschylus,
Euripides, and Sophocles to us,
Pacuvius, Accius, him of Cordova dead,
To life again, to hear thy buskin tread,
And shake a stage. Or, when thy socks were on,
Leave thee alone for the comparison
Of all that insolent Greece or haughty Rome
Sent forth, or since did from their ashes come.
Triumph, my Britain ; thou hast one to show,
To whom all scenes of Europe homage owe.
He was not of an age but for all time !
And all the Muses still were in their prime,
When, like Apollo, he came forth to warm

Our ears, or like a Mercury to charm !
Nature herself was proud of his designs,
And joy'd to wear the dressing of his lines,
Which were so richly spun, and woven so fit,
As, since, she will vouchsafe no other wit.
The merry Greek, tart Aristophanes,
Neat Terence, witty Plautus, now not please ;
But antiquated and deserted lie,
As they were not of Nature's family.
Yet must I not give Nature all. Thy art,
My gentle Shakespeare, must enjoy a part.
For though the poet's matter nature be,
His art doth give the fashion ; and that he
Who casts to write a living line must sweat,
(Such as thine are) and strike the second heat
Upon the Muses' anvil, turn the same,
And himself with it, that he thinks to frame,
Or for the laurel he may gain a scorn ;
For a good poet 's made as well as born.
And such wert thou. Look how the father's face
Lives in his issue ; even so the race
Of Shakespeare's mind and manners brightly shines
In his well-turnèd and true-filèd lines ;
In each of which he seems to shake a lance,
As brandish'd at the eyes of ignorance.
Sweet swan of Avon ! what a sight it were
To see thee in our waters yet appear,
And make those flights upon the banks of Thames
That so did take Eliza, and our James !
But stay, I see thee in the hemisphere
Advanc'd, and made a constellation there !
Shine forth, thou star of poets, and with rage,
Or influence, chide, or cheer the drooping stage,

Which, since thy flight from hence, hath mourn'd like night,
And despairs day, but for thy volume's light.

AN EPITAPH

ON SALATHIEL PAVY, A CHILD OF
QUEEN ELIZABETH'S CHAPEL

Weep with me, all you that read
    This little story :
And know, for whom a tear you shed,
    Death's self is sorry.
'Twas a child, that so did thrive
    In grace and feature,
As heaven and nature seem'd to strive
    Which own'd the creature.
Years he numbered scarce thirteen,
    When Fates turn'd cruel,
Yet three fill'd zodiacs had he been
    The stage's jewel ;
And did act (what now we moan)
    Old men so duly,
As, sooth, the Parcae thought him one,
    He play'd so truly.
So, by error, to his fate
    They all consented ;
But viewing him since (alas, too late)
    They have repented,
And have sought, to give new birth,
    In baths to steep him ;
But being so much too good for earth,
    Heaven vows to keep him.

THE SEVENTEENTH CENTURY

Herrick to Dryden

ROBERT HERRICK

(1591–1674)

AN ODE FOR [BEN JONSON]

Ah Ben !
Say how, or when
Shall we, thy guests,
Meet at those lyric feasts,
Made at the Sun,
The Dog, the Triple Tun ?
Where we such clusters had,
As made us nobly wild, not mad ;
And yet each verse of thine
Outdid the meat, outdid the frolic wine.

My Ben !
Or come again ;
Or send to us,
Thy wit's great overplus.
But teach us yet
Wisely to husband it ;
Lest we that talent spend.
And having once brought to an end
That precious stock ; the store
Of such a wit the world should have no more.

TO DAFFODILS

Fair daffodils, we weep to see
   You haste away so soon :
As yet the early-rising Sun
   Has not attain'd his noon.
     Stay, stay,
   Until the hasting day
     Has run
   But to the evensong ;
And, having pray'd together, we
   Will go with you along.

We have short time to stay as you ;
   We have as short a spring ;
As quick a growth to meet decay,
   As you, or anything.
     We die,
   As your hours do, and dry
     Away,
   Like to the summer's rain ;
Or as the pearls of morning's dew,
   Ne'er to be found again.

TO THE VIRGINS,
TO MAKE MUCH OF TIME

Gather ye rosebuds while ye may,
   Old Time is still a-flying ;
And this same flower that smiles to-day,
   To-morrow will be dying.

The glorious lamp of heaven, the Sun,
　The higher he 's a getting,
The sooner will his race be run,
　And nearer he 's to setting.

That age is best, which is the first,
　When youth and blood are warmer ;
But being spent, the worse, and worst
　Times, still succeed the former.

Then be not coy, but use your time ;
　And, while ye may, go marry.
For, having lost but once your prime,
　You may for ever tarry.

DELIGHT IN DISORDER

A sweet disorder in the dress
Kindles in clothes a wantonness :
A lawn about the shoulders thrown
Into a fine distraction :
An erring lace, which here and there
Enthrals the crimson stomacher :
A cuff neglectful, and thereby
Ribbands to flow confusedly :
A winning wave, deserving note,
In the tempestuous petticoat :
A careless shoe-string, in whose tie
I see a wild civility :
Do more bewitch me than when art
Is too precise in every part.

UPON JULIA'S CLOTHES

When as in silks my Julia goes,
Then, then, me thinks, how sweetly flows
That liquefaction of her clothes.

Next, when I cast mine eyes, and see
That brave vibration, each way free ;
O how that glittering taketh me !

THE NIGHT-PIECE : TO JULIA

Her eyes the glow worm lend thee ;
The shooting stars attend thee ;
   And the elves also,
   Whose little eyes glow,
Like the sparks of fire, befriend thee.

No will-o'-the-wisp mislight thee ;
Nor snake, or slow worm bite thee.
   But on, on thy way,
   Not making a stay,
Since ghost there 's none to affright thee.

Let not the dark thee cumber ;
What though the moon does slumber ?
   The stars of the night
   Will lend thee their light,
Like tapers clear without number.

Then, Julia, let me woo thee,
Thus, thus to come unto me.
   And when I shall meet
   Thy silvery feet,
My soul I 'll pour into thee.

TO ANTHEA

WHO MAY COMMAND HIM ANY THING

Bid me to live, and I will live
   Thy Protestant to be.
Or bid me love, and I will give
   A loving heart to thee :

A heart as soft, a heart as kind,
   A heart as sound and free,
As in the whole world thou canst find,
   That heart I 'll give to thee.

Bid that heart stay, and it will stay,
   To honor thy decree.
Or bid it languish quite away,
   And 't shall do so for thee.

Bid me to weep, and I will weep
   While I have eyes to see.
And having none, yet I will keep
   A heart to weep for thee.

Bid me despair, and I 'll despair,
   Under that cypress tree.

Or bid me die, and I will dare
  E'en death, to die for thee.

Thou art my life, my love, my heart,
  The very eyes of me ;
And hast command of every part,
  To live and die for thee.

ANOTHER GRACE FOR A CHILD

Here a little child I stand,
Heaving up my either hand ;
Cold as paddocks though they be,
Here I lift them up to Thee,
For a benison to fall
On our meat, and on us all. Amen.

GEORGE HERBERT

(1593–1633)

"IMMORTAL LOVE, AUTHOR OF THIS GREAT FRAME"

Immortal Love, author of this great frame,
  Sprung from that beauty which can never fade,
  How hath man parcel'd out Thy glorious name,
And thrown it on that dust which Thou hast made,
While mortal love doth all the title gain !
  Which, siding with invention, they together
  Bear all the sway, possessing heart and brain —

Thy workmanship — and give Thee share in neither.
Wit fancies beauty, beauty raiseth wit ;
   The world is theirs ; they two play out the game,
   Thou standing by. And though Thy glorious name
Wrought our deliverance from the infernal pit,
   Who sings Thy praise ? Only a scarf or glove
   Doth warm our hands, and make them write of love.

THE COLLAR

   I struck the board, and cried, "No more ;
   I will abroad !
   What, shall I ever sigh and pine ?
My lines and life are free ; free as the road,
   Loose as the wind, as large as store.
         Shall I be still in suit ?
   Have I no harvest but a thorn
   To let me blood, and not restore
What I have lost with cordial fruit ?
         Sure there was wine
      Before my sighs did dry it ; there was corn
      Before my tears did drown it.
Is the year only lost to me ?
      Have I no bays to crown it,
No flowers, no garlands gay ? All blasted,
         All wasted ?
   Not so, my heart ! But there is fruit,
         And thou hast hands.
      Recover all thy sigh-blown age
On double pleasures ; leave thy cold dispute
Of what is fit and not ; forsake thy cage,
         Thy rope of sands,

Which petty thoughts have made, and made to thee
   Good cable, to enforce and draw,
       And be thy law,
  While thou didst wink and wouldst not see.
       Away ! Take heed !
       I will abroad !
Call in thy death's head there ; tie up thy fears ;
       He that forbears
   To suit and serve his need
     Deserves his load."
But as I rav'd, and grew more fierce and wild
      At every word,
  Me thoughts I heard one calling, "Child !"
     And I replied, "My Lord."

THE PULLEY

     When God at first made man,
  Having a glass of blessings standing by,
    "Let us," said He, "pour on him all we can ;
  Let the world's riches, which dispersèd lie,
     Contract into a span."

     So strength first made a way ;
  Then beauty flow'd, then wisdom, honor, pleasure ;
    When almost all was out, God made a stay,
  Perceiving that, alone of all His treasure,
     Rest in the bottom lay.

     "For if I should," said He,
  "Bestow this jewel also on My creature,
    He would adore My gifts instead of Me,

And rest in nature, not the God of nature :
    So both should losers be.

    "Yet let him keep the rest,
But keep them with repining restlessness.
    Let him be rich and weary, that at least,
If goodness lead him not, yet weariness
    May toss him to My breast."

VIRTUE

    Sweet day, so cool, so calm, so bright,
      The bridal of the earth and sky ;
    The dew shall weep thy fall to-night,
      For thou must die.

    Sweet rose, whose hue, angry and brave,
      Bids the rash gazer wipe his eye ;
    Thy root is ever in its grave,
      And thou must die.

    Sweet spring, full of sweet days and roses,
      A box where sweets compacted lie ;
    My music shows ye have your closes,
      And all must die.

    Only a sweet and virtuous soul,
      Like season'd timber, never gives ;
    But though the whole world turn to coal,
      Then chiefly lives.

THOMAS CAREW

(1594 or 1595–1639 ?)

SONG

Ask me no more where Jove bestows,
When June is past, the fading rose ;
For in your beauty's orient deep
These flowers, as in their causes, sleep.

Ask me no more whither doth stray
The golden atoms of the day ;
For in pure love heaven did prepare
Those powders to enrich your hair.

Ask me no more whither doth haste
The nightingale when May is past ;
For in your sweet dividing throat
She winters, and keeps warm her note.

Ask me no more where those stars light
That downwards fall in dead of night ;
For in your eyes they sit, and there
Fixèd become as in their sphere.

Ask me no more if east or west
The phoenix builds her spicy nest ;
For unto you at last she flies,
And in your fragrant bosom dies.

JOHN MILTON

(1608–1674)

ON THE MORNING OF CHRIST'S NATIVITY

I

This is the month, and this the happy morn,
Wherein the Son of Heav'ns eternal King,
Of wedded maid and virgin mother born,
Our great redemption from above did bring ;
For so the holy sages once did sing,
   That He our deadly forfeit should release,
And with His Father work us a perpetual peace.

II

That glorious Form, that Light unsufferable,
And that far-beaming blaze of Majesty,
Wherewith He wont at Heav'ns high council-table,
To sit the midst of Trinal Unity,
He laid aside ; and here with us to be,
   Forsook the courts of everlasting day,
And chose with us a darksome house of mortal clay.

III

Say Heav'nly Muse, shall not thy sacred vein
Afford a present to the Infant God ?
Hast thou no verse, no hymn, or solemn strain,
To welcome Him to this His new abode,
Now while the Heav'n, by the Sun's team untrod,

Hath took no print of the approaching light,
And all the spangled host keep watch in squadrons bright ?

IV

See how from far upon the eastern road
The star-led wizards haste with odours sweet.
O run, prevent them with thy humble ode,
And lay it lowly at His blessed feet ;
Have thou the honour first, thy Lord to greet,
   And join thy voice unto the angel quire,
From out His secret altar toucht with hallow'd fire.

THE HYMN

I

It was the winter wild,
While the Heav'n-born-Child,
   All meanly wrapt in the rude manger lies ;
Nature in awe to Him
Had doff't her gaudy trim,
   With her great Master so to sympathize :
It was no season then for her
To wanton with the sun, her lusty paramour.

II

Only with speeches fair
She woos the gentle air
   To hide her guilty front with innocent snow,
And on her naked shame,
Pollute with sinful blame,
   The saintly veil of maiden white to throw,

Confounded, that her Maker's eyes
Should look so near upon her foul deformities.

III

But he, her fears to cease,
Sent down the meek-ey'd Peace ;
   She crown'd with olive green, came softly sliding
Down through the turning sphere,
His ready harbinger,
   With turtle wing the amorous clouds dividing,
And waving wide her myrtle wand,
She strikes a universal peace through sea and land.

IV

No war or battle's sound
Was heard the world around,
   The idle spear and shield were high up hung ;
The hooked chariot stood
Unstain'd with hostile blood ;
   The trumpet spake not to the armed throng,
And kings sat still with awful eye,
As if they surely knew their sovran Lord was by.

V

But peaceful was the night
Wherein the Prince of Light
   His reign of peace upon the earth began :
The winds, with wonder whist,
Smoothly the waters kiss't,
   Whispering new joys to the mild Ocean,
Who now hath quite forgot to rave,
While birds of calm sit brooding on the charmed wave.

VI

The stars with deep amaze
Stand fixt in steadfast gaze,
  Bending one way their precious influence,
And will not take their flight,
For all the morning light,
  Or Lucifer that often warn'd them thence ;
But in their glimmering orbs did glow,
Until their Lord himself bespake, and bid them go.

VII

And though the shady gloom
Had given day her room,
  The sun himself withheld his wonted speed,
And hid his head for shame,
As his inferior flame,
  The new-enlightn'd world no more should need ;
He saw a greater sun appear
Than his bright throne or burning axle-tree could bear.

VIII

The shepherds on the lawn,
Or ere the point of dawn,
  Sat simply chatting in a rustic row ;
Full little thought they than
That the mighty Pan
  Was kindly come to live with them below ;
Perhaps their loves or else their sheep,
Was all that did their silly thoughts so busy keep.

IX

When such music sweet
Their hearts and ears did greet,
   As never was by mortal finger strook,
Divinely warbled voice
Answering the stringed noise,
   As all their souls in blissful rapture took.
The air such pleasure loth to lose,
With thousand echoes still prolongs each heav'nly close.

X

Nature that heard such sound
Beneath the hollow round
   Of Cynthia's seat, the airy region thrilling,
Now was almost won
To think her part was done,
   And that her reign had here its last fulfilling ;
She knew such harmony alone
Could hold all Heav'n and Earth in happier union.

XI

At last surrounds their sight
A Globe of circular light,
   That with long beams the shame-fac't night array'd,
The helmed cherubim
And sworded seraphim
   'Are seen in glittering ranks with wings display'd,
Harping in loud and solemn quire,
With unexpressive notes to Heav'ns new-born Heir.

XII

Such Music (as 'tis said)
Before was never made,
  But when of old the sons of morning sung,
While the Creator great
His constellations set,
  And the well-balanc't world on hinges hung,
And cast the dark foundations deep,
And bid the weltring waves their oozy channel keep.

XIII

Ring out, ye crystal spheres,
Once bless our human ears,
  (If ye have power to touch our senses so)
And let your silver chime
Move in melodious time ;
  And let the bass of Heav'ns deep organ blow ;
And with your ninefold harmony
Make up full consort to th' angelic symphony.

XIV

For if such holy song
Enwrap our fancy long,
  Time will run back and fetch the age of gold,
And speckl'd vanity
Will sicken soon, and die,
  And leprous sin will melt from earthly mould,
And Hell itself will pass away
And leave her dolorous mansions to the peering day.

XV

Yea, Truth and Justice then
Will down return to men,
   Orb'd in a rainbow ; and, like glories wearing,
Mercy will sit between,
Thron'd in celestial sheen,
   With radiant feet the tissued clouds down steering,
And Heav'n as at some festival,
Will open wide the gates of her high palace hall.

XVI

But wisest Fate says no,
This must not yet be so,
   The Babe lies yet in smiling Infancy,
That on the bitter cross
Must redeem our loss ;
   So both himself and us to glorify :
Yet first to those ychain'd in sleep,
The wakeful trump of doom must thunder through the
    deep,

XVII

With such a horrid clang
As on mount Sinai rang
   While the red fire, and smould'ring clouds out brake ;
The aged Earth aghast
With terror of that blast,
   Shall from the surface to the centre shake ;
When at the world's last session,
The dreadful Judge in middle air shall spread his throne.

XVIII

And then at last our bliss
Full and perfect is,
  But now begins ; for from this happy day
Th' old Dragon under ground
In straiter limits bound,
  Not half so far casts his usurped sway,
And wrath to see his kingdom fail,
Swinges the scaly horror of his folded tail.

XIX

The Oracles are dumb,
No voice or hideous hum
  Runs through the arched roof in words deceiving.
Apollo from his shrine
Can no more divine,
  With hollow shriek the steep of Delphos leaving.
No nightly trance, or breathed spell,
Inspires the pale-ey'd priest from the prophetic cell.

XX

The lonely mountains o'er,
And the resounding shore,
  A voice of weeping heard, and loud lament ;
From haunted spring and dale,
Edg'd with poplar pale,
  The parting Genius is with sighing sent ;
With flow'r-inwov'n tresses torn
The Nymphs in twilight shade of tangled thickets mourn.

XXI

In consecrated earth,
And on the holy hearth,

The Lars, and Lemures moan with midnight plaint ;
In urns and altars round,
A drear and dying sound
   Affrights the Flamens at their service quaint ;
And the chill marble seems to sweat,
While each peculiar power forgoes his wonted seat.

XXII

Peor and Baalim
·Forsake their temples dim,
   With that twice-batter'd god of Palestine;
And mooned Ashtaroth,
Heav'ns queen and mother both,
   Now sits not girt with tapers' holy shine ;
The Libyc Hammon shrinks his horn,
In vain the Tyrian maids their wounded Thammuz mourn.

XXIII

And Sullen Moloch fled,
Hath left in shadows dread,
   His burning Idol all of blackest hue ;
In vain with cymbals' ring
They call the grisly king,
   In dismal dance about the furnace blue ;
The brutish gods of Nile as fast,
Isis and Orus, and the Dog Anubis haste.

XXIV

Nor is Osiris seen
In Memphian grove or green,
   Trampling the unshowr'd grass with lowings loud :
Nor can he be at rest

Within his sacred chest,
   Naught but profoundest Hell can be his shroud ;
In vain with timbrel'd anthems dark
The sable-stoled sorcerers bear his worshipt ark.

XXV

He feels from Juda's Land
The dreaded Infant's hand,
   The rays of Bethlehem blind his dusky eyn ;
Nor all the gods beside,
Longer dare abide,
   Nor Typhon huge ending in snaky twine ;
Our Babe, to show his Godhead true,
Can in his swaddling bands control the damnèd crew.

XXVI

So when the sun in bed,
Curtain'd with cloudy red,
   Pillows his chin upon an orient wave,
The flocking shadows pale
   Troop to th' infernal jail,
   Each fetter'd ghost slips to his several grave,
And the yellow-skirted fays
Fly after the night-steeds, leaving their moon-lov'd maze.

XXVII

But see, the Virgin blest,
Hath laid her Babe to rest.
   Time is our tedious song should here have ending,
Heav'ns youngest teemed star
Hath fixt her polisht car,
   Her sleeping Lord with handmaid lamp attending ;

And all about the courtly stable,
Bright-harness'd angels sit in order serviceable.

"HOW SOON HATH TIME,
THE SUBTLE THIEF OF YOUTH"

How soon hath Time, the subtle thief of youth,
    Stol'n on his wing my three-and-twentieth year !
    My hasting days fly on with full career,
    But my late spring no bud or blossom shew'th.
Perhaps my semblance might deceive the truth
    That I to manhood am arriv'd so near,
    And inward ripeness doth much less appear,
    That some more timely-happy spirits endu'th.
Yet be it less or more, or soon or slow,
    It shall be still in strictest measure eev'n
    To that same lot, however mean, or high,
Toward which Time leads me, and the will of Heav'n ;
    All is, if I have grace to use it so,
    As ever in my great task Master's eye.

LYCIDAS

In this Monody the Author bewails a learned Friend, unfortunately
drown'd in his Passage from *Chester* on the *Irish* Seas, 1637. And by occa-
sion foretells the ruine of our corrupted Clergy then in their height.

Yet once more, O ye Laurels, and once more
Ye Myrtles brown, with Ivy never-sere,
I come to pluck your Berries harsh and crude,
And with forc'd fingers rude,
Shatter your leaves before the mellowing year.
Bitter constraint, and sad occasion dear,

Compels me to disturb your season due :
For *Lycidas* is dead, dead ere his prime
Young *Lycidas*, and hath not left his peer :
Who would not sing for *Lycidas* ? he knew
Himself to sing, and build the lofty rhyme.
He must not float upon his watry bier
Unwept, and welter to the parching wind,
Without the meed of some melodious tear.

Begin then, Sisters of the sacred well,
That from beneath the seat of *Jove* doth spring,
Begin, and somewhat loudly sweep the string.
Hence with denial vain, and coy excuse,
So may some gentle Muse
With lucky words favour my destin'd Urn,
And as he passes turn,
And bid fair peace be to my sable shrowd.
For we were nurst upon the self-same hill,
Fed the same flock, by fountain, shade, and rill.

Together both, ere the high Lawns appear'd
Under the opening eye-lids of the morn,
We drove a field, and both together heard
What time the Gray-fly winds her sultry horn,
Batt'ning our flocks with the fresh dews of night,
Oft till the Star that rose, at Ev'ning, bright
Toward Heav'ns descent had slop'd his westering wheel.
Mean while the Rural ditties were not mute,
Temper'd to th'Oaten Flute ;
Rough *Satyrs* danc'd, and *Fauns* with clov'n heel,
From the glad sound would not be absent long,
And old *Damaetas* lov'd to hear our song.

But O the heavy change, now thou art gone,
Now thou art gone, and never must return !
Thee Shepherd, thee the Woods, and desert Caves,

With wild Thyme and the gadding Vine o'ergrown,
And all their echoes mourn.
The Willows, and the Hazel Copses green,
Shall now no more be seen,
Fanning their joyous Leaves to thy soft lays.
As killing as the Canker to the Rose,
Or Taint-worm to the weanling Herds that graze,
Or Frost to Flowers, that their gay wardrop wear,
When first the White thorn blows —
Such, *Lycidas*, thy loss to Shepherd's ear.

Where were ye Nymphs when the remorseless deep
Clos'd o're the head of your lov'd *Lycidas?*
For neither were ye playing on the steep,
Where your old *Bards*, the famous *Druids* lie,
Nor on the shaggy top of *Mona* high,
Nor yet where *Deva* spreads her wizard stream :
Ay me, I fondly dream !
Had ye been there — for what could that have done ?
What could the Muse her self that *Orpheus* bore,
The Muse her self, for her inchanting son
Whom Universal nature did lament,
When by the rout that made the hideous roar,
His gory visage down the stream was sent,
Down the swift *Hebrus* to the *Lesbian* shore.

Alas ! What boots it with uncessant care
To tend the homely slighted Shepherd's trade,
And strictly meditate the thankless Muse ?
Were it not better done as others use,
To sport with *Amaryllis* in the shade,
Or with the tangles of *Neaera's* hair ?
Fame is the spur that the clear spirit doth raise
(That last infirmity of Noble mind)
To scorn delights, and live laborious days ;

But the fair Guerdon when we hope to find,
And think to burst out into sudden blaze,
Comes the blind *Fury* with th'abhorred shears,
And slits the thin-spun life. — But not the praise,
Phoebus repli'd, and touch'd my trembling ears ;
Fame is no plant that grows on mortal soil,
Nor in the glistering foil
Set off to th'world, nor in broad rumour lies,
But lives and spreads aloft by those pure eyes
And perfet witness of all judging *Jove* ;
As he pronounces lastly on each deed,
Of so much fame in Heav'n expect thy meed.

O Fountain *Arethuse*, and thou honour'd flood,
Smooth-sliding *Mincius,* crown'd with vocal reeds,
That strain I heard was of a higher mood :
But now my Oat proceeds,
And listens to the Herald of the Sea
That came in *Neptune's* plea.
He ask'd the Waves, and ask'd the Felon winds,
What hard mishap hath doom'd this gentle swain ?
And question'd every gust of rugged wings
That blows from off each beaked Promontory —
They knew not of his story,
And sage *Hippotades* their answer brings,
That not a blast was from his dungeon stray'd,
The Air was calm, and on the level brine,
Sleek *Panope* with all her sisters play'd.
It was that fatal and perfidious Bark,
Built in th'eclipse, and rigg'd with curses dark,
That sunk so low that sacred head of thine.

Next *Camus,* reverend Sire, went footing slow,
His Mantle hairy, and his Bonnet sedge,
Inwrought with figures dim, and on the edge

Like to that sanguine flower inscrib'd with woe.
Ah ! Who hath reft (quoth he) my dearest pledge ?
Last came, and last did go,
The Pilot of the *Galilean* lake.
Two massy Keys he bore of metals twain,
(The Golden opes, the Iron shuts amain).
He shook his Miter'd locks, and stern bespake,
How well could I have spar'd for thee, young swain,
Anow of such as for their bellies' sake,
Creep and intrude, and climb into the fold ?
Of other care they little reck'ning make,
Than how to scramble at the shearers' feast,
And shove away the worthy bidden guest.
Blind mouths ! that scarce themselves know how to hold
A Sheep-hook, or have learn'd aught else the least
That to the faithful Herdman's art belongs !
What recks it them ? What need they ? They are sped ;
And when they list, their lean and flashy songs
Grate on their scrannel Pipes of wretched straw,
The hungry Sheep look up, and are not fed,
But swoln with wind, and the rank mist they draw,
Rot inwardly, and foul contagion spread :
Besides what the grim Wolf with privy paw
Daily devours apace, and nothing said ;
But that two-handed engine at the door,
Stands ready to smite once, and smite no more.
Return *Alpheus*, the dread voice is past,
That shrunk thy streams ; Return *Sicilian* Muse,
And call the Vales, and bid them hither cast
Their Bells, and Flourets of a thousand hues.
Ye valleys low where the mild whispers use,
Of shades and wanton winds, and gushing brooks,
On whose fresh lap the swart Star sparely looks,

Throw hither all your quaint enameld eyes,
That on the green turf suck the honied showres,
And purple all the ground with vernal flowers.
Bring the rathe Primrose that forsaken dies,
The tufted Crow-toe, and pale Gessamine,
The white Pink, and the Pansie freakt with jet,
The glowing Violet.
The Musk-rose, and the well attir'd Woodbine,
With Cowslips wan that hang the pensive head,
And every flower that sad embroidery wears :
Bid *Amaranthus* all his beauty shed,
And Daffadillies fill their cups with tears,
To strew the Laureat Herse where *Lycid* lies.
For so to interpose a little ease,
Let our frail thoughts dally with false surmise.
Ay me ! Whilst thee the shores, and sounding Seas
Wash far away, where ere thy bones are hurld,
Whether beyond the stormy Hebrides,
Where thou perhaps under the whelming tide
Visit'st the bottom of the monstrous world ;
Or whether thou to our moist vows deny'd,
Sleep'st by the fable of *Bellerus* old,
Where the great vision of the guarded Mount
Looks toward *Namancos* and *Bayona's* hold ;
Look homeward Angel now, and melt with ruth.
And, O ye *Dolphins*, waft the haples youth.
    Weep no more, woeful Shepherds weep no more.
For *Lycidas* your sorrow is not dead,
Sunk though he be beneath the watry floor,
So sinks the day-star in the Ocean bed,
And yet anon repairs his drooping head,
And tricks his beams, and with new spangled Ore,
Flames in the forehead of the morning sky :

So *Lycidas* sunk low, but mounted high,
Through the dear might of him that walk'd the waves,
Where other groves, and other streams along,
With *Nectar* pure his oozy Locks he laves,
And hears the unexpressive nuptial Song,
In the blest Kingdoms meek of joy and love.
There entertain him all the Saints above,
In solemn troops, and sweet Societies
That sing, and singing in their glory move,
And wipe the tears for ever from his eyes.
Now *Lycidas* the Shepherds weep no more ;
Hence forth thou art the Genius of the shore,
In thy large recompense, and shalt be good
To all that wander in that perilous flood.
  Thus sang the uncouth Swain to th'Oaks and rills,
While the still morn went out with Sandals gray.
He touch'd the tender stops of various Quills,
With eager thought warbling his *Doric* lay :
And now the Sun had stretch'd out all the hills,
And now was dropt into the Western bay ;
At last he rose, and twitch'd his Mantle blue :
To-morrow to fresh Woods, and Pastures new.

ON THE LATE MASSACRE IN PIEMONT

Avenge O Lord thy slaughter'd Saints, whose bones
  Lie scatter'd on the Alpine mountains cold,
  Ev'n them who kept thy truth so pure of old
  When all our Fathers worship't Stocks and Stones,
Forget not : in thy book record their groans
  Who were thy Sheep and in their ancient Fold
  Slain by the bloody *Piemontese* that roll'd

Mother with Infant down the Rocks. Their moans
The Vales redoubl'd to the Hills, and they
    To Heav'n. Their martyr'd blood and ashes sow
O're all th'*Italian* fields where still doth sway
The triple Tyrant : that from these may grow
    A hundred-fold, who having learnt thy way
    Early may fly the *Babylonian* woe.

"WHEN I CONSIDER
HOW MY LIGHT IS SPENT"

When I consider how my light is spent,
    Ere half my days, in this dark world and wide,
    And that one Talent which is death to hide,
    Lodg'd with me useless, though my Soul more bent
To serve therewith my Maker, and present
    My true account, lest he returning chide —
    Doth God exact day-labour, light deny'd,
    I fondly ask ; But patience to prevent
That murmur, soon replies, God doth not need
    Either man's work or his own gifts, who best
    Bear his mild yoke, they serve him best, his State
Is Kingly. Thousands at his bidding speed
    And post o're Land and Ocean without rest :
    They also serve who only stand and wait.

"METHOUGHT I SAW MY LATE
ESPOUSED SAINT"

Methought I saw my late espoused Saint
    Brought to me like *Alcestis* from the grave,

Whom *Jove's* great Son to her glad Husband gave,
  Rescu'd from death by force though pale and faint.
Mine as whom washt from spot of child-bed taint,
  Purification in the old Law did save,
  And such, as yet once more I trust to have
Full sight of her in Heaven without restraint,
Came vested all in white, pure as her mind :
  Her face was veil'd, yet to my fancied sight,
  Love, sweetness, goodness, in her person shin'd
So clear, as in no face with more delight.
  But O as to embrace me she inclin'd
  I wak'd, she fled, and day brought back my night.

closing passages from
SAMSON AGONISTES

Chorus. O dearly-bought revenge, yet glorious !
Living or dying thou hast fulfill'd
The work for which thou wast foretold
To *Israel,* and now ly'st victorious
Among thy slain self-kill'd
Not willingly, but tangl'd in the fold
Of dire necessity, whose law in death conjoin'd
Thee with thy slaughter'd foes in number more
Than all thy life had slain before.
Semichorus. While thir hearts were jocund and sublime,
Drunk with Idolatry, drunk with Wine,
And fat regorg'd of Bulls and goats,
Chaunting thir Idol, and preferring
Before our living Dread who dwells
In *Silo* his bright Sanctuary :
Among them he a spirit of phrenzy sent,

Who hurt thir minds,
And urg'd them on with mad desire
To call in haste for thir destroyer ;
They only set on sport and play
Unweetingly importun'd
Thir own destruction to come speedy upon them.
So fond are mortal men
Fall'n into wrath divine,
As thir own ruin on themselves to invite,
Insensate left, or to sense reprobate,
And with blindness internal struck.
    Semichorus. But he though blind of sight,
Despis'd and thought extinguish't quite,
With inward eyes illuminated
His fierie virtue rous'd
From under ashes into sudden flame,
And as an ev'ning Dragon came,
Assailant on the perched roosts,
And nests in order rang'd
Of tame villatic Fowl ; but as an Eagle
His cloudless thunder bolted on thir heads.
So virtue giv'n for lost,
Deprest, and overthrown, as seem'd,
Like that self-begott'n bird
In the *Arabian* woods embost,
That no second knows nor third,
And lay e're while a Holocaust,
From out her ashy womb now teem'd,
Revives, reflourishes, then vigorous most
When most unactive deem'd,
And though her body die, her fame survives,
A secular bird ages of lives.
    Manoa. Come, come, no time for lamentation now,

Nor much more cause, *Samson* hath quit himself
Like *Samson*, and heroicly hath finish'd
A life Heroic, on his Enemies
Fully reveng'd, hath left them years of mourning,
And lamentation to the Sons of *Caphtor*
Through all *Philistian* bounds. To *Israel*
Honour hath left, and freedom, let but them
Find courage to lay hold on this occasion ;
To himself and Father's house eternal fame ;
And which is best and happiest yet, all this
With God not parted from him, as was feard,
But favouring and assisting to the end.
Nothing is here for tears, nothing to wail
Or knock the breast, no weakness, no contempt,
Dispraise, or blame, nothing but well and fair,
And what may quiet us in a death so noble.
Let us go find the body where it lies
Soak't in his enemies' blood, and from the stream
With lavers pure and cleansing herbs wash off
The clotted gore. I with what speed the while
(*Gaza* is not in plight to say us nay)
Will send for all my kindred, all my friends
To fetch him hence and solemnly attend
With silent obsequie and funeral train
Home to his Father's house : there will I build him
A Monument, and plant it round with shade
Of Laurel ever green, and branching Palm,
With all his Trophies hung, and Acts enroll'd
In copious Legend, or sweet Lyric Song.
Thither shall all the valiant youth resort,
And from his memory inflame thir breasts
To matchless valour, and adventures high :
The Virgins also shall on feastful days

Visit his Tomb with flowers, only bewailing
His lot unfortunate in nuptial choice,
From whence captivity and loss of eyes.
   Chorus. All is best, though we oft doubt,
What th' unsearchable dispose
Of highest wisdom brings about,
And ever best found in the close.
Oft he seems to hide his face,
But unexpectedly returns
And to his faithful Champion hath in place
Bore witness gloriously ; whence *Gaza* mourns
And all that band them to resist
His uncontrollable intent,
His servants he with new acquist
Of true experience from this great event
With peace and consolation hath dismist,
And calm of mind all passion spent.

SIR JOHN SUCKLING

(1609–1642)

SONG

Why so pale and wan, fond lover ?
   Prithee, why so pale ?
Will, when looking well can't move her,
   Looking ill prevail ?
   Prithee, why so pale ?

Why so dull and mute, young sinner ?
   Prithee, why so mute ?

Will, when speaking well can't win her,
   Saying nothing do 't ?
   Prithee, why so mute ?

Quit, quit, for shame ! This will not move,
   This cannot take her.
If of herself she will not love,
   Nothing can make her.
   The devil take her !

"OUT UPON IT ! I HAVE LOVED"

Out upon it ! I have loved
   Three whole days together ;
And am like to love three more,
   If it prove fair weather.

Time shall molt away his wings,
   Ere he shall discover,
In the whole wide world again,
   Such a constant lover.

But the spite on 't is, no praise
   Is due at all to me.
Love with me had made no stays,
   Had it any been but she.

Had it any been but she,
   And that very face,
There had been at least ere this
   A dozen dozen in her place.

RICHARD CRASHAW

(1612–1649)

from
THE FLAMING HEART

Upon the book and picture of the seraphical Saint Teresa, as she is
usually expressed with a seraphim beside her

O heart ! the equal poise of love's both parts,
Big alike with wounds and darts.
Live in these conquering leaves ; live all the same,
And walk through all tongues one triumphant flame ;
Live here, great heart, and love and die and kill,
And bleed and wound, and yield and conquer still.
Let this immortal life, where'er it comes,
Walk in a crowd of loves and martyrdoms.
Let mystic deaths wait on 't, and wise souls be
The love-slain witnesses of this life of thee.
O sweet incendiary ! show here thy art,
Upon this carcass of a hard, cold heart,
Let all thy scatter'd shafts of light, that play
Among the leaves of thy large books of day,
Combin'd against this breast, at once break in
And take away from me my self and sin ;
This gracious robbery shall thy bounty be,
And my best fortunes such fair spoils of me.
O thou undaunted daughter of desires !
By all thy dower of lights and fires ;
By all the eagle in thee, all the dove ;
By all thy lives and deaths of love ;
By thy large draughts of intellectual day,

And by thy thirsts of love more large than they ;
By all thy brim-fill'd bowls of fierce desire,
By thy last morning's draught of liquid fire ;
By the full kingdom of that final kiss
That seiz'd thy parting soul, and sealed thee his ;
By all the heav'ns thou hast in him,
Fair sister of the seraphim !
By all of him we have in thee ;
Leave nothing of myself in me.
Let me so read thy life, that I
Unto all life of mine may die.

A SONG

Lord, when the sense of thy sweet grace
Sends up my soul to seek thy face :
Thy blessèd eyes breed such desire,
I die in love's delicious fire.
   O love, I am thy sacrifice.
Be still triumphant, blessèd eyes :
Still shine on me, fair suns ! that I
Still may behold, though still I die.

Though still I die, I live again,
Still longing so to be still slain ;
So gainful is such loss of breath,
I die even in desire of death.
   Still live in me this loving strife
Of living death and dying life :
For while thou sweetly slayest me
Dead to myself, I live in thee.

RICHARD LOVELACE

(1618–1656 or 1657)

TO ALTHEA, FROM PRISON

When Love with unconfinèd wings
　　Hovers within my gates,
And my divine Althea brings
　　To whisper at the grates ;
When I lie tangled in her hair,
　　And fettered to her eye,
The gods that wanton in the air
　　Know no such liberty.

When flowing cups run swiftly round,
　　With no allaying Thames,
Our careless heads with roses bound,
　　Our hearts with loyal flames ;
When thirsty grief in wine we steep,
　　When healths and draughts go free,
Fishes that tipple in the deep
　　Know no such liberty.

When, like committed linnets, I
　　With shriller throat shall sing
The sweetness, mercy, majesty,
　　And glories of my king ;
When I shall voice aloud, how good
　　He is, how great should be,
Enlargèd winds that curl the flood
　　Know no such liberty.

Stone walls do not a prison make,
    Nor iron bars a cage ;
Minds innocent and quiet take
    That for an hermitage ;
If I have freedom in my love,
    And in my soul am free,
Angels alone, that soar above
    Enjoy such liberty.

TO LUCASTA.
GOING TO THE WARS

Tell me not, sweet, I am unkind,
    That from the nunnery
Of thy chaste breast and quiet mind,
    To war and arms I fly.

True, a new mistress now I chase,
    The first foe in the field ;
And with a stronger faith embrace
    A sword, a horse, a shield.

Yet this inconstancy is such
    As you too shall adore —
I could not love thee, dear, so much,
    Lov'd I not honor more.

ANDREW MARVELL

(1621–1678)

BERMUDAS

Where the remote Bermudas ride
In th' ocean's bosom unespy'd,
From a small boat that rowed along,
The list'ning winds receiv'd this song :

"What should we do but sing His praise,
That led us through the watery maze,
Unto an isle so long unknown,
And yet far kinder than our own ?
Where He the huge sea-monsters wracks,
That lift the deep upon their backs.
He lands us on a grassy stage,
Safe from the storms, and prelate's rage.
He gave us this eternal spring,
Which here enamels everything,
And sends the fowls to us in care,
On daily visits through the air.
He hangs in shades the orange bright,
Like golden lamps in a green night,
And does in the pomgranates close
Jewels more rich than Ormus shows.
He makes the figs our mouths to meet,
And throws the melons at our feet.
But apples plants of such a price,
No tree could ever bear them twice.

With cedars, chosen by His hand,
From Lebanon, He stores the land,
And makes the hollow seas, that roar,
Proclaim the ambergris on shore.
He cast (of which we rather boast)
The gospel's pearl upon our coast,
And in these rocks for us did frame
A temple, where to sound His name.
Oh let our voice His praise exalt,
Till it arrive at heaven's vault,
Which thence, perhaps, rebounding, may
Echo beyond the Mexique Bay."

    Thus sung they, in the English boat,
An holy and a cheerful note ;
And all the way, to guide their chime,
With falling oars they kept the time.

THE GARDEN

How vainly men themselves amaze
To win the palm, the oak, or bays,
And their incessant labors see
Crown'd from some single herb or tree,
Whose short and narrow vergèd shade
Does prudently their toils upbraid ;
While all flow'rs and all trees do close
To weave the garlands of repose.

Fair Quiet, have I found thee here,
And Innocence, thy sister dear !
Mistaken long, I sought you then

In busy companies of men.
Your sacred plants, if here below,
Only among the plants will grow.
Society is all but rude,
To this delicious solitude.

No white nor red was ever seen
So am'rous as this lovely green.
Fond lovers, cruel as their flame,
Cut in these trees their mistress' name ;
Little, Alas, they know, or heed,
How far these beauties hers exceed !
Fair trees, where s'eer your barks I wound
No name shall but your own be found.

When we have run our passion's heat,
Love hither makes his best retreat.
The gods that mortal beauty chase,
Still in a tree did end their race :
Apollo hunted Daphne so,
Only that she might laurel grow ;
And Pan did after Syrinx speed,
Not as a nymph, but for a reed.

What wond'rous life in this I lead !
Ripe apples drop about my head ;
The luscious clusters of the vine
Upon my mouth do crush their wine ;
The nectaren and curious peach
Into my hands themselves do reach ;
Stumbling on melons, as I pass,
Insnar'd with flowers, I fall on grass.

Meanwhile the mind, from pleasure less,
Withdraws into its happiness ;
The mind, that ocean where each kind
Does straight its own resemblance find,
Yet it creates, transcending these,
Far other worlds and other seas,
Annihilating all that 's made
To a green thought in a green shade.

Here at the fountain's sliding foot,
Or at some fruit tree's mossy root,
Casting the body's vest aside,
My soul into the boughs does glide ;
There, like a bird, it sits and sings,
Then whets and combs its silver wings,
And till prepared for longer flight,
Waves in its plumes the various light.

Such was that happy garden-state,
While man there walked without a mate ;
After a place so pure and sweet,
What other help could yet be meet !
But 'twas beyond a mortal's share
To wander solitary there :
Two paradises 'twere, in one,
To live in paradise alone.

How well the skilful gardner drew
Of flowers and herbs this dial new,
Where, from above, the milder sun
Does through a fragrant zodiac run ;
And as it works, th' industrious bee

Computes its time as well as we.
How could such sweet and wholesome hours
Be reckon'd but with herbs and flow'rs ?

TO HIS COY MISTRESS

Had we but world enough, and time,
This coyness, lady, were no crime.
We would sit down, and think which way
To walk, and pass our long love's day.
Thou by the Indian Ganges' side
Should'st rubies find ; I by the tide
Of Humber would complain. I would
Love you ten years before the flood,
And you should, if you please, refuse
Till the conversion of the Jews.
My vegetable love should grow
Vaster than empires, and more slow ;
An hundred years should go to praise
Thine eyes, and on thy forehead gaze ;
Two hundred to adore each breast,
But thirty thousand to the rest.
An age at least to every part,
And the last age should show your heart.
For, lady, you deserve this state,
Nor would I love at lower rate.
   But at my back I always hear
Time's wingèd chariot hurrying near :
And yonder all before us lie
Deserts of vast eternity.
Thy beauty shall no more be found,
Nor in thy marble vault shall sound

My echoing song ; then worms shall try
That long preserv'd virginity,
And your quaint honor turn to dust,
And into ashes all my lust.
The grave's a fine and private place,
But none, I think, do there embrace.
　　Now therefore, while the youthful hue
Sits on thy skin like morning glew,
And while thy willing soul transpires
At every pore with instant fires,
Now let us sport us while we may,
And now, like am'rous birds of prey,
Rather at once our time devour
Than languish in his slow-chapt pow'r.
Let us roll all our strength, and all
Our sweetness, up into one ball,
And tear our pleasures with rough strife
Thorough the iron gates of life.
Thus, though we cannot make our sun
Stand still, yet we will make him run.

HENRY VAUGHAN

(1622–1695)

THE RETREAT

Happy those early days, when I
Shin'd in my angel-infancy !
Before I understood this place
Appointed for my second race,
Or taught my soul to fancy aught

But a white, celestial thought ;
When yet I had not walkt above
A mile or two from my first love,
And looking back (at that short space)
Could see a glimpse of His bright face ;
When on some gilded cloud, or flower,
My gazing soul would dwell an hour,
And in those weaker glories spy
Some shadows of eternity ;
Before I taught my tongue to wound
My conscience with a sinful sound,
Or had the black art to dispense
A sev'ral sin to ev'ry sense,
But felt through all this fleshly dress
Bright shoots of everlastingness.
O how I long to travel back,
And tread again that ancient track !
That I might once more reach that plain,
Where first I left my glorious train,
From whence th' enlightned spirit sees
That shady City of Palm Trees ;
But, ah ! my soul with too much stay
Is drunk, and staggers in the way :
Some men a forward motion love,
But I by backward steps would move,
And when this dust falls to the urn,
In that state I came return.

THE WATER FALL

With what deep murmurs through time's silent stealth
Doth thy transparent, cool, and wat'ry wealth

Here flowing fall,
  And chide, and call,
As if his liquid, loose retínue stayed
Ling'ring, and were of this steep place afraid,
  The common pass
  Where, clear as glass,
  All must descend
  Not to an end —
But quicknèd by this deep and rocky grave,
Rise to a longer course more bright and brave.

Dear stream ! dear bank, where often I
Have sat, and pleas'd my pensive eye,
Why, since each drop of thy quick store
Runs thither, whence it flow'd before,
Should poor souls fear a shade or night,
Who came (sure) from a sea of light ?
Or since those drops are all sent back
So sure to thee, that none doth lack,
Why should frail flesh doubt any more
That what God takes he 'll not restore ?

O useful element and clear !
My sacred wash and cleanser here,
My first consigner unto those
Fountains of life, where the Lamb goes.
What sublime truths and wholesome themes,
Lodge in thy mystical deep streams !
Such as dull man can never find
Unless that spirit lead his mind,
Which first upon thy face did move,
And hatch'd all with his quick'ning love.
As this loud brook's incessant fall

In streaming rings restagnates àll,
Which reach by course the bank, and then
Are no more seen, just so pass men.
O my invisible estate,
My glorious liberty, still late !
Thou art the channel my soul seeks,
Not this with cataracts and creeks.

THE WORLD

I saw Eternity the other night,
Like a great ring of pure and endless light,
    All calm, as it was bright ;
And round beneath it, Time in hours, days, years,
    Driv'n by the spheres,
Like a vast shadow mov'd, in which the world
    And all her train were hurl'd.
The doting lover in his quaintest strain
    Did there complain ;
Near him, his lute, his fancy, and his flights,
    Wit's sour delights,
With gloves and knots, the silly snares of pleasure,
    Yet his dear treasure,
All scatter'd lay, while he his eyes did pour
    Upon a flower.

The darksome statesman, hung with weights and woe,
Like a thick midnight-fog, mov'd there so slow
    He did nor stay, nor go ;
Condemning thoughts (like sad eclipses) scowl
    Upon his soul,

And clouds of crying witnesses without
        Pursu'd him with one shout.
Yet dig'd the mole, and lest his ways be found,
        Workt under ground,
Where he did clutch his prey ; but one did see
        That policy —
Churches and altars fed him, perjuries
        Were gnats and flies,
It rain'd about him blood and tears ; but he
        Drank them as free.

The fearful miser on a heap of rust
Sat pining all his life there, did scarce trust
        His own hands with the dust ;
Yet would not place one piece above, but lives
        In fear of thieves.
Thousands there were as frantic as himself,
        And hug'd each one his pelf :
The down-right epicure plac'd heav'n in sense,
        And scorn'd pretense ;
While others, slipt into a wide excess,
        Said little less ;
The weaker sort slight, trivial wares inslave,
        Who think them brave ;
And poor, despisèd Truth sat counting by
        Their victory.

Yet some, who all this while did weep and sing,
And sing, and weep, soar'd up into the ring ;
        But most would use no wing.
"O fools !" said I, "thus to prefer dark night
        Before true light !

To live in grots and caves, and hate the day
    Because it shows the way,
The way which from this dead and dark abode
    Leads up to God,
A way where you might tread the sun, and be
    More bright than he !"
But as I did their madness so discuss,
    One whisper'd thus,
"This ring the Bridegroom did for none provide
    But for His bride."

"THEY ARE ALL GONE"

They are all gone into the world of light !
    And I alone sit ling'ring here ;
Their very memory is fair and bright,
    And my sad thoughts doth clear.

It glows and glitters in my cloudy breast
    Like stars upon some gloomy grove,
Or those faint beams in which this hill is dresst,
    After the sun's remove.

I see them walking in an air of glory,
    Whose light doth trample on my days —
My days, which are at best but dull and hoary,
    Mere glimmering and decays.

O holy hope ! and high humility,
    High as the heavens above !
These are your walks, and you have show'd them me
    To kindle my cold love.

Dear, beauteous death ! the jewel of the just,
  Shining no where, but in the dark ;
What mysteries do lie beyond thy dust,
  Could man outlook that mark !

He that hath found some fledg'd bird's nest, may know
  At first sight, if the bird be flown ;
But what fair well or grove he sings in now,
  That is to him unknown.

And yet, as angels in some brighter dreams
  Call to the soul, when man doth sleep :
So some strange thoughts transcend our wonted themes,
  And into glory peep.

If a star were confin'd into a tomb,
  Her captive flames must needs burn there ;
But when the hand that lockt her up, gives room,
  She 'll shine through all the sphere.

O Father of eternal life, and all
  Created glories under Thee !
Resume Thy spirit from this world of thrall
  Into true liberty.

Either disperse these mists, which blot and fill
  My perspective, still, as they pass,
Or else remove me hence unto that hill,
  Where I shall need no glass.

THOMAS TRAHERNE
(1636–1674)

WONDER

How like an angel came I down !
    How bright are all things here !
When first among his works I did appear
    O, how their glory did me crown !
The world resembled his eternity,
        In which my soul did walk ;
    And evry thing that I did see
        Did with me talk.

The skies in their magnificence,
    The lovely, lively air,
O, how divine, how soft, how sweet, how fair !
    The stars did entertain my sense,
And all the works of God so bright and pure,
        So rich and great, did seem,
    As if they ever must endure,
        In my esteem.

A native health and innocence
    Within my bones did grow,
And while my God did all his glories show,
    I felt a vigor in my sense
That was all spirit. I within did flow
        With seas of life, like wine ;
    I nothing in the world did know,
    But 'twas divine.

Harsh rugged objects were conceal'd ;
  Oppressions, tears, and cries,
Sins, griefs, complaints, dissensions, weeping eyes,
  Were hid : and only things reveal'd
Which heav'nly spirits and the angels prize :
   The state of innocence
  And bliss, not trades and poverties,
   Did fill my sense.

  The streets seemed pav'd with golden stones,
   The boys and girls all mine —
To me how did their lovely faces shine !
   The sons of men all holy ones,
In joy and beauty, then appear'd to me ;
   And evry thing I found,
  While like an angel I did see,
   Adorn'd the ground.

  Rich diamonds, and pearl, and gold
   Might evry where be seen ;
Rare colors, yellow, blue, red, white, and green,
  Mine eyes on evry side behold.
All that I saw a wonder did appear,
   Amazement was my bliss —
That and my wealth met evry where
   No joy to this !

  Curs'd, ill-devis'd proprieties,
   With envy, avarice,
And fraud, those fiends that spoil ev'n paradise,
  Were not the object of mine eyes ;
Nor hedges, ditches, limits, narrow bounds.
   I dreamt not aught of those,

But in surveying all men's grounds
I found repose.

For property itself was mine,
And hedges, ornaments.
Walls, houses, coffers, and their rich contents,
To make me rich, combine.
Clothes, costly jewels, laces, I esteem'd
My wealth, by others worn,
For me they all to wear them seem'd,
When I was born.

JOHN DRYDEN

(1631–1700)

MAC FLECKNOE, OR A SATIRE
UPON THE TRUE-BLUE-PROTESTANT POET,
T.S.

BY THE AUTHOR OF *Absalom and Achitophel*

All human things are subject to decay,
And when Fate summons, monarchs must obey.
This Flecknoe found, who, like Augustus, young
Was call'd to empire, and had govern'd long ;
In prose and verse, was own'd without dispute,
Thro' all the realms of *Nonsense,* absolute.
This agèd prince, now flourishing in peace,
And blest with issue of a large increase,
Worn out with business, did at length debate
To settle the succession of the State ;
And, pond'ring which of all his sons was fit
To reign, and wage immortal war with wit,

Cried : " 'T is resolv'd ; for Nature pleads, that he
Should only rule, who most resembles me.
Sh—— alone my perfect image bears,
Mature in dulness from his tender years :
Sh—— alone, of all my sons, is he
Who stands confirm'd in full stupidity.
The rest to some faint meaning make pretense,
But Sh—— never deviates into sense.
Some beams of wit on other souls may fall,
Strike through, and make a lucid interval ;
But Sh——'s genuine night admits no ray,
His rising fogs prevail upon the day.
Besides, his goodly fabric fills the eye,
And seems design'd for thoughtless majesty —
Thoughtless as monarch oaks that shade the plain,
And, spread in solemn state, supinely reign.
Heywood and Shirley were but types of thee,
Thou last great prophet of tautology.
Even I, a dunce of more renown than they,
Was sent before but to prepare thy way :
And coarsely clad in Norwich drugget came
To teach the nations in thy greater name.
My warbling lute, the lute I whilom strung,
When to King John of Portugal I sung,
Was but the prelude to that glorious day,
When thou on silver Thames didst cut thy way,
With well-tim'd oars before the royal barge,
Swell'd with the pride of thy celestial charge ;
And big with hymn, commander of a host,
The like was ne'er in Epsom blankets toss'd.
Methinks I see the new Arion sail,
The lute still trembling underneath thy nail.
At thy well-sharpen'd thumb from shore to shore

The treble squeaks for fear, the basses roar ;
Echoes from Pissing Alley Sh—— call,
And Sh—— they resound from Aston Hall.
About thy boat the little fishes throng,
As at the morning toast that floats along.
Sometimes, as prince of thy harmonious band,
Thou wield'st thy papers in thy threshing hand.
St. André's feet ne'er kept more equal time,
Not ev'n the feet of thy own *Psyche's* rhyme ;
Tho' they in number as in sense excel,
So just, so like tautology, they fell,
That, pale with envy, Singleton forswore   ⎫
The lute and sword, which he in triumph bore, ⎬
And vow'd he ne'er would act Villerius more." ⎭
Here stopp'd the good old sire, and wept for joy
In silent raptures of the hopeful boy.
All arguments, but most his plays, persuade,
That for anointed dulness he was made.

   Close to the walls which fair Augusta bind,
(The fair Augusta much to fears inclin'd)
An ancient fabric rais'd t' inform the sight,
There stood of yore, and Barbican it hight :
A watchtower once ; but now, so fate ordains,
Of all the pile an empty name remains.
From its old ruins brothel-houses rise,
Scenes of lewd loves, and of polluted joys,
Where their vast courts the mother-strumpets keep,
And, undisturb'd by watch, in silence sleep.
Near these a Nursery erects its head,
Where queens are form'd, and future heroes bred ;
Where unfledg'd actors learn to laugh and cry, ⎫
Where infant punks their tender voices try,   ⎬
And little Maximins the gods defy.   ⎭

Great Fletcher never treads in buskins here,
Nor greater Jonson dares in socks appear ;
But gentle Simkin just reception finds
Amidst this monument of vanish'd minds :
Pure clinches the suburbian Muse affords,
And Panton waging harmless war with words.
Here Flecknoe, as a place to fame well known,
Ambitiously design'd his Sh——'s throne ;
For ancient Dekker prophesied long since,
That in this pile should reign a mighty prince,
Born for a scourge of wit, and flail of sense,
To whom true dulness should some *Psyches* owe,
But worlds of *Misers* from his pen should flow ;
Humorists and hypocrites it should produce,
Whole Raymond families, and tribes of Bruce.
  Now Empress Fame had publish'd the renown
Of Sh——'s coronation through the town.
Rous'd by report of Fame, the nations meet,
From near Bunhill, and distant Watling Street.
No Persian carpets spread th' imperial way,
But scatter'd limbs of mangled poets lay ;
From dusty shops neglected authors come,
Martyrs of pies, and relics of the bum.
Much Heywood, Shirley, Ogleby there lay,
But loads of Sh—— almost chok'd the way.
Bilk'd stationers for yeomen stood prepar'd
And Herringman was captain of the guard.
The hoary prince in majesty appear'd,
High on a throne of his own labors rear'd.
At his right hand our young Ascanius sat,
Rome's other hope, and pillar of the State.
His brows thick fogs, instead of glories, grace,
And lambent dulness play'd around his face.

As Hannibal did to the altars come,
Sworn by his sire a mortal foe to Rome ;
So Sh—— swore, nor should his vow be vain,
That he till death true dulness would maintain ;
And, in his father's right, and realm's defense,
Ne'er to have peace with wit, nor truce with sense.
The king himself the sacred unction made,
As king by office, and as priest by trade.
In his sinister hand, instead of ball,
He plac'd a mighty mug of potent ale ;
Love's Kingdom to his right he did convey,
At once his scepter, and his rule of sway ;
Whose righteous lore the prince had practic'd young
And from whose loins recorded *Psyche* sprung.
His temples, last, with poppies were o'erspread,
That nodding seem'd to consecrate his head :
Just at that point of time, if fame not lie,
On his left hand twelve reverend owls did fly.
So Romulus, 't is sung, by Tiber's brook,
Presage of sway from twice six vultures took.
Th' admiring throng loud acclamations make,
And omens of his future empire take.
The sire then shook the honors of his head,
And from his brows damps of oblivion shed
Full on the filial dulness : long he stood,
Repelling from his breast the raging god ;
At length burst out in this prophetic mood :
  "Heavens bless my son, from Ireland let him reign
To far Barbadoes on the western main ;
Of his dominion may no end be known,
And greater than his father's be his throne ;
Beyond *Love's Kingdom* let him stretch his pen !"
He paus'd, and all the people cried, "Amen !"

Then thus continued he : "My son, advance
Still in new impudence, new ignorance.
Success let others teach, learn thou from me
Pangs without birth, and fruitless industry.
Let *Virtuosos* in five years be writ ;
Yet not one thought accuse thy toil of wit.
Let gentle George in triumph tread the stage,
Make Dorimant betray, and Loveit rage ;
Let Cully, Cockwood, Fopling, charm the pit,
And in their folly shew the writer's wit.
Yet still thy fools shall stand in thy defense,
And justify their author's want of sense.
Let 'em be all by thy own model made
Of dulness, and desire no foreign aid,
That they to future ages may be known,
Not copies drawn, but issue of thy own.
Nay, let thy men of wit too be the same,
All full of thee, and differing but in name.
But let no alien S—dl—y interpose,
To lard with wit thy hungry *Epsom* prose.
And when false flowers of rhetoric thou wouldst cull,
Trust nature, do not labor to be dull ;
But write thy best, and top ; and, in each line,
Sir Formal's oratory will be thine :
Sir Formal, though unsought, attends thy quill,
And does thy northern dedications fill.
Nor let false friends seduce thy mind to fame,
By arrogating Jonson's hostile name.
Let father Flecknoe fire thy mind with praise,
And uncle Ogleby thy envy raise.
Thou art my blood, where Jonson has no part :
What share have we in nature, or in art ?
Where did his wit on learning fix a brand,

And rail at arts he did not understand?
Where made he love in Prince Nicander's vein,
Or swept the dust in *Psyche's* humble strain?
Where sold he bargains, 'whip-stitch, kiss my arse,'
Promis'd a play and dwindled to a farce?
When did his Muse from Fletcher scenes purloin,
As thou whole Eth'rege dost transfuse to thine?
But so transfus'd, as oil on water's flow,
His always floats above, thine sinks below.
This is thy province, this thy wondrous way,
New humors to invent for each new play:
This is that boasted bias of thy mind,
By which one way, to dulness, 't is inclin'd,
Which makes thy writings lean on one side still,
And, in all changes, that way bends thy will.
Nor let thy mountain-belly make pretense
Of likeness; thine 's a tympany of sense.
A tun of man in thy large bulk is writ,
But sure thou 'rt but a kilderkin of wit.
Like mine, thy gentle numbers feebly creep;
Thy tragic Muse gives smiles, thy comic sleep.
With whate'er gall thou sett'st thyself to write,
Thy inoffensive satires never bite.
In thy felonious heart though venom lies,
It does but touch thy Irish pen, and dies.
Thy genius calls thee not to purchase fame
In keen iambics, but mild anagram.
Leave writing plays, and choose for thy command
Some peaceful province in acrostic land.
There thou may'st wings display and altars raise,
And torture one poor word ten thousand ways.
Or, if thou wouldst thy diff'rent talents suit,
Set thy own songs, and sing them to thy lute."

He said. But his last words were scarcely heard ; ⎫
For Bruce and Longvil had a trap prepar'd, ⎬
And down they sent the yet declaiming bard. ⎭
Sinking he left his drugget robe behind,
Borne upwards by a subterranean wind.
The mantle fell to the young prophet's part,
With double portion of his father's art.

THE EIGHTEENTH CENTURY

Pope to Blake

ALEXANDER POPE

(1688–1744)

THE RAPE OF THE LOCK

An Heroi-Comical Poem

Nolueram, Belinda, tuos violare capillos,
Sed juvat hoc precibus me tribuisse tuis.

— Martial.

CANTO I

What dire Offence from Am'rous Causes springs,
What mighty Contests rise from trivial Things,
I sing — This Verse to CARYL, Muse ! is due ;
This, ev'n Belinda may vouchsafe to view.
Slight is the Subject, but not so the Praise,
If She inspire, and He approve my lays.
    Say what strange Motive, Goddess ! could compel
A well-bred Lord t' assault a gentle Belle ?
Oh say what stranger Cause, yet unexplor'd,
Could make a gentle Belle reject a Lord ?
In Tasks so bold, can Little Men engage,
And in soft Bosoms dwells such mighty Rage ?
    Sol thro' white Curtains shot a tim'rous Ray,
And op'd those Eyes that must eclipse the Day ;
Now Lap-dogs give themselves the rousing Shake,
And sleepless Lovers, just at Twelve, awake.
Thrice rung the Bell, the Slipper knock'd the Ground,

And the press'd Watch return'd a silver Sound.
Belinda still her downy Pillow prest,
Her Guardian SYLPH prolong'd the balmy Rest :
'Twas he had summon'd to her silent Bed
The Morning-Dream that hover'd o'er her Head :
A Youth more glitt'ring than a Birth-night Beau,
(That ev'n in Slumber caus'd her Cheek to glow)
Seem'd to her Ear his winning Lips to lay,
And thus in Whispers said, or seem'd to say :
    "Fairest of Mortals, thou distinguish'd Care
Of thousand bright Inhabitants of Air !
If e'er one Vision touch'd thy infant Thought,
Of all the Nurse and all the Priest have taught,
Of airy Elves by Moonlight Shadows seen,
The silver Token, and the circled Green,
Or Virgins visited by Angel-Pow'rs,
With Golden Crowns and Wreaths of heav'nly Flow'rs,
Hear and believe ! thy own Importance know,
Nor bound thy narrow Views to Things below.
Some secret Truths, from Learnèd Pride conceal'd,
To Maids alone and Children are reveal'd.
What tho' no Credit doubting Wits may give ?
The Fair and Innocent shall still believe.
Know, then, unnumber'd Spirits round thee fly,
The light Militia of the lower Sky :
These, tho' unseen, are ever on the Wing,
Hang o'er the Box, and hover round the Ring.
Think what an Equipage thou hast in Air,
And view with scorn Two Pages and a Chair.
As now your own, our Beings were of old,
And once inclos'd in Woman's beauteous Mould ;
Thence, by a soft Transition, we repair
From earthly Vehicles to these of Air.

Think not, when Woman's transient Breath is fled,
That all her Vanities at once are dead —
Succeeding Vanities she still regards,
And tho' she plays no more, o'erlooks the Cards ;
Her Joy in gilded Chariots, when alive,
And Love of Ombre, after Death survive.
For when the Fair in all their Pride expire,
To their first Elements their Souls retire :
The Sprites of fiery Termagants in Flame
Mount up, and take a Salamander's name.
Soft yielding Minds to Water glide away,
And sip, with Nymphs, their Elemental Tea.
The graver Prude sinks downward to a Gnome,
In search of Mischief still on Earth to roam.
The light Coquettes in Sylphs aloft repair,
And sport and flutter in the Fields of Air.

"Know further yet ; Whoever fair and chaste
Rejects Mankind, is by some Sylph embrac'd,
For Spirits, freed from mortal Laws, with ease
Assume what Sexes and what Shapes they please.
What guards the Purity of melting Maids,
In Courtly Balls, and Midnight Masquerades,
Safe from the treach'rous Friend, the daring Spark,
The Glance by Day, the Whisper in the Dark,
When kind Occasion prompts their warm Desires,
When Music softens, and when Dancing fires ?
'Tis but their Sylph, the wise Celestials know,
Tho' Honour is the word with Men below.

"Some Nymphs there are, too conscious of their Face,
For Life predestin'd to the Gnomes' Embrace.
These swell their Prospects and exalt their Pride,
When Offers are disdain'd, and Love deny'd.
Then gay Ideas crowd the vacant Brain,

While Peers, and Dukes, and all their sweeping Train,
And Garters, Stars, and Coronets appear,
And in soft Sounds, 'Your Grace' salutes their Ear.
'Tis these that early taint the Female Soul,
Instruct the Eyes of young Coquettes to roll,
Teach Infant-Cheeks a bidden Blush to know,
And little Hearts to flutter at a Beau.

   "Oft, when the World imagine Women stray,
The Sylphs thro' mystic Mazes guide their Way,
Thro' all the giddy Circle they pursue,
And old Impertinence expel by new.
What tender Maid but must a Victim fall
To one Man's Treat, but for another's Ball ?
When Florio speaks what Virgin could withstand,
If gentle Damon did not squeeze her Hand ?
With varying Vanities, from ev'ry Part,
They shift the moving Toyshop of their Heart ;
Where Wigs with Wigs, with Sword-knots Sword-knots strive,
Beaus banish Beaus, and Coaches Coaches drive.
This erring Mortals Levity may call —
Oh blind to Truth ! the Sylphs contrive it all.

   "Of these am I, who thy Protection claim,
A watchful sprite, and Ariel is my Name.
Late, as I rang'd the Crystal Wilds of Air,
In the clear Mirror of thy ruling Star
I saw, alas ! some dread Event impend,
Ere to the Main this Morning Sun descend ;
But Heav'n reveals not what, or how, or where.
Warn'd by the Sylph, oh Pious Maid, beware !
This to disclose is all thy Guardian can.
Beware of all, but most beware of Man !"

   He said ; when Shock, who thought she slept too long,
Leapt up, and wak'd his Mistress with his Tongue.

'Twas then, Belinda ! if Report say true,
Thy Eyes first open'd on a Billet-doux ;
Wounds, Charms, and Ardors were no sooner read,
But all the Vision vanish'd from thy Head.
   And now, unveil'd, the Toilet stands display'd,
Each Silver Vase in mystic Order laid.
First, rob'd in White, the Nymph intent adores,
With Head uncover'd, the Cosmetic Pow'rs.
A heav'nly Image in the Glass appears,
To that she bends, to that her Eyes she rears ;
Th' inferior Priestess, at her Altar's side,
Trembling begins the sacred Rites of Pride.
Unnumber'd Treasures ope at once, and here
The various Off'rings of the World appear ;
From each she nicely culls with curious Toil,
And decks the Goddess with the glitt'ring Spoil.
This Casket India's glowing Gems unlocks,
And all Arabia breathes from yonder Box.
The Tortoise here and Elephant unite,
Transform'd to Combs, the speckled, and the white.
Here Files of Pins extend their shining Rows,
Puffs, Powders, Patches, Bibles, Billet-doux.
Now awful Beauty puts on all its Arms ;
The Fair each moment rises in her Charms,
Repairs her Smiles, awakens ev'ry Grace,
And calls forth all the Wonders of her Face ;
Sees by Degrees a purer Blush arise,
And keener Lightnings quicken in her Eyes.
The busy Sylphs surround their darling Care,
These set the Head, and those divide the Hair,
Some fold the Sleeve, whilst others plait the Gown ;
And Betty 's prais'd for Labours not her own.

CANTO II

Not with more Glories, in th' Etherial Plain,
The Sun first rises o'er the purpled Main,
Than, issuing forth, the Rival of his Beams
Launch'd on the Bosom of the Silver Thames.
Fair Nymphs, and well-drest Youths around her shone,
But ev'ry Eye was fix'd on her alone.
On her white Breast a sparkling Cross she wore,
Which Jews might kiss, and Infidels adore.
Her lively Looks a sprightly Mind disclose,
Quick as her Eyes, and as unfix'd as those.
Favours to none, to all she Smiles extends ;
Oft she rejects, but never once offends.
Bright as the Sun, her Eyes the Gazers strike,
And, like the Sun, they shine on all alike.
Yet graceful Ease, and Sweetness void of Pride,
Might hide her Faults, if Belles had Faults to hide :
If to her share some Female Errors fall,
Look on her Face, and you 'll forget 'em all.
    This Nymph, to the Destruction of Mankind,
Nourish'd two Locks, which graceful hung behind
In equal Curls, and well conspir'd to deck
With shining Ringlets the smooth Iv'ry Neck.
Love in these Labyrinths his Slaves detains,
And mighty Hearts are held in slender Chains.
With hairy Sprindges we the Birds betray,
Slight Lines of Hair surprize the Finny Prey,
Fair Tresses Man's Imperial Race ensnare,
And Beauty draws us with a single Hair.
    Th' Advent'rous Baron the bright Locks admir'd ;
He saw, he wish'd, and to the Prize aspir'd.
Resolv'd to win, he meditates the way,

By Force to ravish, or by Fraud betray ;
For when Success a Lover's Toil attends,
Few ask, if Fraud or Force attain'd his Ends.
   For this, ere Phoebus rose, he had implor'd
Propitious Heav'n, and ev'ry Pow'r ador'd,
But chiefly Love — to Love an Altar built,
Of twelve vast French Romances, neatly gilt.
There lay three Garters, half a Pair of Gloves ;
And all the Trophies of his former Loves ;
With tender Billet-doux he lights the Pyre,
And breathes three am'rous Sighs to raise the Fire.
Then prostrate falls, and begs with ardent Eyes
Soon to obtain, and long possess the Prize :
The Pow'rs gave Ear, and granted half his Pray'r,
The rest, the Winds dispers'd in empty Air.
   But now secure the painted Vessel glides,
The Sun-beams trembling on the floating Tides ;
While melting Music steals upon the Sky,
And soften'd Sounds along the Waters die ;
Smooth flow the Waves, the Zephyrs gently play,
Belinda smil'd, and all the World was gay.
All but the Sylph — with careful Thoughts opprest,
Th' impending Woe sat heavy on his Breast.
He summons strait his Denizens of Air ;
The lucid Squadrons round the Sails repair :
Soft o'er the Shrouds Aërial Whispers breathe,
That seem'd but Zephyrs to the Train beneath.
Some to the Sun their Insect-Wings unfold,
Waft on the Breeze, or sink in Clouds of Gold ;
Transparent Forms, too fine for mortal Sight,
Their fluid Bodies half dissolv'd in Light.
Loose to the Wind their airy Garments flew,
Thin glitt'ring Textures of the filmy Dew,

Dipt in the richest Tincture of the Skies,
Where Light disports in ever-mingling Dyes,
While ev'ry Beam new transient Colours flings,
Colours that change whene'er they wave their Wings.
Amid the Circle, on the gilded Mast,
Superior by the Head, was Ariel plac'd ;
His Purple Pinions opening to the Sun,
He rais'd his Azure Wand, and thus begun :
   "Ye Sylphs and Sylphids, to your Chief give Ear !
Fays, Fairies, Genii, Elves, and Daemons, hear !
Ye know the Spheres and various Tasks assign'd
By Laws Eternal to th' Aërial Kind.
Some in the fields of purest Æther play,
And bask and whiten in the Blaze of Day.
Some guide the Course of wand'ring Orbs on high,
Or roll the Planets thro' the boundless Sky.
Some less refin'd, beneath the Moon's pale Light
Pursue the Stars that shoot athwart the Night,
Or suck the Mists in grosser Air below,
Or dip their Pinions in the painted Bow,
Or brew fierce Tempests on the wintry Main,
Or o'er the Glebe distil the kindly Rain.
Others on Earth o'er human Race preside,
Watch all their Ways, and all their Actions guide.
Of these the Chief the Care of Nations own,
And guard with Arms Divine the British Throne.
   "Our humbler Province is to tend the Fair,
Not a less pleasing, tho' less glorious Care ;
To save the Powder from too rude a Gale,
Nor let th' imprison'd Essences exhale ;
To draw fresh Colours from the vernal Flow'rs ;
To steal from Rainbows ere they drop in Show'rs
A brighter Wash ; to curl their waving Hairs,

Assist their Blushes, and inspire their Airs ;
Nay oft, in Dreams, Invention we bestow,
To change a Flounce, or add a Furbelow.

"This Day, black Omens threat the brightest Fair,
That e'er deserv'd a watchful Spirit's Care ;
Some dire Disaster, or by Force, or Slight ;
But what, or where, the Fates have wrapt in Night.
Whether the Nymph shall break Diana's Law,
Or some frail China Jar receive a Flaw,
Or stain her Honour or her new Brocade ;
Forget her Prayers, or miss a Masquerade,
Or lose her Heart or Necklace at a Ball ;
Or whether Heav'n has doom'd that Shock must fall.
Haste, then, ye spirits ! to your Charge repair :
The flutt'ring Fan be Zephyretta's Care ;
The Drops to thee, Brillante, we consign ;
And, Momentilla, let the Watch be thine ;
Do thou, Crispissa, tend her fav'rite Lock ;
Ariel himself shall be the Guard of Shock.

"To Fifty chosen Sylphs, of special Note,
We trust th' important Charge, the Petticoat :
Oft have we known that sevenfold Fence to fail,
Tho' stiff with Hoops, and arm'd with Ribs of Whale ;
Form a strong Line about the Silver Bound,
And guard the wide Circumference around.

"Whatever Spirit, careless of his Charge,
His Post neglects, or leaves the Fair at large,
Shall feel sharp Vengeance soon o'ertake his Sins,
Be stop'd in Vials, or transfix'd with Pins ;
Or plung'd in Lakes of bitter Washes lie,
Or wedg'd whole Ages in a Bodkin's Eye :
Gums and Pomatums shall his Flight restrain,
While clog'd he beats his silken Wings in vain ;

Or Alum-Styptics with contracting Power
Shrink his thin Essence like a rivell'd Flower :
Or, as Ixion fix'd, the Wretch shall feel
The giddy Motion of the whirling Mill,
In Fumes of burning Chocolate shall glow,
And tremble at the Sea that froths below !"
　　He spoke ; the Spirits from the Sails descend ;
Some, Orb in Orb, around the Nymph extend ;
Some thrid the mazy Ringlets of her Hair ;
Some hang upon the Pendants of her Ear :
With beating Hearts the dire Event they wait,
Anxious, and trembling for the Birth of Fate.

CANTO III

Close by those Meads, for ever crown'd with Flow'rs,
Where Thames with Pride surveys his rising Tow'rs,
There stands a Structure of Majestic Frame,
Which from the neighb'ring Hampton takes its Name.
Here Britain's Statesmen oft the Fall foredoom
Of Foreign Tyrants and of Nymphs at home ;
Here Thou, Great ANNA ! whom three Realms obey,
Dost sometimes Counsel take — and sometimes Tea.
　　Hither the Heroes and the Nymphs resort,
To taste awhile the Pleasures of a Court ;
In various Talk th' instructive hours they past,
Who gave the Ball, or paid the Visit last.
One speaks the Glory of the British Queen,
And one describes a charming Indian Screen ;
A third interprets Motions, Looks, and Eyes ;
At ev'ry Word a Reputation dies.
Snuff, or the Fan, supply each Pause of Chat,
With singing, laughing, ogling, *and all that.*

Mean while, declining from the Noon of Day,
The Sun obliquely shoots his burning Ray ;
The hungry Judges soon the Sentence sign,
And Wretches hang that Jury-men may Dine ;
The Merchant from th' Exchange returns in Peace,
And the long Labours of the Toilet cease.
Belinda now, whom Thirst of Fame invites,
Burns to encounter two adventrous Knights,
At Ombre singly to decide their Doom ;
And swells her Breast with Conquests yet to come.
Straight the three Bands prepare in Arms to join,
Each Band the number of the Sacred Nine.
Soon as she spreads her Hand, th' Aërial Guard
Descend, and sit on each important Card :
First Ariel perch'd upon a Matadore,
Then each, according to the Rank they bore ;
For Sylphs, yet mindful of their ancient Race,
Are, as when Women, wondrous fond of Place.
 Behold, four Kings in Majesty rever'd,
With hoary Whiskers and a forky Beard ;
And four fair Queens whose hands sustain a Flow'r,
Th' expressive Emblem of their softer Pow'r ;
Four Knaves in Garbs succinct, a trusty Band,
Caps on their heads, and Halberts in their hand ;
And Particolour'd Troops, a shining Train,
Draw forth to Combat on the Velvet Plain.
 The skilful Nymph reviews her Force with Care ;
"Let Spades be Trumps !" she said, and Trumps they were.
 Now move to War her Sable Matadores,
In Show like Leaders of the swarthy Moors.
Spadillio first, unconquerable Lord !
Led off two captive Trumps, and swept the Board.
As many more Manillio forc'd to yield,

And march'd a Victor from the verdant Field.
Him Basto follow'd, but his Fate more hard
Gain'd but one Trump and one Plebeian Card.
With his broad Sabre next, a Chief in Years,
The hoary Majesty of Spades appears ;
Puts forth one manly Leg, to sight reveal'd,
The rest, his many-colour'd Robe conceal'd.
The Rebel Knave, who dares his Prince engage,
Proves the just Victim of his Royal Rage.
Ev'n mighty Pam, that Kings and Queens o'erthrew
And mow'd down Armies in the Fights of Lu,
Sad Chance of War ! now destitute of Aid,
Falls undistinguish'd by the Victor Spade !
  Thus far both Armies to Belinda yield ;
Now to the Baron Fate inclines the Field.
His warlike Amazon her Host invades,
Th' Imperial Consort of the Crown of Spades.
The Club's black Tyrant first her Victim dy'd,
Spite of his haughty Mien, and barb'rous Pride :
What boots the Regal Circle on his Head,
His Giant Limbs in State unwieldy spread :
That long behind he trails his pompous Robe,
And, of all Monarchs, only grasps the Globe ?
  The Baron now his Diamonds pours apace ;
Th' embroider'd King who shows but half his Face,
And his refulgent Queen, with Pow'rs combin'd
Of broken Troops an easy Conquest find.
Clubs, Diamonds, Hearts, in wild Disorder seen,
With Throngs promiscuous strow the level Green.
Thus when dispers'd a routed Army runs,
Of Asia's Troops, and Afric's Sable Sons,
With like Confusion different Nations fly,
Of various Habit, and of various Dye,

The pierc'd Battalions dis-united fall,
In Heaps on Heaps ; one Fate o'erwhelms them all.
  The Knave of Diamonds tries his wily Arts,
And wins (oh shameful Chance !) the Queen of Hearts.
At this the Blood the Virgin's Cheek forsook,
A livid Paleness spreads o'er all her Look ;
She sees, and trembles at th' approaching Ill,
Just in the Jaws of Ruin, and Codille,
And now (as oft in some distempered State)
On one nice Trick depends the gen'ral Fate.
An Ace of Hearts steps forth : The King unseen
Lurk'd in her Hand, and mourn'd his captive Queen.
He springs to Vengeance with an eager pace,
And falls like Thunder on the prostrate Ace.
The Nymph exulting fills with Shouts the Sky ;
The Walls, the Woods, and long Canals reply.
  Oh thoughtless Mortals ! ever blind to Fate,
Too soon dejected, and too soon elate !
Sudden, these Honours shall be snatch'd away,
And curs'd for ever this Victorious Day.
  For lo ! the Board with Cups and Spoons is crown'd,
The Berries crackle, and the Mill turns round ;
On shining Altars of Japan they raise
The silver Lamp ; the fiery Spirits blaze.
From silver Spouts the grateful Liquors glide,
While China's Earth receives the smoking Tide.
At once they gratify their Scent and Taste,
And frequent Cups prolong the rich Repast.
Straight hover round the Fair her Airy Band ;
Some, as she sipp'd, the fuming Liquor fann'd,
Some o'er her Lap their careful Plumes display'd,
Trembling, and conscious of the rich Brocade.
Coffee (which makes the Politician wise,

And see thro' all things with his half-shut Eyes)
Sent up in Vapours to the Baron's Brain
New Stratagems, the radiant Lock to gain.
Ah cease, rash Youth ! desist ere 'tis too late,
Fear the just Gods, and think of Scylla's Fate !
Chang'd to a Bird, and sent to flit in Air,
She dearly pays for Nisus' injur'd Hair !

But when to Mischief Mortals bend their Will,
How soon they find fit Instruments of Ill !
Just then, Clarissa drew with tempting Grace
A two-edg'd Weapon from her shining Case :
So Ladies in Romance assist their Knight,
Present the Spear, and arm him for the Fight.
He takes the Gift with rev'rence, and extends
The little Engine on his Fingers' Ends ;
This just behind Belinda's Neck he spread,
As o'er the fragrant Steams she bends her Head.
Swift to the Lock a thousand Sprites repair,
A thousand Wings, by turns, blow back the Hair,
And thrice they twitch'd the Diamond in her Ear,
Thrice she look'd back, and thrice the Foe drew near.
Just in that instant, anxious Ariel sought
The close Recesses of the Virgin's Thought ;
As on the Nosegay in her Breast reclin'd,
He watch'd th' Ideas rising in her Mind,
Sudden he view'd, in spite of all her Art,
An Earthly Lover lurking at her Heart.
Amaz'd, confus'd, he found his Pow'r expir'd,
Resign'd to Fate, and with a Sigh retir'd.

The Peer now spreads the glitt'ring Forfex wide,
T' inclose the Lock ; now joins it, to divide.
Ev'n then, before the fatal Engine clos'd,
A wretch'd Sylph too fondly interpos'd ;

Fate urg'd the Shears, and cut the Sylph in twain,
(But Airy Substance soon unites again)
The meeting Points the sacred Hair dissever
From the fair Head, for ever, and for ever !

Then flash'd the living Lightning from her Eyes,
And Screams of Horror rend th' affrighted Skies.
Not louder Shrieks to pitying Heav'n are cast,
When Husbands or when Lap-dogs breathe their last ;
Or when rich China Vessels, fall'n from high,
In glitt'ring Dust and painted Fragments lie !

"Let Wreaths of Triumph now my Temples twine,
(The Victor cry'd) the glorious Prize is mine !
While Fish in Streams, or Birds delight in Air,
Or in a Coach and Six the British Fair,
As long as Atalantis shall be read,
Or the small Pillow grace a Lady's Bed,
While Visits shall be paid on solemn Days,
When num'rous Wax-lights in bright Order blaze,
While Nymphs take Treats, or Assignations give,
So long my Honour, Name, and Praise shall live !"

What Time would spare, from Steel receives its date,
And Monuments, like Men, submit to Fate !
Steel could the Labour of the Gods destroy,
And strike to Dust th' Imperial Tow'rs of Troy ;
Steel could the Works of mortal Pride confound,
And hew Triumphal Arches to the Ground.
What Wonder then, fair Nymph ! thy Hairs should feel
The conq'ring Force of unresisted Steel ?

CANTO IV

But anxious Cares the pensive Nymph oppress'd,
And secret Passions labour'd in her Breast.

Not youthful Kings in Battle seiz'd alive,
Not scornful Virgins who their Charms survive,
Not ardent Lovers robb'd of all their Bliss,
Not ancient Ladies when refus'd a Kiss,
Not Tyrants fierce that unrepenting die,
Not Cynthia when her Manteau's pinn'd awry,
E'er felt such Rage, Resentment, and Despair,
As Thou, sad Virgin ! for thy ravish'd Hair.

    For, that sad moment, when the Sylphs withdrew,
And Ariel weeping from Belinda flew,
Umbriel, a dusky, melancholy Sprite,
As ever sully'd the fair face of Light,
Down to the Central Earth, his proper Scene,
Repair'd to search the gloomy Cave of Spleen.

    Swift on his sooty Pinions flits the Gnome,
And in a Vapour reach'd the dismal Dome.
No cheerful Breeze this sullen Region knows,
The dreaded East is all the Wind that blows.
Here in a Grotto, shelter'd close from Air,
And screen'd in Shades from Day's detested Glare,
She sighs for ever on her pensive Bed,
Pain at her Side and Megrim at her Head.

    Two Handmaids wait the Throne : Alike in Place,
But diff'ring far in Figure and in Face.
Here stood Ill-nature like an ancient Maid,
Her wrinkled Form in Black and White array'd ;
With store of Prayers, for Mornings, Nights, and Noons,
Her Hand is fill'd ; her Bosom with Lampoons.

    There Affectation, with a sickly Mien,
Shows in her Cheek the Roses of Eighteen,
Practis'd to Lisp, and hang the Head aside,
Faints into Airs, and languishes with Pride,
On the rich Quilt sinks with becoming Woe,

Wrapt in a Gown, for Sickness, and for Show.
The Fair-ones feel such Maladies as these,
When each new Night-Dress gives a new Disease.

   A constant Vapour o'er the Palace flies ;
Strange Phantoms rising as the Mists arise ;
Dreadful as Hermit's Dreams in haunted Shades,
Or bright as Visions of expiring Maids.
Now glaring Fiends, and Snakes on rolling Spires,
Pale Spectres, gaping Tombs, and Purple Fires ;
Now Lakes of liquid Gold, Elysian Scenes,
And Crystal Domes, and Angels in Machines.

   Unnumber'd Throngs on ev'ry side are seen,
Of Bodies chang'd to various Forms by Spleen.
Here living Teapots stand, one Arm held out,
One bent ; the Handle this, and that the Spout :
A Pipkin there, like Homer's Tripod walks ;
Here sighs a Jar, and there a Goose-pye talks ;
Men prove with Child, as pow'rful Fancy works,
And Maids turn'd Bottles, call aloud for Corks.

   Safe past the Gnome thro' this fantastic Band,
A Branch of healing Spleenwort in his hand.
Then thus address'd the power : "Hail, wayward Queen !
Who rule the Sex to Fifty from Fifteen ;
Parent of Vapours and of Female Wit,
Who give th' Hysteric or Poetic fit,
On various Tempers act by various ways,
Make some take Physic, others scribble Plays ;
Who cause the Proud their Visits to delay,
And send the Godly in a Pet to pray.
A Nymph there is, that all thy Pow'r disdains,
And thousands more in equal Mirth maintains.
But oh ! if e'er thy Gnome could spoil a Grace,
Or raise a Pimple on a beauteous Face,

Like Citron-Waters Matrons' Cheeks inflame,
Or change Complexions at a losing Game ;
If e'er with airy Horns I planted Heads,
Or rumpled Petticoats, or tumbled Beds,
Or caus'd Suspicion when no Soul was rude,
Or discompos'd the Head-dress of a Prude,
Or e'er to costive Lap-dog gave Disease,
Which not the Tears of brightest Eyes could ease :
Hear me, and touch Belinda with Chagrin —
That single Act gives half the World the Spleen."
  The Goddess with a discontented Air
Seems to reject him, tho' she grants his Pray'r.
A wondrous Bag with both her Hands she binds,
Like that where once Ulysses held the Winds ;
There she collects the Force of Female Lungs,
Sighs, Sobs, and Passions, and the War of Tongues.
A Vial next she fills with fainting Fears,
Soft Sorrows, melting Griefs, and flowing Tears.
The Gnome, rejoicing, bears her Gifts away,
Spreads his black Wings, and slowly mounts to Day.
  Sunk in Thalestris' Arms the Nymph he found,
Her Eyes dejected and her Hair unbound.
Full o'er their Heads the swelling Bag he rent,
And all the Furies issu'd at the Vent.
Belinda burns with more than mortal Ire,
And fierce Thalestris fans the rising Fire.
"Oh wretched Maid !" she spread her Hands, and cried,
(While Hampton's Echoes, "Wretched Maid !" reply'd)
"Was it for this you took such constant Care
The Bodkin, Comb, and Essence to prepare ?
For this your Locks in Paper-Durance bound,
For this with tort'ring Irons wreath'd around ?
For this with Fillets strain'd your tender Head,

And bravely bore the double Loads of Lead ?
Gods ! shall the Ravisher display your Hair,
While the Fops envy, and the Ladies stare !
Honour forbid ! at whose unrival'd Shrine
Ease, Pleasure, Virtue, All, our Sex resign.
Methinks already I your Tears survey,
Already hear the horrid things they say,
Already see you a degraded Toast,
And all your Honour in a Whisper lost !
How shall I, then, your helpless Fame defend ?
'Twill then be Infamy to seem your Friend !
And shall this Prize, th' inestimable Prize,
Expos'd thro' Crystal to the gazing Eyes,
And heighten'd by the Diamond's circling Rays,
On that Rapacious Hand for ever blaze ?
Sooner shall Grass in Hyde-Park Circus grow
And wits take Lodgings in the Sound of Bow ;
Sooner let Earth, Air, Sea, to Chaos fall,
Men, Monkeys, Lap-dogs, Parrots, perish all !"
  She said ; then raging to Sir Plume repairs,
And bids her Beau demand the precious Hairs :
(Sir Plume, of Amber Snuff-box justly vain,
And the nice Conduct of a clouded Cane)
With earnest Eyes and round unthinking Face,
He First the Snuff-box open'd, then the Case,
And thus broke out — "My Lord, why, what the devil ?
Z—ds ! damn the Lock ! 'fore Gad, you must be civil !
Plague on't ! 'tis past a Jest — nay prithee, Pox !
Give her the Hair" — he spoke, and rapp'd his Box.
"It grieves me much (reply'd the Peer again)
Who speaks so well should ever speak in vain.
But by this Lock, this sacred Lock I swear,
(Which never more shall join its parted Hair ;

Which never more its Honours shall renew,
Clipt from the lovely Head where late it grew)
That while my Nostrils draw the vital Air,
This Hand, which won it, shall for ever wear."
He spoke, and speaking, in proud Triumph spread
The long-contended Honours of her Head.

But Umbriel, hateful Gnome ! forbears not so ;
He breaks the Vial whence the Sorrows flow.
Then see ! the nymph in beauteous Grief appears,
Her Eyes half-languishing, half-drown'd in Tears ;
On her heav'd Bosom hung her drooping Head,
Which, with a Sigh, she rais'd ; and thus she said :

"For ever curs'd be this detested Day,
Which snatch'd my best, my fav'rite Curl away !
Happy ! ah ten times happy had I been,
If Hampton-Court these Eyes had never seen !
Yet am not I the first mistaken Maid,
By Love of Courts to num'rous Ills betrayed.
Oh had I rather un-admir'd remain'd
In some lone Isle, or distant Northern Land ;
Where the gilt Chariot never marks the Way,
Where none learn Ombre, none e'er taste Bohea !
There kept my Charms conceal'd from mortal Eye,
Like Roses that in Deserts bloom and die.
What mov'd my Mind with youthful Lords to roam ?
Oh had I stay'd, and said my Pray'rs at home !
'Twas this, the Morning Omens seem'd to tell :
Thrice from my trembling hand the Patch-box fell ;
The tott'ring China shook without a Wind,
Nay, Poll sat mute, and Shock was most Unkind !
A Sylph too warn'd me of the Threats of Fate,
In mystic Visions, now believ'd too late !
See the poor Remnants of these slighted Hairs !

My hands shall rend what ev'n thy Rapine spares.
These in two sable Ringlets taught to break,
Once gave new Beauties to the snowy Neck ;
The Sister-Lock now sits uncouth, alone,
And in its Fellow's Fate foresees its own ;
Uncurl'd it hangs, the fatal Shears demands,
And tempts once more thy sacrilegious Hands.
Oh hadst thou, Cruel ! been content to seize
Hairs less in sight, or any Hairs but these !"

CANTO V

She said : the pitying Audience melt in Tears.
But Fate and Jove had stopp'd the Baron's Ears.
In vain Thalestris with Reproach assails,
For who can move when fair Belinda fails ?
Not half so fixt the Trojan could remain,
While Anna begg'd and Dido rag'd in vain.
Then grave Clarissa graceful wav'd her Fan ;
Silence ensu'd, and thus the Nymph began :
    "Say, why are Beauties prais'd and honour'd most,
The wise Man's Passion, and the vain Man's Toast ?
Why deck'd with all that Land and Sea afford,
Why Angels call'd, and Angel-like ador'd ?
Why round our Coaches croud the white-glov'd Beaus,
Why bows the Side-box from its inmost Rows ?
How vain are all these Glories, all our Pains,
Unless good Sense preserve what Beauty gains :
That Men may say, when we the Front-box grace,
Behold the first in Virtue as in Face !
Oh ! if to dance all Night, and dress all Day,
Charm'd the Small-pox, or chas'd old Age away ;
Who would not scorn what Housewife's Cares produce,

Or who would learn one earthly Thing of Use ?
To patch, nay ogle, might become a Saint,
Nor could it sure be such a Sin to paint.
But since, alas ! frail Beauty must decay,
Curl'd or uncurl'd, since Locks will turn to grey ;
Since painted, or not painted, all shall fade,
And she who scorns a Man, must die a Maid ;
What then remains but well our Pow'r to use,
And keep good Humour still whate'er we lose ?
And trust me, Dear ! good Humour can prevail,
When Airs, and Flights, and Screams, and Scolding fail.
Beauties in vain their pretty Eyes may roll ;
Charms strike the Sight, but Merit wins the Soul."

   So spoke the Dame, but no Applause ensu'd ;
Belinda frown'd, Thalestris call'd her Prude.
"To Arms, to Arms !" the fierce Virago cries,
And swift as Lightning to the Combat flies.
All side in Parties, and begin th' Attack ;
Fans clap, Silks russle, and tough Whalebones crack ;
Heroes' and Heroines' Shouts confus'dly rise,
And bass and treble Voices strike the Skies.
No common Weapons in their Hands are found,
Like Gods they fight, nor dread a mortal Wound.

   So when bold Homer makes the Gods engage,
And heav'nly Breasts with human Passions rage,
'Gainst Pallas, Mars ; Latona, Hermes arms,
And all Olympus rings with loud Alarms ;
Jove's Thunder roars, Heav'n trembles all around,
Blue Neptune storms, the bellowing Deeps resound ;
Earth shakes her nodding Tow'rs, the Ground gives way,
And the pale Ghosts start at the Flash of Day !

    Triumphant Umbriel on a Sconce's Height
Clapt his glad Wings, and sate to view the Fight :

Propt on their Bodkin Spears, the Sprites survey
The growing Combat, or assist the Fray.

  While thro' the Press enrag'd Thalestris flies,
And scatters Deaths around from both her Eyes,
A Beau and Witling perish'd in the Throng,
One dy'd in Metaphor, and one in Song.
"O cruel Nymph ! a living Death I bear,"
Cry'd Dapperwit, and sunk beside his Chair.
A mournful Glance Sir Fopling upwards cast,
"Those eyes are made so killing" — was his last.
Thus on Maeander's flow'ry Margin lies
Th' expiring Swan, and as he sings he dies.

  When bold Sir Plume had drawn Clarissa down,
Chloe stepp'd in, and killed him with a Frown ;
She smil'd to see the doughty Hero slain,
But, at her Smile, the Beau reviv'd again.

  Now Jove suspends his golden Scales in Air,
Weighs the Men's Wits against the Lady's Hair ;
The doubtful Beam long nods from side to side ;
At length the Wits mount up, the Hairs subside.

  See fierce Belinda on the Baron flies,
With more than usual Lightning in her Eyes :
Nor fear'd the Chief th' unequal Fight to try,
Who sought no more than on his Foe to die.
But this bold Lord with manly Strength endu'd,
She with one Finger and a Thumb subdu'd :
Just where the Breath of Life his Nostrils drew,
A Charge of Snuff the wily Virgin threw ;
The Gnomes direct, to ev'ry Atom just,
The pungent Grains of titillating Dust.
Sudden, with starting Tears each Eye o'er flows,
And the high Dome re-echoes to his Nose.

  "Now meet thy Fate !" incens'd Belinda cry'd,

And drew a deadly Bodkin from her Side.
(The same, his ancient Personage to deck,
Her great great Grandsire wore about his Neck,
In three Seal-Rings ; which after, melted down,
Form'd a vast Buckle for his Widow's Gown :
Her infant Grandame's Whistle next it grew,
The Bells she jingl'd, and the Whistle blew ;
Then in a Bodkin grac'd her Mother's Hairs,
Which long she wore, and now Belinda wears.)
　"Boast not my Fall (he cry'd) insulting Foe !
Thou by some other shalt be laid as low,
Nor think, to die dejects my lofty Mind :
All that I dread is leaving you behind !
Rather than so, ah let me still survive,
And burn in Cupid's Flames — but burn alive."
　"Restore the Lock !" she cries ; and all around,
"Restore the Lock !" the vaulted Roofs rebound.
Not fierce Othello in so loud a Strain
Roar'd for the Handkerchief that caus'd his Pain.
But see how oft Ambitious Aims are cross'd,
And Chiefs contend 'till all the Prize is lost !
The Lock, obtain'd with Guilt, and kept with Pain,
In ev'ry place is sought, but sought in vain :
With such a Prize no Mortal must be blest,
So Heav'n decrees ! with Heav'n who can contest ?
　Some thought it mounted to the Lunar sphere,
Since all things lost on Earth are treasur'd there.
There Heroes' Wits are kept in pond'rous Vases,
And Beaus' in Snuff-boxes and Tweezer-Cases.
There broken Vows and Death-bed Alms are found,
And Lovers' Hearts with Ends of Riband bound,
The Courtier's Promises, and Sick Man's Pray'rs,
The Smiles of Harlots, and the Tears of Heirs,

Cages for Gnats, and Chains to Yoke a Flea,
Dry'd Butterflies, and Tomes of Casuistry.
   But trust the Muse — she saw it upward rise,
Though mark'd by none but quick, Poetic Eyes :
(So Rome's great Founder to the Heav'ns withdrew,
To Proculus alone confess'd in view)
A sudden Star, it shot thro' liquid Air,
And drew behind a radiant Trail of Hair.
Not Berenice's Locks first rose so bright,
The Heav'ns bespangling with dishevell'd Light.
The Sylphs behold it kindling as it flies,
And pleas'd pursue its Progress thro' the Skies.
   This the Beau-monde shall from the Mall survey,
And hail with Music its propitious Ray.
This the blest Lover shall for Venus take,
And send up Vows from Rosamonda's Lake.
This Partridge soon shall view in cloudless Skies,
When next he looks thro' Galileo's Eyes ;
And hence th' Egregious Wizard shall foredoom
The Fate of Louis, and the Fall of Rome.
   Then cease, bright Nymph ! to mourn thy ravish'd Hair,
Which adds new Glory to the shining Sphere !
Not all the Tresses that fair Head can boast,
Shall draw such Envy as the Lock you lost.
For, after all the Murders of your Eye,
When, after Millions slain, your self shall die ;
When those fair Suns shall set, as set they must,
And all those Tresses shall be laid in Dust,
This Lock, the Muse shall consecrate to Fame,
And 'midst the Stars inscribe Belinda's Name.

THOMAS GRAY

(1716–1771)

ODE ON A DISTANT PROSPECT OF ETON COLLEGE

Ye distant spires, ye antique towers,
That crown the watery glade,
Where grateful Science still adores
Her Henry's holy Shade ;
And ye, that from the stately brow
Of Windsor's heights th' expanse below
Of grove, of lawn, of mead survey,
Whose turf, whose shade, whose flowers among
Wanders the hoary Thames along
His silver-winding way.

Ah, happy hills ! ah, pleasing shade !
Ah, fields beloved in vain !
Where once my careless childhood stray'd,
A stranger yet to pain !
I feel the gales, that from ye blow,
A momentary bliss bestow,
As, waving fresh their gladsome wing,
My weary soul they seem to soothe,
And, redolent of joy and youth,
To breathe a second spring.

Say, Father Thames, for thou hast seen
Full many a sprightly race

Disporting on thy margent green
The paths of pleasure trace,
Who foremost now delight to cleave
With pliant arm thy glassy wave ?
The captive linnet which enthrall ?
What idle progeny succeed
To chase the rolling circle's speed,
Or urge the flying ball ?

While some on earnest business bent
Their murm'ring labors ply
'Gainst graver hours, that bring constraint
To sweeten liberty ;
Some bold adventurers disdain
The limits of their little reign,
And unknown regions dare descry —
Still as they run they look behind,
They hear a voice in every wind,
And snatch a fearful joy.

Gay hope is theirs by fancy fed,
Less pleasing when possest ;
The tear forgot as soon as shed,
The sunshine of the breast ;
Theirs buxom health of rosy hue,
Wild wit, invention ever-new,
And lively cheer of vigor born ;
The thoughtless day, the easy night,
The spirits pure, the slumbers light,
That fly th' approach of morn.

Alas, regardless of their doom,
The little victims play !

No sense have they of ills to come,
Nor care beyond to-day.
Yet see how all around 'em wait
The ministers of human fate,
And black Misfortune's baleful train !
Ah, show them where in ambush stand
To seize their prey the murth'rous band !
Ah, tell them, they are men !

These shall the fury Passions tear,
The vultures of the mind,
Disdainful Anger, pallid Fear,
And Shame that skulks behind ;
Or pining Love shall waste their youth,
Or Jealousy with rankling tooth,
That inly gnaws the secret heart,
And Envy wan, and faded Care,
Grim-visag'd comfortless Despair,
And Sorrow's piercing dart.

Ambition this shall tempt to rise,
Then whirl the wretch from high,
To bitter Scorn a sacrifice,
And grinning Infamy.
The stings of Falsehood those shall try,
And hard Unkindness' alter'd eye,
That mocks the tear it forc'd to flow ;
And keen Remorse with blood defil'd,
And moody Madness laughing wild
Amid severest woe.

Lo, in the vale of years beneath
A grisly troop are seen,

The painful family of Death,
More hideous than their queen :
This racks the joints, this fires the veins,
That every laboring sinew strains,
Those in the deeper vitals rage ;
Lo, Poverty, to fill the band,
That numbs the soul with icy hand,
And slow-consuming Age.

To each his suff'rings : all are men,
Condemn'd alike to groan,
The tender for another's pain ;
Th' unfeeling for his own.
Yet ah ! why should they know their fate ?
Since sorrow never comes too late,
And happiness too swiftly flies.
Thought would destroy their paradise.
No more ; where ignorance is bliss,
'Tis folly to be wise.

ELEGY

WRITTEN IN A COUNTRY CHURCH-YARD

The curfew tolls the knell of parting day,
    The lowing herd wind slowly o'er the lea,
The ploughman homeward plods his weary way,
    And leaves the world to darkness and to me.

Now fades the glimmering landscape on the sight,
    And all the air a solemn stillness holds,
Save where the beetle wheels his droning flight,
    And drowsy tinklings lull the distant folds ;

Save that from yonder ivy-mantled tow'r
　　The moping owl does to the moon complain
Of such, as wandering near her secret bow'r,
　　Molest her ancient solitary reign.

Beneath those rugged elms, that yew-tree's shade,
　　Where heaves the turf in many a mold'ring heap,
Each in his narrow cell for ever laid,
　　The rude forefathers of the hamlet sleep.

The breezy call of incense-breathing morn,
　　The swallow twitt'ring from the straw-built shed,
The cock's shrill clarion, or the echoing horn,
　　No more shall rouse them from their lowly bed.

For them no more the blazing hearth shall burn,
　　Or busy housewife ply her evening care :
No children run to lisp their sire's return,
　　Or climb his knees the envied kiss to share.

Oft did the harvest to their sickle yield,
　　Their furrow oft the stubborn glebe has broke ;
How jocund did they drive their team afield !
　　How bow'd the woods beneath their sturdy stroke !

Let not Ambition mock their useful toil,
　　Their homely joys, and destiny obscure ;
Nor Grandeur hear with a disdainful smile
　　The short and simple annals of the poor.

The boast of heraldry, the pomp of pow'r,
　　And all that beauty, all that wealth e'er gave,
Awaits alike th' inevitable hour —
　　The paths of glory lead but to the grave.

Nor you, ye proud, impute to these the fault,
  If Mem'ry o'er their tomb no trophies raise,
Where through the long-drawn aisle and fretted vault
  The pealing anthem swells the note of praise.

Can storied urn or animated bust
  Back to its mansion call the fleeting breath ?
Can Honor's voice provoke the silent dust,
  Or Flatt'ry soothe the dull cold ear of Death ?

Perhaps in this neglected spot is laid
  Some heart once pregnant with celestial fire ;
Hands, that the rod of empire might have sway'd,
  Or wak'd to ecstasy the living lyre.

But Knowledge to their eyes her ample page,
  Rich with the spoils of time did ne'er unroll ;
Chill Penury repress'd their noble rage,
  And froze the genial current of the soul.

Full many a gem of purest ray serene,
  The dark unfathom'd caves of ocean bear :
Full many a flower is born to blush unseen,
  And waste its sweetness on the desert air.

Some village Hampden, that with dauntless breast
  The little tyrant of his fields withstood ;
Some mute, inglorious Milton here may rest,
  Some Cromwell guiltless of his country's blood.

Th' applause of list'ning senates to command,
  The threats of pain and ruin to despise,
To scatter plenty o'er a smiling land,
  And read their hist'ry in a nation's eyes,

Their lot forbade : nor circumscrib'd alone
　　Their growing virtues, but their crimes confin'd ;
Forbade to wade through slaughter to a throne,
　　And shut the gates of mercy on mankind ;

The struggling pangs of conscious truth to hide,
　　To quench the blushes of ingenuous shame,
Or heap the shrine of Luxury and Pride
　　With incense kindled at the Muse's flame.

Far from the madding crowd's ignoble strife,
　　Their sober wishes never learn'd to stray ;
Along the cool sequester'd vale of life
　　They kept the noiseless tenor of their way.

Yet ev'n these bones from insult to protect
　　Some frail memorial still erected nigh,
With uncouth rhymes and shapeless sculpture deck'd,
　　Implores the passing tribute of a sigh.

Their name, their years, spelt by th' unletter'd Muse,
　　The place of fame and elegy supply ;
And many a holy text around she strews,
　　That teach the rustic moralist to die.

For who, to dumb forgetfulness a prey,
　　This pleasing anxious being e'er resign'd,
Left the warm precincts of the cheerful day,
　　Nor cast one longing ling'ring look behind ?

On some fond breast the parting soul relies,
　　Some pious drops the closing eye requires ;

Ev'n from the tomb the voice of Nature cries,
　　Ev'n in our ashes live their wonted fires.

For thee who, mindful of th' unhonor'd dead,
　　Dost in these lines their artless tale relate ;
If chance, by lonely contemplation led,
　　Some kindred spirit shall inquire thy fate,

Haply some hoary-headed swain may say,
　　"Oft have we seen him at the peep of dawn
Brushing with hasty steps the dews away,
　　To meet the sun upon the upland lawn.

"There at the foot of yonder nodding beech
　　That wreathes its old fantastic roots so high,
His listless length at noontide would he stretch,
　　And pore upon the brook that babbles by.

"Hard by yon wood, now smiling as in scorn,
　　Mutt'ring his wayward fancies he would rove ;
Now drooping, woeful wan, like one forlorn,
　　Or craz'd with care, or cross'd in hopeless love.

"One morn I miss'd him on the custom'd hill,
　　Along the heath, and near his fav'rite tree ;
Another came ; nor yet beside the rill,
　　Nor up the lawn, nor at the wood was he ;

"The next, with dirges due, in sad array,
　　Slow through the church-way path we saw him borne.
Approach and read (for thou canst read) the lay,
　　Grav'd on the stone beneath yon aged thorn."

THE EPITAPH

Here rests his head upon the lap of earth
  A youth to Fortune and to Fame unknown.
Fair Science frown'd not on his humble birth,
  And Melancholy mark'd him for her own.

Large was his bounty, and his soul sincere,
  Heav'n did a recompence as largely send :
He gave to Mis'ry all he had, a tear,
  He gain'd from Heav'n ('twas all he wish'd) a friend.

No farther seek his merits to disclose,
  Or draw his frailties from their dread abode,
(There they alike in trembling hope repose,)
  The bosom of his Father and his God.

WILLIAM COLLINS

(1721–1759)

ODE TO EVENING

If aught of oaten stop, or pastoral song
May hope, chaste Eve, to soothe thy modest ear,
  Like thy own solemn springs,
  Thy springs and dying gales,
O nymph reserv'd, while now the bright-hair'd sun
Sits in yon western tent, whose cloudy skirts,
  With brede ethereal wove,
  O'erhang his wavy bed :

Now air is hush'd, save where the weak-ey'd bat,
With short shrill shriek flits by on leathern wing ;
 Or where the beetle winds
 His small but sullen horn,
As oft he rises 'midst the twilight path,
Against the pilgrim borne in heedless hum :
 Now teach me, maid compos'd,
 To breathe some soften'd strain,
Whose numbers, stealing through thy darkning vale,
May not unseemly with its stillness suit,
 As musing slow, I hail
 Thy genial lov'd return !
For when thy folding-star arising shows
His paly circlet, at his warning lamp
 The fragrant Hours, and elves
 Who slept in flowers the day,
And many a nymph who wreathes her brows with sedge,
And sheds the fresh'ning dew, and, lovelier still,
 The pensive Pleasures sweet
 Prepare thy shadowy car.
Then lead, calm vot'ress, where some sheety lake
Cheers the lone heath, or some time-hallow'd pile,
 Or upland fallows gray
 Reflect its last cool gleam.
But when chill blust'ring winds or driving rain
Forbid my willing feet, be mine the hut
 That from the mountain's side
 Views wilds, and swelling floods,
And hamlets brown, and dim-discover'd spires,
And hears their simple bell, and marks o'er all
 Thy dewy fingers draw
 The gradual dusky veil.

While Spring shall pour his show'rs, as oft he wont,
And bathe thy breathing tresses, meekest Eve !
　　While Summer loves to sport
　　Beneath thy ling'ring light ;
While sallow Autumn fills thy lap with leaves ;
Or Winter, yelling through the troublous air,
　　Affrights thy shrinking train,
　　And rudely rends thy robes ;
So long, sure-found beneath the sylvan shed,
Shall Fancy, Friendship, Science, rose-lip'd Health,
　　Thy gentlest influence own,
　　And hymn thy fav'rite name !

WILLIAM COWPER

(1731–1800)

THE SHRUBBERY

WRITTEN IN A TIME OF AFFLICTION

Oh, happy shades — to me unblest !
　　Friendly to peace, but not to me !
How ill the scene that offers rest,
　　And heart that cannot rest, agree !

This glassy stream, that spreading pine,
　　Those alders quiv'ring to the breeze,
Might soothe a soul less hurt than mine,
　　And please, if anything could please.

But fix'd unalterable care
　　Foregoes not what she feels within,

Shows the same sadness ev'ry where,
 And slights the season and the scene.

For all that pleas'd in wood or lawn,
 While peace possess'd these silent bow'rs,
Her animating smile withdrawn,
 Has lost its beauties and its pow'rs.

The saint or moralist should tread
 This moss-grown alley, musing, slow ;
They seek, like me, the secret shade,
 But not, like me, to nourish woe !

Me fruitful scenes and prospects waste
 Alike admonish not to roam ;
These tell me of enjoyments past,
 And those of sorrows yet to come.

THE CASTAWAY

Obscurest night involv'd the sky,
 Th' Atlantic billows roar'd,
When such a destin'd wretch as I,
 Wash'd headlong from on board,
Of friends, of hope, of all bereft,
His floating home forever left.

No braver chief could Albion boast
 Than he with whom he went,
Nor ever ship left Albion's coast,
 With warmer wishes sent.
He lov'd them both, but both in vain,
Nor him beheld, nor her again.

Not long beneath the whelming brine,
    Expert to swim, he lay ;
Nor soon he felt his strength decline,
    Or courage die away ;
But wag'd with death a lasting strife,
Supported by despair of life.

He shouted : nor his friends had fail'd
    To check the vessel's course,
But so the furious blast prevail'd,
    That, pitiless perforce,
They left their outcast mate behind,
And scudded still before the wind.

Some succour yet they could afford ;
    And, such as storms allow,
The cask, the coop, the floated cord,
    Delay'd not to bestow.
But he (they knew) nor ship, nor shore,
Whate'er they gave, should visit more.

Nor, cruel as it seem'd, could he
    Their haste himself condemn,
Aware that flight, in such a sea,
    Alone could rescue them ;
Yet bitter felt it still to die
Deserted, and his friends so nigh.

He long survives, who lives an hour
    In ocean, self-upheld ;
And so long he, with unspent power,
    His destiny repell'd ;
And ever, as the minutes flew,
Entreated help, or cried, Adieu !

At length, his transient respite past,
 His comrades, who before
Had heard his voice in ev'ry blast,
 Could catch the sound no more.
For then, by toil subdued, he drank
The stifling wave, and then he sank.

No poet wept him : but the page
 Of narrative sincere,
That tells his name, his worth, his age,
 Is wet with Anson's tear.
And tears by bards or heroes shed
Alike immortalize the dead.

I therefore purpose not, or dream,
 Descanting on his fate,
To give the melancholy theme
 A more enduring date :
But misery still delights to trace
Its semblance in another's case.

No voice divine the storm allay'd,
 No light propitious shone,
When, snatch'd from all effectual aid,
 We perish'd, each alone —
But I beneath a rougher sea,
And whelm'd in deeper gulfs than he.

WILLIAM BLAKE

(1757–1827)

TO THE EVENING STAR

Thou fair-hair'd angel of the evening,
Now, whilst the sun rests on the mountains, light
Thy bright torch of love ; thy radiant crown
Put on, and smile upon our evening bed !
Smile on our loves, and while thou drawest the
Blue curtains of the sky, scatter thy silver dew
On every flower that shuts its sweet eyes
In timely sleep. Let thy west wind sleep on
The lake ; speak silence with thy glimmering eyes,
And wash the dusk with silver. Soon, full soon,
Dost thou withdraw ; then the wolf rages wide,
And the lion glares through the dun forest :
The fleeces of our flocks are cover'd with
Thy sacred dew : protect them with thine influence.

THE LAMB

Little Lamb, who made thee ?
Dost thou know who made thee ?
Gave thee life and bid thee feed
By the stream and o'er the mead ;
Gave thee clothing of delight,
Softest clothing, woolly, bright ;
Gave thee such a tender voice,
Making all the vales rejoice ?

Little Lamb, who made thee ?
Dost thou know who made thee ?

Little Lamb, I 'll tell thee,
Little Lamb, I 'll tell thee —
He is callèd by thy name,
For he calls himself a Lamb.
He is meek, and he is mild ;
He became a little child.
I a child and thou a lamb,
We are callèd by his name.
Little Lamb, God bless thee !
Little Lamb, God bless thee !

THE TIGER

Tiger ! Tiger ! burning bright
In the forests of the night,
What immortal hand or eye
Could frame thy fearful symmetry ?

In what distant deeps or skies
Burnt the fire of thine eyes ?
On what wings dare he aspire ?
What the hand dare seize the fire ?

And what shoulder, and what art,
Could twist the sinews of thy heart ?
And when thy heart began to beat,
What dread hand ? and what dread feet ?

What the hammer ? what the chain ?
In what furnace was thy brain ?

What the anvil ? what dread grasp
Dare its deadly terrors clasp ?

When the stars threw down their spears,
And water'd heaven with their tears,
Did he smile his work to see ?
Did he who made the Lamb make thee ?

Tiger ! Tiger ! burning bright
In the forests of the night,
What immortal hand or eye,
Dare frame thy fearful symmetry ?

THE SICK ROSE

O Rose, thou art sick !
The invisible worm
That flies in the night,
In the howling storm,

Has found out thy bed
Of crimson joy,
And his dark secret love
Does thy life destroy.

LONDON

I wander through each charter'd street,
Near where the charter'd Thames does flow,
And mark in every face I meet
Marks of weakness, marks of woe.

In every cry of every Man,
In every Infant's cry of fear,
In every voice, in every ban,
The mind-forg'd manacles I hear.

How the chimney-sweeper's cry
Every black'ning church appals ;
And the hapless soldier's sigh
Runs in blood down palace walls.

But most through midnight streets I hear
How the youthful harlot's curse
Blasts the new-born infant's tear,
And blights with plagues the marriage hearse.

THE NINETEENTH CENTURY

Wordsworth to Housman

Poetry close to everyday speech
1. Photographic language
Written in blank verse — no rhyme

WILLIAM WORDSWORTH

(1770–1850)

Was on a walking trip with his sister

LINES

COMPOSED A FEW MILES ABOVE TINTERN ABBEY, ON REVISIT-
ING THE BANKS OF THE WYE DURING A TOUR. JULY 13, 1798

Five years have past ; five summers, with the length
Of five long winters ! and again I hear
These waters, rolling from their mountain-springs
With a soft inland murmur. — Once again
Do I behold these steep and lofty cliffs,
That on a wild, secluded scene impress
Thoughts of more deep seclusion, and connect
The landscape with the quiet of the sky.
The day is come when I again repose
Here, under this dark sycamore, and view
These plots of cottage-ground, these orchard-tufts,
Which at this season, with their unripe fruits,
Are clad in one green hue, and lose themselves
'Mid groves and copses. Once again I see
These hedge-rows, hardly hedge-rows, little lines
Of sportive wood run wild : these pastoral farms,
Green to the very door ; and wreaths of smoke
Sent up, in silence, from among the trees !
With some uncertain notice, as might seem
Of vagrant dwellers in the houseless woods,
Or of some Hermit's cave, where by his fire
The Hermit sits alone.

says again the scene he saw five yrs. ago

isolated

describes the scene

tree

                        These beauteous forms,
Through a long absence, have not been to me
As is a landscape to a blind man's eye :
But oft, in lonely rooms, and 'mid the din
Of towns and cities, I have owed to them,
In hours of weariness, sensations sweet,
Felt in the blood, and felt along the heart ;
And passing even into my purer mind,
With tranquil restoration : — feelings too
Of unremembered pleasure : such, perhaps,
As have no slight or trivial influence
On that best portion of a good man's life,
His little, nameless, unremembered acts
Of kindness and of love. Nor less, I trust,
To them I may have owed another gift,
Of aspect more sublime ; that blessed mood,
In which the burden of the mystery,
In which the heavy and the weary weight
Of all this unintelligible world,
Is lightened : — that serene and blessed mood,
In which the affections gently lead us on, —
Until, the breath of this corporeal frame
And even the motion of our human blood
Almost suspended, we are laid asleep
In body, and become a living soul
While with an eye made quiet by the power
Of harmony, and the deep power of joy,
We see into the life of things.
                        If this
Be but a vain belief, yet, oh ! how oft —
In darkness and amid the many shapes
Of joyless daylight ; when the fretful stir
Unprofitable, and the fever of the world,

[handwritten marginal notes:]
how these them has registered in him during the last 5 yrs.
renews
(objective) actual language
key separation
imaginative language (emotional)
key words
my feelings may be alone

Have hung upon the beatings of my heart —
How oft, in spirit, have I turned to thee,
O sylvan Wye ! thou wanderer through the woods,
How often has my spirit turned to thee !

And now, with gleams of half-extinguished thought,
With many recognitions dim and faint,
And somewhat of a sad perplexity,
The picture of the mind revives again :
While here I stand, not only with the sense
Of present pleasure, but with pleasing thoughts
That in this moment there is life and food
For future years. And so I dare to hope,
Though changed, no doubt, from what I was when first
I came among these hills ; when like a roe
I bounded o'er the mountains, by the sides
Of the deep rivers, and the lonely streams,
Wherever nature led : more like a man
Flying from something that he dreads, than one
Who sought the thing he loved. For nature then
(The coarser pleasures of my boyish days
And their glad animal movements all gone by)
To me was all in all. — I cannot paint
What then I was. The sounding cataract
Haunted me like a passion : the tall rock,
The mountain, and the deep and gloomy wood,
Their colors and their forms, were then to me
An appetite ; a feeling and a love,
That had no need of a remoter charm
By thoughts supplied, nor any interest
Unborrowed from the eye. — That time is past,
And all its aching joys are now no more,
And all its dizzy raptures. Not for this

Faint I, nor mourn nor murmur ; other gifts
Have followed ; for such loss, I would believe,
Abundant recompense. For I have learned
To look on nature, not as in the hour
Of thoughtless youth ; but hearing oftentimes
The still, sad music of humanity,
Nor harsh nor grating, though of ample power
To chasten and subdue. And I have felt
A presence that disturbs me with the joy
Of elevated thoughts ; a sense sublime
Of something far more deeply interfused,
Whose dwelling is the light of setting suns,
And the round ocean, and the living air,
And the blue sky, and in the mind of man :
A motion and a spirit, that impels
All thinking things, all objects of all thought,
And rolls through all things. Therefore am I still
A lover of the meadows and the woods,
And mountains ; and of all that we behold
From this green earth ; of all the mighty world
Of eye, and ear, — both what they half create,
And what perceive ; well pleased to recognize
In nature and the language of the sense,
The anchor of my purest thoughts, the nurse,
The guide, the guardian of my heart, and soul
Of all my moral being. ————————
                         Nor perchance,
If I were not thus taught, should I the more
Suffer my genial spirits to decay :
For thou art with me here upon the banks
Of this fair river ; thou my dearest Friend,
My dear, dear Friend ; and in thy voice I catch
The language of my former heart, and read

My former pleasures in the shooting lights
Of thy wild eyes. O yet a little while
May I behold in thee what I was once,
My dear, dear Sister ! and this prayer I make,
Knowing that Nature never did betray
The heart that loved her ; 't is her privilege,
Through all the years of this our life, to lead
From joy to joy : for she can so inform
The mind that is within us, so impress
With quietness and beauty, and so feed
With lofty thoughts, that neither evil tongues,
Rash judgments, nor the sneers of selfish men,
Nor greetings where no kindness is, nor all
The dreary intercourse of daily life,
Shall e'er prevail against us, or disturb
Our cheerful faith, that all which we behold
Is full of blessings. Therefore let the moon
Shine on thee in thy solitary walk ;
And let the misty mountain-winds be free
To blow against thee : and, in after years,
When these wild ecstasies shall be matured
Into a sober pleasure ; when thy mind
Shall be a mansion for all lovely forms,
Thy memory be as a dwelling-place
For all sweet sounds and harmonies ; O, then,
If solitude, or fear, or pain, or grief,
Should be thy portion, with what healing thoughts
Of tender joy wilt thou remember me,
And these my exhortations ! Nor, perchance, —
If I should be where I no more can hear
Thy voice, nor catch from thy wild eyes these gleams
Of past existence, — wilt thou then forget
That on the banks of this delightful stream

We stood together ; and that I, so long
A worshipper of Nature, hither came
Unwearied in that service : rather say
With warmer love, — oh ! with far deeper zeal
Of holier love. Nor wilt thou then forget,
That after many wanderings, many years
Of absence, these steep woods and lofty cliffs,
And this green pastoral landscape, were to me
More dear, both for themselves and for thy sake !

"SHE DWELT AMONG THE UNTRODDEN WAYS"

She dwelt among the untrodden ways
    Beside the springs of Dove,
A maid whom there were none to praise
    And very few to love :

A violet by a mossy stone
    Half hidden from the eye !
Fair as a star, when only one
    Is shining in the sky.

She lived unknown, and few could know
    When Lucy ceased to be ;
But she is in her grave, and oh !
    The difference to me !

"A SLUMBER DID MY SPIRIT SEAL"

A slumber did my spirit seal ;
   I had no human fears :
She seemed a thing that could not feel
   The touch of earthly years.

No motion has she now, no force ;
   She neither hears nor sees ;
Rolled round in earth's diurnal course,
   With rocks, and stones, and trees.

"MY HEART LEAPS UP WHEN I BEHOLD"

My heart leaps up when I behold
   A rainbow in the sky :
So was it when my life began ;
So is it now I am a man ;
So be it when I shall grow old,
   Or let me die !
The Child is father of the Man ;
And I could wish my days to be
Bound each to each by natural piety.

[handwritten margin notes: Process of developement in nature - part of a divine process (religious)]

[handwritten note: sense]

[handwritten note: Nationalistic pride - is the explosion / Milton - is a symbol for Nat. pride]

LONDON, 1802

Milton ! thou shouldst be living at this hour :
England hath need of thee : she is a fen
Of stagnant waters : altar, sword, and pen,

[handwritten notes: boggy, lying district; church army; writers]

Fireside, the heroic wealth of hall and bower,
Have forfeited their ancient English dower
Of inward happiness. We are selfish men ;
O, raise us up, return to us again ;
And give us manners, virtue, freedom, power !
Thy soul was like a Star, and dwelt apart :
Thou hadst a voice whose sound was like the sea :
Pure as the naked heavens, majestic, free,
So didst thou travel on life's common way,
In cheerful godliness ; and yet thy heart
The lowliest duties on herself did lay.

COMPOSED UPON WESTMINSTER BRIDGE, SEPT. 3, 1802

Earth has not anything to show more fair :
Dull would he be of soul who could pass by
A sight so touching in its majesty :
This City now doth, like a garment, wear
The beauty of the morning ; silent, bare,
Ships, towers, domes, theatres, and temples lie
Open unto the fields, and to the sky,
All bright and glittering in the smokeless air.
Never did sun more beautifully steep,
In his first splendor, valley, rock, or hill ;
Ne'er saw I, never felt, a calm so deep !
The river glideth at his own sweet will :
Dear God ! the very houses seem asleep ;
And all that mighty heart is lying still !

"IT IS A BEAUTEOUS EVENING,
CALM AND FREE"

His solemn feelings

It is a beauteous evening, calm and free,
The holy time is quiet as a Nun
Breathless with adoration ; the broad sun
Is sinking down in its tranquillity ;
The gentleness of heaven broods o'er the Sea.
Listen ! the mighty Being is awake,
And doth with his eternal motion make
A sound like thunder — everlastingly.

child emotions of joy

Dear Child ! dear Girl ! that walkest with me here,
If thou appear untouched by solemn thought,
Thy nature is not therefore less divine :

father of the Hebrews

Thou liest in Abraham's bosom all the year ;
And worshipp'st at the Temple's inner shrine
God being with thee when we know it not.

Philosophical (Wordsworth)

p-190

THE SOLITARY REAPER

Behold her, single in the field,
Yon solitary Highland Lass !
Reaping and singing by herself ;
Stop here, or gently pass !
Alone she cuts and binds the grain,
And sings a melancholy strain ;
O listen ! for the Vale profound
Is overflowing with the sound.

symbol described

No Nightingale did ever chant
More welcome notes to weary bands

Of travellers in some shady haunt,
Among Arabian sands :
A voice so thrilling ne'er was heard .
In spring-time from the Cuckoo-bird,
Breaking the silence of the seas
Among the farthest Hebrides.

Will no one tell me what she sings ? —
Perhaps the plaintive numbers flow
For old, unhappy, far-off things,
And battles long ago :
Or is it some more humble lay,
Familiar matter of to-day ?
Some natural sorrow, loss, or pain,
That has been, and may be again ?

Whate'er the theme, the Maiden sang
As if her song could have no ending ;
I saw her singing at her work,
And o'er the sickle bending ; —
I listened, motionless and still ;
And, as I mounted up the hill,
The music in my heart I bore,
Long after it was heard no more.

TO THE CUCKOO

O Blithe New-comer ! I have heard,
I hear thee and rejoice.
O Cuckoo ! shall I call thee Bird,
Or but a wandering Voice ?

While I am lying on the grass
Thy twofold shout I hear,
From hill to hill it seems to pass,
At once far off, and near.

Though babbling only to the Vale,
Of sunshine and of flowers,
Thou bringest unto me a tale
Of visionary hours.

Thrice welcome, darling of the Spring !
Even yet thou art to me
No bird, but an invisible thing,
A voice, a mystery ;

The same whom in my schoolboy days
I listened to ; that cry
Which made me look a thousand ways,
In bush, and tree, and sky.

To seek thee did I often rove
Through woods and on the green ;
And thou wert still a hope, a love ;
Still longed for, never seen.

And I can listen to thee yet ;
Can lie upon the plain
And listen, till I do beget
That golden time again.

O blessed Bird ! the earth we pace
Again appears to be
An unsubstantial, faery place ;
That is fit home for thee !

Bring out:
1. Theory of Joy
2. Nature

Philosophical p. 187

Wordsworth is a great poet of happiness

"I WANDERED LONELY AS A CLOUD"

I wandered lonely as a cloud
That floats on high o'er vales and hills,
When all at once I saw a crowd,
A host, of golden daffodils ;
Beside the lake, beneath the trees,
Fluttering and dancing in the breeze.

Continuous as the stars that shine
And twinkle on the milky way,
They stretched in never-ending line
Along the margin of a bay :
Ten thousand saw I at a glance,
Tossing their heads in sprightly dance.

remembered of two months

The waves beside them danced ; but they
Outdid the sparkling waves in glee :
A poet could not but be gay,
In such a jocund company :
I gazed, — and gazed, — but little thought
What wealth the show to me had brought :

(remembered incident)

feeling of seeing gaiety

Philosophical conclusion

For oft, when on my couch I lie
In vacant or in pensive mood,
They flash upon that inward eye
Which is the bliss of solitude ;
And then my heart with pleasure fills,
And dances with the daffodils.

lonely again (different type of loneliness)

great feeling of refreshment

Industrialism - forgetting what the world really is - the nature part

"THE WORLD IS TOO MUCH WITH US; LATE AND SOON"

The world is too much with us ; late and soon,
Getting and spending, we lay waste our powers :
Little we see in Nature that is ours ;
We have given our hearts away, a sordid boon !
This Sea that bares her bosom to the moon ;
The winds that will be howling at all hours,
And are up-gathered now like sleeping flowers ;
For this, for everything, we are out of tune ;
It moves us not. — Great God ! I 'd rather be
A Pagan suckled in a creed outworn ;
So might I, standing on this pleasant lea,
Have glimpses that would make me less forlorn ;
Have sight of Proteus rising from the sea,
Or hear old Triton blow his wreathed horn.

We see little in nature

enumeration of the sea

3 sections I II III - timely utterance IV - IX - myth X XI

ODE it rhymes

INTIMATIONS OF IMMORTALITY FROM RECOLLECTIONS OF EARLY CHILDHOOD

The Child is father of the Man ; The poem is uneven
And I could wish my days to be
Bound each to each by natural piety.

I

There was a time when meadow, grove, and stream
The earth, and every common sight,
    To me did seem

Apparelled in celestial light,
The glory and the freshness of a dream.
It is not now as it hath been of yore ; —
Turn wheresoe'er I may,
By night or day,
The things which I have seen I now can see no more.

II

The Rainbow comes and goes,
And lovely is the Rose ;
The Moon doth with delight
Look round her when the heavens are bare ;
Waters on a starry night
Are beautiful and fair ;
The sunshine is a glorious birth ;
But yet I know where'er I go,
That there hath passed away a glory from the earth

III

Now, while the birds thus sing a joyous song,
And while the young lambs bound
As to the tabor's sound,
To me alone there came a thought of grief :
A timely utterance gave that thought relief,
And I again am strong :
The cataracts blow their trumpets from the steep ;
No more shall grief of mine the season wrong ;
I hear the echoes through the mountains throng,
The winds come to me from the fields of sleep,
And all the earth is gay ;
Land and sea
Give themselves up to jollity,

And with the heart of May
Doth every beast keep holiday ; —
Thou Child of Joy,
Shout round me, let me hear thy shouts, thou happy *Rfs : to a child*
Shepherd-boy !

Skip to sec. 3

IV

Ye blessed Creatures, I have heard the call
Ye to each other make ; I see
The heavens laugh with you in your jubilee ;
My heart is at your festival,
My head hath its coronal, *crown*
The fulness of your bliss, I feel, I feel it all.
O evil day ! if I were sullen
While Earth herself is adorning,
This sweet May-morning,
And the Children are culling
On every side,
In a thousand valleys far and wide,
Fresh flowers ; while the sun shines warm,
And the Babe leaps up on his Mother's arm : —
I hear, I hear, with joy I hear !
— But there 's a Tree, of many, one,
A single Field which I have looked upon,
Both of them speak of something that is gone :
The pansy at my feet
Doth the same tale repeat :
Whither is fled the visionary gleam ?
Where is it now, the glory and the dream ?

as if statements IV → IX

Does W. W. believe what he has written? 1. It complicates the poem

Quintana wouldn't read these lines

Sudden realization of the loss that has come upon him

V

Our birth is but a sleep and a forgetting :
The Soul that rises with us, our life's Star,

Birth death

Hath had elsewhere its setting,
   And cometh from afar :
Not in entire forgetfulness,
   And not in utter nakedness,
But trailing clouds of glory, do we come
   From God, who is our home :
Heaven lies about us in our infancy !
Shades of the prison-house begin to close
   Upon the growing Boy,
But he beholds the light, and whence it flows,
   He sees it in his joy ;
The Youth, who daily farther from the east
   Must travel, still is Nature's Priest,
   And by the vision splendid
   Is on his way attended ;
At length the Man perceives it die away,
And fade into the light of common day.

VI

Earth fills her lap with pleasures of her own ;
Yearnings she hath in her own natural kind,
And, even with something of a Mother's mind,
   And no unworthy aim,
   The homely Nurse doth all she can
To make her Foster-child, her Inmate Man,
   Forget the glories he hath known,
And that imperial palace whence he came.

VII

Behold the Child among his new-born blisses,
A six years' Darling of a pigmy size !
See, where 'mid work of his own hand he lies,

Fretted by sallies of his mother's kisses,
With light upon him from his father's eyes !
See, at his feet, some little plan or chart,
Some fragment from his dream of human life,
Shaped by himself with newly-learned art ;
    A wedding or a festival,
    A mourning or a funeral ;
        And this hath now his heart,
    And unto this he frames his song :
        Then will he fit his tongue
To dialogues of business, love, or strife ;
    But it will not be long
    Ere this be thrown aside,
    And with new joy and pride
The little Actor cons another part ;
Filling from time to time his "humorous stage"
With all the Persons, down to palsied Age,
That Life brings with her in her equipage ;
    As if his whole vocation
    Were endless imitation.

                    VIII

Thou, whose exterior semblance doth belie
        Thy Soul's immensity ;
Thou best Philosopher, who yet dost keep
Thy heritage, thou Eye among the blind,
That, deaf and silent, read'st the eternal deep,
Haunted for ever by the eternal mind,—
        Mighty Prophet ! Seer blest !
        On whom those truths do rest,
Which we are toiling all our lives to find,
In darkness lost, the darkness of the grave ;

Thou, over whom thy Immortality
Broods like the Day, a Master o'er a Slave,
A Presence which is not to be put by ;
Thou little Child, yet glorious in the might
Of heaven-born freedom on thy being's height,
Why with such earnest pains dost thou provoke
The years to bring the inevitable yoke,
Thus blindly with thy blessedness at strife ?
Full soon thy Soul shall have her earthly freight,
And custom lie upon thee with a weight,
Heavy as frost, and deep almost as life !

IX

O joy ! that in our embers
Is something that doth live,
That Nature yet remembers
What was so fugitive !
The thought of our past years in me doth breed
Perpetual benediction : not indeed
For that which is most worthy to be blest ;
Delight and liberty, the simple creed
Of Childhood, whether busy or at rest,
With new-fledged hope still fluttering in his breast : —
    Not for these I raise
    The song of thanks and praise ;
    But for those obstinate questionings
    Of sense and outward things,
    Fallings from us, vanishings ;
    Blank misgivings of a Creature
Moving about in worlds not realized,
High instincts before which our mortal Nature

Did tremble like a guilty thing surprised :
　　But for those first affections,
　　Those shadowy recollections,
　Which, be they what they may,
Are yet the fountain light of all our day,
Are yet a master light of all our seeing ;
　　Uphold us, cherish, and have power to make
Our noisy years seem moments in the being
Of the eternal Silence : truths that wake,
　　　To perish never ;
Which neither listlessness, nor mad endeavor,
　　　Nor Man nor Boy,
Nor all that is at enmity with joy,
Can utterly abolish or destroy !
　　Hence in a season of calm weather
　　Though inland far we be,
Our souls have sight of that immortal sea
　　Which brought us hither,
　Can in a moment travel thither,
And see the Children sport upon the shore,
And hear the mighty waters rolling evermore.

　　　　　　X

Then sing, ye Birds, sing, sing a joyous song !
　　And let the young Lambs bound
　　As to the tabor's sound !
We in thought will join your throng,
　　Ye that pipe and ye that play,
　　Ye that through your hearts to-day
　　Feel the gladness of the May !
What though the radiance which was once so bright

Be now for ever taken from my sight,
    Though nothing can bring back the hour
Of splendor in the grass, of glory in the flower;
    We will grieve not, rather find
    Strength in what remains behind;
    In the primal sympathy *real interest*
    Which, having been, must ever be;
    In the soothing thoughts that spring
    Out of human suffering;
    In the faith that looks through death,
In years that bring the philosophic mind.

XI

And O ye Fountains, Meadows, Hills, and Groves, *Cycle of life*
Forebode not any severing of our loves!
Yet in my heart of hearts I feel your might;
I only have relinquished one delight
To live beneath your more habitual sway.
I love the Brooks which down their channels fret,
Even more than when I tripped lightly as they;
The innocent brightness of a new-born Day
    Is lovely yet;
The Clouds that gather round the setting sun
Do take a sober coloring from an eye
That hath kept watch o'er man's mortality;
Another race hath been, and other palms are won,
Thanks to the human heart by which we live,
Thanks to its tenderness, its joys, and fears,
To me the meanest flower that blows can give
Thoughts that do often lie too deep for tears.

THOUGHT OF A BRITON ON THE SUBJUGATION OF SWITZERLAND

Two Voices are there ; one is of the sea,   *Manufactured too much.*
One of the mountains ; each a mighty Voice :
In both from age to age thou didst rejoice,
They were thy chosen music, Liberty !
There came a Tyrant, and with holy glee
Thou fought'st against him ; but hast vainly striven :
Thou from thy Alpine holds at length art driven,
Where not a torrent murmurs heard by thee.
Of one deep bliss thine ear hath been bereft :
Then cleave, O cleave to that which still is left ;
For, high-souled Maid, what sorrow would it be
That Mountain floods should thunder as before,
And Ocean bellow from his rocky shore,
And neither awful Voice be heard by thee !

SAMUEL TAYLOR COLERIDGE

(1772–1834)

KUBLA KHAN

In Xanadu did Kubla Khan
   A stately pleasure-dome decree :
Where Alph, the sacred river, ran
Through caverns measureless to man
   Down to a sunless sea.
So twice five miles of fertile ground
With walls and towers were girdled round :

And there were gardens bright with sinuous rills
Where blossomed many an incense-bearing tree ;
And here were forests ancient as the hills,
Enfolding sunny spots of greenery.

But oh ! that deep romantic chasm which slanted
Down the green hill athwart a cedarn cover !
A savage place ! as holy and enchanted
As e'er beneath a waning moon was haunted
By woman wailing for her demon-lover !
And from this chasm, with ceaseless turmoil seething,
As if this earth in fast thick pants were breathing,
A mighty fountain momently was forced :
Amid whose swift half-intermitted burst
Huge fragments vaulted like rebounding hail,
Or chaffy grain beneath the thresher's flail :
And 'mid these dancing rocks at once and ever
It flung up momently the sacred river.
Five miles meandering with a mazy motion
Through wood and dale the sacred river ran,
Then reached the caverns measureless to man,
And sank in tumult to a lifeless ocean :
And 'mid this tumult Kubla heard from far
Ancestral voices prophesying war !

The shadow of the dome of pleasure
    Floated mid-way on the waves ;
Where was heard the mingled measure
    From the fountain and the caves.
It was a miracle of rare device,
A sunny pleasure-dome with caves of ice !

A damsel with a dulcimer
    In a vision once I saw :

It was an Abyssinian maid,
    And on her dulcimer she played,
Singing of Mount Abora.
Could I revive within me,
    Her symphony and song,
To such a deep delight 'twould win me,
That with music loud and long,
I would build that dome in air,
That sunny dome ! those caves of ice !
And all who heard should see them there,
And all should cry, Beware ! Beware !
His flashing eyes, his floating hair !
Weave a circle round him thrice,
    And close your eyes with holy dread,
    For he on honey-dew hath fed,
And drunk the milk of Paradise.

from
ZAPOLYA

SONG

by Glycine

A sunny shaft did I behold,
    From sky to earth it slanted :
And poised therein a bird so bold —
    Sweet bird, thou wert enchanted !

He sunk, he rose, he twinkled, he trolled
    Within that shaft of sunny mist ;
His eyes of fire, his beak of gold,
    All else of amethyst !

And thus he sang : "Adieu ! adieu !
Love's dreams prove seldom true.
The blossoms, they make no delay :
The sparkling dewdrops will not stay.
Sweet month of May,
We must away ;
Far, far away !
To-day ! to-day !"

PERCY BYSSHE SHELLEY

(1792–1822)

ODE TO THE WEST WIND

I

O wild West Wind, thou breath of Autumn's being,
Thou, from whose unseen presence the leaves dead
Are driven, like ghosts from an enchanter fleeing,

Yellow, and black, and pale, and hectic red,
Pestilence-stricken multitudes : O thou,
Who chariotest to their dark wintry bed

The wingèd seeds, where they lie cold and low,
Each like a corpse within its grave, until
Thine azure sister of the Spring shall blow

Her clarion o'er the dreaming earth, and fill
(Driving sweet buds like flocks to feed in air)
With living hues and odours plain and hill :

Wild Spirit, which art moving everywhere ; *e*
Destroyer and preserver ; hear, oh, hear ! *ᴦ*

II

Thou on whose stream, mid the steep sky's commotion,
Loose clouds like earth's decaying leaves are shed,
Shook from the tangled boughs of Heaven and Ocean,

Angels of rain and lightning : there are spread
On the blue surface of thine aëry surge,
Like the bright hair uplifted from the head

Of some fierce Maenad, even from the dim verge
Of the horizon to the zenith's height,
The locks of the approaching storm. Thou dirge

Of the dying year, to which this closing night
Will be the dome of a vast sepulchre,
Vaulted with all thy congregated might

Of vapours, from whose solid atmosphere
Black rain, and fire, and hail will burst : oh, hear !

III

Thou who didst waken from his summer dreams
The blue Mediterranean, where he lay,
Lulled by the coil of his crystàlline streams,

Beside a pumice isle on Baiæ's bay,
And saw in sleep old palaces and towers
Quivering within the wave's intenser day,

All overgrown with azure moss and flowers
So sweet, the sense faints picturing them ! Thou
For whose path the Atlantic's level powers

Cleave themselves into chasms, while far below
The sea-blooms and the oozy woods which wear
The sapless foliage of the ocean, know

Thy voice, and suddenly grow gray with fear,
And tremble and despoil themselves : oh, hear !

IV

If I were a dead leaf thou mightest bear ;
If I were a swift cloud to fly with thee ;
A wave to pant beneath thy power, and share

The impulse of thy strength, only less free
Than thou, O uncontrollable ! If even
I were as in my boyhood, and could be

The comrade of thy wanderings over Heaven,
As then, when to outstrip thy skiey speed
Scarce seemed a vision ; I would ne'er have striven

As thus with thee in prayer in my sore need.
Oh, lift me as a wave, a leaf, a cloud !
I fall upon the thorns of life ! I bleed !

A heavy weight of hours has chained and bowed
One too like thee : tameless, and swift, and proud.

V

Make me thy lyre, even as the forest is :
What if my leaves are falling like its own !
The tumult of thy mighty harmonies

Will take from both a deep, autumnal tone,
Sweet though in sadness. Be thou, Spirit fierce,
My spirit ! Be thou me, impetuous one !

Drive my dead thoughts over the universe
Like withered leaves to quicken a new birth !
And, by the incantation of this verse,

Scatter, as from an unextinguished hearth
Ashes and sparks, my words among mankind !
Be through my lips to unawakened earth

The trumpet of a prophecy ! O, Wind,
If Winter comes, can Spring be far behind ?

TO A SKYLARK

Hail to thee, blithe Spirit !
  Bird thou never wert,
That from Heaven, or near it,
  Pourest thy full heart
In profuse strains of unpremeditated art.

Higher still and higher
  From the earth thou springest

Like a cloud of fire ;
   The blue deep thou wingest,
And singing still dost soar, and soaring ever singest.

   In the golden lightning
     Of the sunken sun,
   O'er which clouds are bright'ning,
     Thou dost float and run ;
Like an unbodied joy whose race is just begun.

   The pale purple even
     Melts around thy flight ;
   Like a star of Heaven,
     In the broad daylight
Thou art unseen, but yet I hear thy shrill delight,

   Keen as are the arrows
     Of that silver sphere,
   Whose intense lamp narrows
     In the white dawn clear
Until we hardly see — we feel that it is there.

   All the earth and air
     With thy voice is loud,
   As, when night is bare,
     From one lonely cloud
The moon rains out her beams, and Heaven is overflowed.

   What thou art we know not ;
     What is most like thee ?
   From rainbow clouds there flow not
     Drops so bright to see
As from thy presence showers a rain of melody.

Like a Poet hidden
   In the light of thought,
Singing hymns unbidden,
   Till the world is wrought
To sympathy with hopes and fears it heeded not :

Like a high-born maiden
   In a palace-tower
Soothing her love-laden
   Soul in secret hour
With music sweet as love, which overflows her bower :

Like a glow-worm golden
   In a dell of dew,
Scattering unbeholden
   Its aëreal hue
Among the flowers and grass, which screen it from the view !

Like a rose embowered
   In its own green leaves,
By warm winds deflowered,
   Till the scent it gives
Makes faint with too much sweet those heavy-wingèd thieves :

Sound of vernal showers
   On the twinkling grass,
Rain-awakened flowers,
   All that ever was
Joyous, and clear, and fresh, thy music doth surpass :

Teach us, Sprite or Bird,
   What sweet thoughts are thine :

I have never heard
    Praise of love or wine
That panted forth a flood of rapture so divine.

Chorus Hymeneal,
    Or triumphal chant,
Matched with thine would be all
    But an empty vaunt,
A thing wherein we feel there is some hidden want.

What objects are the fountains
    Of thy happy strain ?
What fields, or waves, or mountains ?
    What shapes of sky or plain ?
What love of thine own kind ? what ignorance of pain ?

With thy clear keen joyance
    Languor cannot be :
Shadow of annoyance
    Never came near thee :
Thou lovest — but ne'er knew love's sad satiety.

Waking or asleep,
    Thou of death must deem
Things more true and deep
    Than we mortals dream,
Or how could thy notes flow in such a crystal stream ?

We look before and after,
    And pine for what is not :
Our sincerest laughter
    With some pain is fraught ;
Our sweetest songs are those that tell of saddest thought.

Yet if we could scorn
    Hate, and pride, and fear ;
If we were things born
    Not to shed a tear,
I know not how thy joy we ever should come near.

Better than all measures
    Of delightful sound,
Better than all treasures
    That in books are found,
Thy skill to poet were, thou scorner of the ground !

Teach me half the gladness
    That thy brain must know,
Such harmonious madness
    From my lips would flow
The world should listen then — as I am listening now.

JOHN KEATS
(1795–1821)

ON FIRST LOOKING INTO
CHAPMAN'S HOMER

Much have I travell'd in the realms of gold,
    And many goodly states and kingdoms seen ;
    Round many western islands have I been
Which bards in fealty to Apollo hold.
Oft of one wide expanse had I been told
    That deep-brow'd Homer ruled as his demesne ;
    Yet did I never breathe its pure serene

Till I heard Chapman speak out loud and bold :
Then felt I like some watcher of the skies
    When a new planet swims into his ken ;
Or like stout Cortez when with eagle eyes
    He stared at the Pacific — and all his men
Look'd at each other with a wild surmise —
    Silent, upon a peak in Darien.

ON SEEING THE ELGIN MARBLES
FOR THE FIRST TIME

My spirit is too weak — mortality
    Weighs heavily on me like unwilling sleep,
    And each imagin'd pinnacle and steep
Of godlike hardship, tells me I must die
Like a sick Eagle looking at the sky.
    Yet 'tis a gentle luxury to weep
    That I have not the cloudy winds to keep,
Fresh for the opening of the morning's eye.
Such dim-conceived glories of the brain
    Bring round the heart an undescribable feud ;
So do these wonders a most dizzy pain,
    That mingles Grecian grandeur with the rude
Wasting of old Time — with a billowy main —
    A sun — a shadow of a magnitude.

ON THE SEA

It keeps eternal whisperings around
    Desolate shores, and with its mighty swell
    Gluts twice ten thousand Caverns, till the spell

Of Hecate leaves them their old shadowy sound.
Often 'tis in such gentle temper found,
   That scarcely will the very smallest shell
   Be mov'd for days from where it sometime fell,
When last the winds of Heaven were unbound.
Oh ye ! who have your eye-balls vex'd and tir'd,
   Feast them upon the wideness of the Sea ;
      Oh ye ! whose ears are dinn'd with uproar rude,
    Or fed too much with cloying melody —
      Sit ye near some old Cavern's Mouth, and brood
Until ye start, as if the sea-nymphs quir'd !

"WHEN I HAVE FEARS
THAT I MAY CEASE TO BE"

When I have fears that I may cease to be
   Before my pen has glean'd my teeming brain,
Before high-piled books, in charactery,
   Hold like rich garners the full ripen'd grain ;
When I behold, upon the night's starr'd face,
   Huge cloudy symbols of a high romance,
And think that I may never live to trace
   Their shadows, with the magic hand of chance ;
And when I feel, fair creature of an hour,
   That I shall never look upon thee more,
Never have relish in the faery power
   Of unreflecting love ; — then on the shore
Of the wide world I stand alone, and think
Till love and fame to nothingness do sink.

HYPERION : A FRAGMENT

BOOK I

Deep in the shady sadness of a vale
Far sunken from the healthy breath of morn,
Far from the fiery noon, and eve's one star,
Sat gray-hair'd Saturn, quiet as a stone,
Still as the silence round about his lair ;
Forest on forest hung about his head
Like cloud on cloud. No stir of air was there,
Not so much life as on a summer's day
Robs not one light seed from the feather'd grass,
But where the dead leaf fell, there did it rest.
A stream went voiceless by, still deadened more
By reason of his fallen divinity
Spreading a shade : the Naiad 'mid her reeds
Press'd her cold finger closer to her lips.

Along the margin-sand large foot-marks went,
No further than to where his feet had stray'd,
And slept there since. Upon the sodden ground
His old right hand lay nerveless, listless, dead,
Unsceptred ; and his realmless eyes were closed ;
While his bow'd head seem'd list'ning to the Earth,
His ancient mother, for some comfort yet.

It seem'd no force could wake him from his place ;
But there came one, who with a kindred hand
Touch'd his wide shoulders, after bending low
With reverence, though to one who knew it not.
She was a Goddess of the infant world ;

By her in stature the tall Amazon
Had stood a pigmy's height : she would have ta'en
Achilles by the hair and bent his neck ;
Or with a finger stay'd Ixion's wheel.
Her face was large as that of Memphian sphinx,
Pedestal'd haply in a palace court,
When sages look'd to Egypt for their lore.
But oh ! how unlike marble was that face :
How beautiful, if sorrow had not made
Sorrow more beautiful than Beauty's self.
There was a listening fear in her regard,
As if calamity had but begun ;
As if the vanward clouds of evil days
Had spent their malice, and the sullen rear
Was with its stored thunder labouring up.
One hand she press'd upon that aching spot
Where beats the human heart, as if just there,
Though an immortal, she felt cruel pain :
The other upon Saturn's bended neck
She laid, and to the level of his ear
Leaning with parted lips, some words she spake
In solemn tenour and deep organ tone :
Some mourning words, which in our feeble tongue
Would come in these like accents ; O how frail
To that large utterance of the early Gods !
'Saturn, look up ! — though wherefore, poor old King ?
'I have no comfort for thee, no not one :
'I cannot say, "O wherefore sleepest thou ?"
'For heaven is parted from thee, and the earth
'Knows thee not, thus afflicted, for a God ;
'And ocean too, with all its solemn noise,
'Has from thy sceptre pass'd ; and all the air
'Is emptied of thine hoary majesty.

'Thy thunder, conscious of the new command,
'Rumbles reluctant o'er our fallen house ;
'And thy sharp lightning in unpractis'd hands
'Scorches and burns our once serene domain.
'O aching time ! O moments big as years !
'All as ye pass swell out the monstrous truth,
'And press it so upon our weary griefs
'That unbelief has not a space to breathe.
'Saturn, sleep on : — O thoughtless, why did I
'Thus violate thy slumbrous solitude ?
'Why should I ope thy melancholy eyes ?
'Saturn, sleep on ! while at thy feet I weep.'

As when, upon a tranced summer-night,
Those green-rob'd senators of mighty woods,
Tall oaks, branch-charmed by the earnest stars,
Dream, and so dream all night without a stir,
Save from one gradual solitary gust
Which comes upon the silence, and dies off,
As if the ebbing air had but one wave ;
So came these words and went ; the while in tears
She touch'd her fair large forehead to the ground,
Just where her falling hair might be outspread
A soft and silken mat for Saturn's feet.
One moon, with alteration slow, had shed
Her silver seasons four upon the night,
And still these two were postured motionless,
Like natural sculpture in cathedral cavern ;
The frozen God still couchant on the earth,
And the sad Goddess weeping at his feet :
Until at length old Saturn lifted up
His faded eyes, and saw his kingdom gone,
And all the gloom and sorrow of the place,

And that fair kneeling Goddess ; and then spake,
As with a palsied tongue, and while his beard
Shook horrid with such aspen-malady :
'O tender spouse of gold Hyperion,
'Thea, I feel thee ere I see thy face ;
'Look up, and let me see our doom in it ;
'Look up, and tell me if this feeble shape
'Is Saturn's ; tell me, if thou hear'st the voice
'Of Saturn ; tell me, if this wrinkling brow,
'Naked and bare of its great diadem,
'Peers like the front of Saturn. Who had power
'To make me desolate ? whence came the strength ?
'How was it nurtur'd to such bursting forth,
'While Fate seem'd strangled in my nervous grasp ?
'But it is so ; and I am smother'd up,
'And buried from all godlike exercise
'Of influence benign on planets pale,
'Of admonitions to the winds and seas,
'Of peaceful sway above man's harvesting,
'And all those acts which Deity supreme
'Doth ease its heart of love in. — I am gone
'Away from my own bosom : I have left
'My strong identity, my real self,
'Somewhere between the throne, and where I sit
'Here on this spot of earth. Search, Thea, search !
'Open thine eyes eterne, and sphere them round
'Upon all space : space starr'd, and lorn of light ;
'Space region'd with life-air ; and barren void ;
'Spaces of fire, and all the yawn of hell. —
'Search, Thea, search ! and tell me, if thou seest
'A certain shape or shadow, making way
'With wings or chariot fierce to repossess
'A heaven he lost erewhile : it must — it must

'Be of ripe progress — Saturn must be King.
'Yes, there must be a golden victory ;
'There must be Gods thrown down, and trumpets blown
'Of triumph calm, and hymns of festival
'Upon the gold clouds metropolitan,
'Voices of soft proclaim, and silver stir
'Of strings in hollow shells ; and there shall be
'Beautiful things made new, for the surprise
'Of the sky-children ; I will give command :
'Thea ! Thea ! Thea ! where is Saturn ?'

This passion lifted him upon his feet,
And made his hands to struggle in the air,
His Druid locks to shake and ooze with sweat,
His eyes to fever out, his voice to cease.
He stood, and heard not Thea's sobbing deep ;
A little time, and then again he snatch'd
Utterance thus. — 'But cannot I create ?
'Cannot I form ? Cannot I fashion forth
'Another world, another universe,
'To overbear and crumble this to naught ?
'Where is another chaos ? Where ?' — That word
Found way unto Olympus, and made quake
The rebel three. — Thea was startled up,
And in her bearing was a sort of hope,
As thus she quick-voic'd spake, yet full of awe.
'This cheers our fallen house : come to our friends,
'O Saturn ! come away, and give them heart ;
'I know the covert, for thence came I hither.'
Thus brief ; then with beseeching eyes she went
With backward footing through the shade a space :
He follow'd, and she turn'd to lead the way

Through aged boughs, that yielded like the mist
Which eagles cleave upmounting from their nest.

   Meanwhile in other realms big tears were shed,
More sorrow like to this, and such like woe,
Too huge for mortal tongue or pen of scribe :
The Titans fierce, self-hid, or prison-bound,
Groan'd for the old allegiance once more,
And listen'd in sharp pain for Saturn's voice.
But one of the whole mammoth-brood still kept
His sov'reignty, and rule, and majesty ; —
Blazing Hyperion on his orbed fire
Still sat, still snuff'd the incense, teeming up
From man to the sun's God ; yet unsecure :
For as among us mortals omens drear
Fright and perplex, so also shuddered he —
Not at dog's howl, or gloom-bird's hated screech,
Or the familiar visiting of one
Upon the first toll of his passing-bell,
Or prophesyings of the midnight lamp ;
But horrors, portion'd to a giant nerve,
Oft made Hyperion ache. His palace bright
Bastion'd with pyramids of glowing gold,
And touch'd with shade of bronzed obelisks,
Glar'd a blood-red through all its thousand courts,
Arches, and domes, and fiery galleries ;
And all its curtains of Aurorian clouds
Flush'd angerly : while sometimes eagle's wings,
Unseen before by Gods or wondering men,
Darken'd the place ; and neighing steeds were heard,
Not heard before by Gods or wondering men.
Also, when he would taste the spicy wreaths

Of incense, breath'd aloft from sacred hills,
Instead of sweets, his ample palate took
Savour of poisonous brass and metal sick :
And so, when harbour'd in the sleepy west,
After the full completion of fair day, —
For rest divine upon exalted couch
And slumber in the arms of melody,
He pac'd away the pleasant hours of ease
With stride colossal, on from hall to hall ;
While far within each aisle and deep recess,
His winged minions in close clusters stood,
Amaz'd and full of fear ; like anxious men
Who on wide plains gather in panting troops,
When earthquakes jar their battlements and towers.
Even now, while Saturn, rous'd from icy trance,
Went step for step with Thea through the woods,
Hyperion, leaving twilight in the rear,
Came slope upon the threshold of the west ;
Then, as was wont, his palace-door flew ope
In smoothest silence, save what solemn tubes,
Blown by the serious Zephyrs, gave of sweet
And wandering sounds, slow-breathed melodies ;
And like a rose in vermeil tint and shape,
In fragrance soft, and coolness to the eye,
That inlet to severe magnificence
Stood full blown, for the God to enter in.

He enter'd, but he enter'd full of wrath ;
His flaming robes stream'd out beyond his heels,
And gave a roar, as if of earthly fire,
That scar'd away the meek ethereal Hours
And made their dove-wings tremble. On he flared,
From stately nave to nave, from vault to vault,

Through bowers of fragrant and enwreathed light,
And diamond-paved lustrous long arcades,
Until he reach'd the great main cupola ;
There standing fierce beneath, he stamped his foot,
And from the basements deep to the high towers
Jarr'd his own golden region ; and before
The quavering thunder thereupon had ceas'd,
His voice leapt out, despite of godlike curb,
To this result : 'O dreams of day and night !
'O monstrous forms ! O effigies of pain !
'O spectres busy in a cold, cold gloom !
'O lank-ear'd Phantoms of black-weeded pools !
'Why do I know ye ? why have I seen ye ? why
'Is my eternal essence thus distraught
'To see and to behold these horrors new ?
'Saturn is fallen, am I too to fall ?
'Am I to leave this haven of my rest,
'This cradle of my glory, this soft clime,
'This calm luxuriance of blissful light,
'These crystalline pavilions, and pure fanes,
'Of all my lucent empire ? It is left
'Deserted, void, nor any haunt of mine.
'The blaze, the splendor, and the symmetry,
'I cannot see — but darkness, death and darkness.
'Even here, into my centre of repose,
'The shady visions come to domineer,
'Insult, and blind, and stifle up my pomp. —
'Fall ! — No, by Tellus and her briny robes !
'Over the fiery frontier of my realms
'I will advance a terrible right arm
'Shall scare that infant thunderer, rebel Jove,
'And bid old Saturn take his throne again.' —
He spake, and ceas'd, the while a heavier threat

Held struggle with his throat but came not forth ;
For as in theatres of crowded men
Hubbub increases more they call out 'Hush !'
So at Hyperion's words the Phantoms pale
Bestirr'd themselves, thrice horrible and cold ;
And from the mirror'd level where he stood
A mist arose, as from a scummy marsh.
At this, through all his bulk an agony
Crept gradual, from the feet unto the crown,
Like a lithe serpent vast and muscular
Making slow way, with head and neck convuls'd
From over-strained might. Releas'd, he fled
To the eastern gates, and full six dewy hours
Before the dawn in season due should blush,
He breath'd fierce breath against the sleepy portals,
Clear'd them of heavy vapours, burst them wide
Suddenly on the ocean's chilly streams.
The planet orb of fire, whereon he rode
Each day from east to west the heavens through,
Spun round in sable curtaining of clouds ;
Not therefore veiled quite, blindfold, and hid,
But ever and anon the glancing spheres,
Circles, and arcs, and broad-belting colure,
Glow'd through, and wrought upon the muffling dark
Sweet-shaped lightnings from the nadir deep
Up to the zenith, — hieroglyphics old
Which sages and keen-eyed astrologers
Then living on the earth, with labouring thought
Won from the gaze of many centuries :
Now lost, save what we find on remnants huge
Of stone, or marble swart ; their import gone,
Their wisdom long since fled. — Two wings this orb
Possess'd for glory, two fair argent wings,

Ever exalted at the God's approach :
And now, from forth the gloom their plumes immense
Rose, one by one, till all outspreaded were ;
While still the dazzling globe maintain'd eclipse,
Awaiting for Hyperion's command.
Fain would he have commanded, fain took throne
And bid the day begin, if but for change.
He might not : — No, though a primeval God :
The sacred seasons might not be disturb'd.
Therefore the operations of the dawn
Stay'd in their birth, even as here 'tis told.
Those silver wings expanded sisterly,
Eager to sail their orb ; the porches wide
Open'd upon the dusk demesnes of night ;
And the bright Titan, phrenzied with new woes,
Unus'd to bend, by hard compulsion bent
His spirit to the sorrow of the time ;
And all along a dismal rack of clouds,
Upon the boundaries of day and night,
He stretch'd himself in grief and radiance faint.
There as he lay, the Heaven with its stars
Look'd down on him with pity, and the voice
Of Cœlus, from the universal space,
Thus whisper'd low and solemn in his ear.
'O brightest of my children dear, earth-born
'And sky-engendered, Son of Mysteries
'All unrevealed even to the powers
'Which met at thy creating ; at whose joys
'And palpitations sweet, and pleasures soft,
'I, Cœlus, wonder, how they came and whence ;
'And at the fruits thereof what shapes they be,
'Distinct, and visible ; symbols divine,
'Manifestations of that beauteous life

'Diffus'd unseen throughout eternal space :
'Of these new-form'd art thou, oh brightest child !
'Of these, thy brethren and the Goddesses !
'There is sad feud among ye, and rebellion
'Of son against his sire. I saw him fall,
'I saw my first-born tumbled from his throne !
'To me his arms were spread, to me his voice
'Found way from forth the thunders round his head !
'Pale wox I, and in vapours hid my face.
'Art thou, too, near such doom ? vague fear there is :
'For I have seen my sons most unlike Gods.
'Divine ye were created, and divine
'In sad demeanour, solemn, undisturb'd,
'Unruffled, like high Gods, ye liv'd and ruled :
'Now I behold in you fear, hope, and wrath ;
'Actions of rage and passion ; even as
'I see them, on the mortal world beneath,
'In men who die. — This is the grief, O Son !
'Sad sign of ruin, sudden dismay, and fall !
'Yet do thou strive ; as thou art capable,
'As thou canst move about, an evident God ;
'And canst oppose to each malignant hour
'Ethereal presence : — I am but a voice ;
'My life is but the life of winds and tides,
'No more than winds and tides can I avail : —
'But thou canst. — Be thou therefore in the van
'Of circumstance ; yea, seize the arrow's barb
'Before the tense string murmur. — To the earth !
'For there thou wilt find Saturn, and his woes.
'Meantime I will keep watch on thy bright sun,
'And of thy seasons be a careful nurse.' —
Ere half this region-whisper had come down,
Hyperion arose, and on the stars

Lifted his curved lids, and kept them wide
Until it ceas'd ; and still he kept them wide :
And still they were the same bright, patient stars.
Then with a slow incline of his broad breast,
Like to a diver in the pearly seas,
Forward he stoop'd over the airy shore,
And plung'd all noiseless into the deep night.

BOOK II

Just at the self-same beat of Time's wide wings
Hyperion slid into the rustled air,
And Saturn gain'd with Thea that sad place
Where Cybele and the bruised Titans mourn'd.
It was a den where no insulting light
Could glimmer on their tears ; where their own groans
They felt, but heard not, for the solid roar
Of thunderous waterfalls and torrents hoarse,
Pouring a constant bulk, uncertain where.
Crag jutting forth to crag, and rocks that seem'd
Ever as if just rising from a sleep,
Forehead to forehead held their monstrous horns ;
And thus in thousand hugest phantasies
Made a fit roofing to this nest of woe.
Instead of thrones, hard flint they sat upon,
Couches of rugged stone, and slaty ridge
Stubborn'd with iron. All were not assembled :
Some chain'd in torture, and some wandering.
Cœus, and Gyges, and Briareüs,
Typhon, and Dolor, and Porphyrion,
With many more, the brawniest in assault,
Were pent in regions of laborious breath ;
Dungeon'd in opaque element, to keep

Their clenched teeth still clench'd, and all their limbs
Lock'd up like veins of metal, crampt and screw'd ;
Without a motion, save of their big hearts
Heaving in pain, and horribly convuls'd
With sanguine feverous boiling gurge of pulse.
Mnemosyne was straying in the world ;
Far from her moon had Phœbe wandered ;
And many else were free to roam abroad,
But for the main, here found they covert drear.
Scarce images of life, one here, one there,
Lay vast and edgeways ; like a dismal cirque
Of Druid stones, upon a forlorn moor,
When the chill rain begins at shut of eve,
In dull November, and their chancel vault,
The Heaven itself, is blinded throughout night.
Each one kept shroud, nor to his neighbour gave
Or word, or look, or action of despair.
Creüs was one ; his ponderous iron mace
Lay by him, and a shatter'd rib of rock
Told of his rage, ere he thus sank and pined.
Iäpetus another ; in his grasp,
A serpent's plashy neck ; its barbed tongue
Squeez'd from the gorge, and all its uncurl'd length
Dead ; and because the creature could not spit
Its poison in the eyes of conquering Jove.
Next Cottus : prone he lay, chin uppermost,
As though in pain ; for still upon the flint
He ground severe his skull, with open mouth
And eyes at horrid working. Nearest him
Asia, born of most enormous Caf,
Who cost her mother Tellus keener pangs,
Though feminine, than any of her sons :
More thought than woe was in her dusky face,

For she was prophesying of her glory ;
And in her wide imagination stood
Palm-shaded temples, and high rival fanes,
By Oxus or in Ganges' sacred isles.
Even as Hope upon her anchor leans,
So lent she, not so fair, upon a tusk
Shed from the broadest of her elephants.
Above her, on a crag's uneasy shelve,
Upon his elbow rais'd, all prostrate else,
Shadow'd Enceladus ; once tame and mild
As grazing ox unworried in the meads ;
Now tiger-passion'd, lion-thoughted, wroth,
He meditated, plotted, and even now
Was hurling mountains in that second war,
Not long delay'd, that scar'd the younger Gods
To hide themselves in forms of beast and bird.
Not far hence Atlas ; and beside him prone
Phorcus, the sire of Gorgons. Neighbour'd close
Oceanus, and Tethys, in whose lap
Sobb'd Clymene among her tangled hair.
In midst of all lay Themis, at the feet
Of Ops the queen all clouded round from sight ;
No shape distinguishable, more than when
Thick night confounds the pine-tops with the clouds :
And many else whose names may not be told.
For when the Muse's wings are air-ward spread,
Who shall delay her flight ? And she must chaunt
Of Saturn, and his guide, who now had climb'd
With damp and slippery footing from a depth
More horrid still. Above a sombre cliff
Their heads appear'd, and up their stature grew
Till on the level height their steps found ease :
Then Thea spread abroad her trembling arms

Upon the precincts of this nest of pain,
And sidelong fix'd her eye on Saturn's face :
There saw she direst strife ; the supreme God
At war with all the frailty of grief,
Of rage, of fear, anxiety, revenge,
Remorse, spleen, hope, but most of all despair.
Against these plagues he strove in vain ; for Fate
Had pour'd a mortal oil upon his head,
A disanointing poison : so that Thea,
Affrighted, kept her still, and let him pass
First onwards in, among the fallen tribe.

    As with us mortal men, the laden heart
Is persecuted more, and fever'd more,
When it is nighing to the mournful house
Where other hearts are sick of the same bruise ;
So Saturn, as he walk'd into the midst,
Felt faint, and would have sunk among the rest,
But that he met Enceladus's eye,
Whose mightiness, and awe of him, at once
Came like an inspiration ; and he shouted,
'Titans, behold your God !' at which some groan'd ;
Some started on their feet ; some also shouted ;
Some wept, some wail'd, all bow'd with reverence :
And Ops, uplifting her black folded veil,
Show'd her pale cheeks, and all her forehead wan,
Her eye-brows thin and jet, and hollow eyes.
There is a roaring in the bleak-grown pines
When Winter lifts his voice ; there is a noise
Among immortals when a God gives sign,
With hushing finger, how he means to load
His tongue with the full weight of utterless thought.
With thunder, and with music, and with pomp :

Such noise is like the roar of bleak-grown pines :
Which, when it ceases in this mountain'd world,
No other sound succeeds ; but ceasing here,
Among these fallen, Saturn's voice therefrom
Grew up like organ, that begins anew
Its strain, when other harmonies, stopt short,
Leave the dinn'd air vibrating silverly.
Thus grew it up — 'Not in my own sad breast,
'Which is its own great judge and searcher out,
'Can I find reason why ye should be thus :
'Not in the legends of the first of days,
'Studied from that old spirit-leaved book
'Which starry Uranus with finger bright
'Sav'd from the shores of darkness, when the waves
'Low-ebb'd still hid it up in shallow gloom ; —
'And the which book ye know I ever kept
'For my firm-based footstool : — Ah, infirm !
'Not there, nor in sign, symbol, or portent
'Of element, earth, water, air, and fire, —
'At war, at peace, or inter-quarreling
'One against one, or two, or three, or all
'Each several one against the other three,
'As fire with air loud warring when rain-floods
'Drown both, and press them both against earth's face,
'Where, finding sulphur, a quadruple wrath
'Unhinges the poor world ; — not in that strife,
'Wherefrom I take strange lore, and read it deep,
'Can I find reason why ye should be thus :
'No, no-where can unriddle, though I search,
'And pore on Nature's universal scroll
'Even to swooning, why ye, Divinities,
'The first-born of all shap'd and palpable Gods
'Should cower beneath what, in comparison,

'Is untremendous might. Yet ye are here,
'O'erwhelm'd, and spurn'd, and batter'd, ye are here !
'O Titans, shall I say, "Arise !" — Ye groan :
'Shall I say "Crouch !" — Ye groan. What can I then ?
'O Heaven wide ! O unseen parent dear !
'What can I ? Tell me, all ye brethren Gods,
'How we can war, how engine our great wrath !
'O speak your counsel now, for Saturn's ear
'Is all a-hunger'd. Thou, Oceanus,
'Ponderest high and deep ; and in thy face
'I see, astonied, that severe content
'Which comes of thought and musing : give us help !'

So ended Saturn ; and the God of the Sea,
Sophist and sage, from no Athenian grove,
But cogitation in his watery shades,
Arose, with locks not oozy, and began,
In murmurs, which his first-endeavouring tongue
Caught infant-like from the far-foamed sands.
'O ye, whom wrath consumes ! who, passion-stung,
'Writhe at defeat, and nurse your agonies !
'Shut up your senses, stifle up your ears,
'My voice is not a bellows unto ire.
'Yet listen, ye who will, whilst I bring proof
'How ye, perforce, must be content to stoop :
'And in the proof much comfort will I give,
'If ye will take that comfort in its truth.
'We fall by course of Nature's law, not force
'Of thunder, or of Jove. Great Saturn, thou
'Hast sifted well the atom-universe ;
'But for this reason, that thou art the King,
'And only blind from sheer supremacy,
'One avenue was shaded from thine eyes,

'Through which I wandered to eternal truth.
'And first, as thou wast not the first of powers,
'So art thou not the last ; it cannot be :
'Thou art not the beginning nor the end.
'From chaos and parental darkness came
'Light, the first fruits of that intestine broil,
'That sullen ferment, which for wondrous ends
'Was ripening in itself. The ripe hour came,
'And with it light, and light, engendering
'Upon its own producer, forthwith touch'd
'The whole enormous matter into life.
'Upon that very hour, our parentage,
'The Heavens and the Earth, were manifest :
'Then thou first born, and we the giant race,
'Found ourselves ruling new and beauteous realms.
'Now comes the pain of truth, to whom 'tis pain ;
'O folly ! for to bear all naked truths,
'And to envisage circumstance, all calm,
'That is the top of sovereignty. Mark well !
'As Heaven and Earth are fairer, fairer far
'Than Chaos and blank Darkness, though once chiefs ;
'And as we show beyond that Heaven and Earth
'In form and shape compact and beautiful,
'In will, in action free, companionship,
'And thousand other signs of purer life ;
'So on our heels a fresh perfection treads,
'A power more strong in beauty, born of us
'And fated to excel us, as we pass
'In glory that old Darkness : nor are we
'Thereby more conquer'd, than by us the rule
'Of shapeless Chaos. Say, doth the dull soil
'Quarrel with the proud forests it hath fed,
'And feedeth still, more comely than itself ?

'Can it deny the chiefdom of green groves ?
'Or shall the tree be envious of the dove
'Because it cooeth, and hath snowy wings
'To wander wherewithal and find its joys ?
'We are such forest-trees, and our fair boughs
'Have bred forth, not pale solitary doves,
'But eagles golden-feather'd, who do tower
'Above us in their beauty, and must reign
'In right thereof ; for 'tis the eternal law
'That first in beauty should be first in might :
'Yea, by that law, another race may drive
'Our conquerors to mourn as we do now.
'Have ye beheld the young God of the Seas,
'My dispossessor ? Have ye seen his face ?
'Have ye beheld his chariot, foam'd along
'By noble winged creatures he hath made ?
'I saw him on the calmed waters scud,
'With such a glow of beauty in his eyes,
'That it enforc'd me to bid sad farewell
'To all my empire : farewell sad I took,
'And hither came, to see how dolorous fate
'Had wrought upon ye ; and how I might best
'Give consolation in this woe extreme.
'Receive the truth, and let it be your balm.'

   Whether through pos'd conviction, or disdain,
They guarded silence, when Oceanus
Left murmuring, what deepest thought can tell ?
But so it was, none answer'd for a space,
Save one whom none regarded, Clymene ;
And yet she answer'd not, only complain'd,
With hectic lips, and eyes up-looking mild,
Thus wording timidly among the fierce :

'O Father, I am here the simplest voice,
'And all my knowledge is that joy is gone,
'And this thing woe crept in among our hearts,
'There to remain for ever, as I fear :
'I would not bode of evil, if I thought
'So weak a creature could turn off the help
'Which by just right should come of mighty Gods ;
'Yet let me tell my sorrow, let me tell
'Of what I heard, and how it made me weep,
'And know that we had parted from all hope.
'I stood upon a shore, a pleasant shore,
'Where a sweet clime was breathed from a land
'Of fragrance, quietness, and trees, and flowers.
'Full of calm joy it was, as I of grief ;
'Too full of joy and soft delicious warmth ;
'So that I felt a movement in my heart
'To chide, and to reproach that solitude
'With songs of misery, music of our woes ;
'And sat me down, and took a mouthed shell
'And murmur'd into it, and made melody —
'O melody no more ! for while I sang,
'And with poor skill let pass into the breeze
'The dull shell's echo, from a bowery strand
'Just opposite, an island of the sea,
'There came enchantment with the shifting wind,
'That did both drown and keep alive my ears.
'I threw my shell away upon the sand,
'And a wave fill'd it, as my sense was fill'd
'With that new blissful golden melody.
'A living death was in each gush of sounds,
'Each family of rapturous hurried notes,
'That fell, one after one, yet all at once,
'Like pearl beads dropping sudden from their string :

'And then another, then another strain,
'Each like a dove leaving its olive perch,
'With music wing'd instead of silent plumes,
'To hover round my head, and make me sick
'Of joy and grief at once. Grief overcame,
'And I was stopping up my frantic ears,
'When, past all hindrance of my trembling hands,
'A voice came sweeter, sweeter than all tune,
'And still it cried, "Apollo ! young Apollo !
' "The morning-bright Apollo ! young Apollo !"
'I fled, it follow'd me, and cried "Apollo !"
'O Father, and O Brethren, had ye felt
'Those pains of mine ; O Saturn, hadst thou felt,
'Ye would not call this too indulged tongue
'Presumptuous, in thus venturing to be heard.'

So far her voice flow'd on, like timorous brook
That, lingering along a pebbled coast,
Doth fear to meet the sea : but sea it met,
And shudder'd ; for the overwhelming voice
Of huge Enceladus swallow'd it in wrath :
The ponderous syllables, like sullen waves
In the half-glutted hollows of reef-rocks,
Came booming thus, while still upon his arm
He lean'd ; not rising, from supreme contempt.
'Or shall we listen to the over-wise,
'Or to the over-foolish, Giant-Gods ?
'Not thunderbolt on thunderbolt, till all
'That rebel Jove's whole armoury were spent,
'Not world on world upon these shoulders piled,
'Could agonize me more than baby-words
'In midst of this dethronement horrible.
'Speak ! roar ! shout ! yell ! ye sleepy Titans all.

'Do ye forget the blows, the buffets vile ?
'Are ye not smitten by a youngling arm ?
'Dost thou forget, sham Monarch of the Waves,
'Thy scalding in the seas ? What, have I rous'd
'Your spleens with so few simple words as these ?
'O joy ! for now I see ye are not lost :
'O joy ! for now I see a thousand eyes
'Wide-glaring for revenge !' — As this he said,
He lifted up his stature vast, and stood,
Still without intermission speaking thus :
'Now ye are flames, I 'll tell you how to burn,
'And purge the ether of our enemies ;
'How to feed fierce the crooked stings of fire,
'And singe away the swollen clouds of Jove,
'Stifling that puny essence in its tent.
'O let him feel the evil he hath done ;
'For though I scorn Oceanus's lore,
'Much pain have I for more than loss of realms :
'The days of peace and slumberous calm are fled ;
'Those days, all innocent of scathing war,
'When all the fair Existences of heaven
'Came open-eyed to guess what we would speak : —
'That was before our brows were taught to frown,
'Before our lips knew else but solemn sounds ;
'That was before we knew the winged thing,
'Victory, might be lost, or might be won.
'And be ye mindful that Hyperion
'Our brightest brother, still is undisgraced —
'Hyperion, lo ! his radiance is here !'

    All eyes were on Enceladus's face,
And they beheld, while still Hyperion's name
Flew from his lips up to the vaulted rocks,

A pallid gleam across his features stern :
Not savage, for he saw full many a God
Wroth as himself. He look'd upon them all,
And in each face he saw a gleam of light,
But splendider in Saturn's, whose hoar locks
Shone like the bubbling foam about a keel
When the prow sweeps into a midnight cove.
In pale and silver silence they remain'd,
Till suddenly a splendour, like the morn,
Pervaded all the beetling gloomy steeps,
All the sad spaces of oblivion,
And every gulf, and every chasm old,
And every height, and every sullen depth,
Voiceless, or hoarse with loud tormented streams :
And all the everlasting cataracts,
And all the headlong torrents far and near,
Mantled before in darkness and huge shade,
Now saw the light and made it terrible.
It was Hyperion : — a granite peak
His bright feet touch'd, and there he stay'd to view
The misery his brilliance had betray'd
To the most hateful seeing of itself.
Golden his hair of short Numidian curl,
Regal his shape majestic, a vast shade
In midst of his own brightness, like the bulk
Of Memnon's image at the set of sun
To one who travels from the dusking East :
Sighs, too, as mournful as that Memnon's harp
He utter'd, while his hands contemplative
He press'd together, and in silence stood.
Despondence seiz'd again the fallen Gods
At sight of the dejected King of Day,
And many hid their faces from the light :

But fierce Enceladus sent forth his eyes
Among the brotherhood ; and, at their glare,
Uprose Iäpetus, and Creüs too,
And Phorcus, sea-born, and together strode
To where he towered on his eminence.
There those four shouted forth old Saturn's name ;
Hyperion from the peak loud answered, 'Saturn !'
Saturn sat near the Mother of the Gods,
In whose face was no joy, though all the Gods
Gave from their hollow throats the name of 'Saturn !'

BOOK III

Thus in alternate uproar and sad peace,
Amazed were those Titans utterly.
O leave them, Muse ! O leave them to their woes ;
For thou art weak to sing such tumults dire :
A solitary sorrow best befits
Thy lips, and antheming a lonely grief.
Leave them, O Muse ! for thou anon wilt find
Many a fallen old Divinity
Wandering in vain about bewildered shores.
Meantime touch piously the Delphic harp,
And not a wind of heaven but will breathe
In aid soft warble from the Dorian flute ;
For lo ! 'tis for the Father of all verse.
Flush every thing that hath a vermeil hue,
Let the rose glow intense and warm the air,
And let the clouds of even and of morn
Float in voluptuous fleeces o'er the hills ;
Let the red wine within the goblet boil,
Cold as a bubbling well ; let faint-lipp'd shells,
On sands, or in great deeps, vermilion turn

Through all their labyrinths ; and let the maid
Blush keenly, as with some warm kiss surpris'd.
Chief isle of the embowered Cyclades,
Rejoice, O Delos, with thine olives green,
And poplars, and lawn-shading palms, and beech,
In which the Zephyr breathes the loudest song,
And hazels thick, dark-stemm'd beneath the shade :
Apollo is once more the golden theme !
Where was he, when the Giant of the Sun
Stood bright, amid the sorrow of his peers ?
Together had he left his mother fair
And his twin-sister sleeping in their bower,
And in the morning twilight wandered forth
Beside the osiers of a rivulet,
Full ankle-deep in lillies of the vale.
The nightingale had ceas'd, and a few stars
Were lingering in the heavens, while the thrush
Began calm-throated. Throughout all the isle
There was no covert, no retired cave
Unhaunted by the murmurous noise of waves,
Though scarcely heard in many a green recess.
He listen'd, and he wept, and his bright tears
Went trickling down the golden bow he held.
Thus with half-shut suffused eyes he stood,
While from beneath some cumbrous boughs hard by
With solemn step an awful Goddess came,
And there was purport in her looks for him,
Which he with eager guess began to read
Perplex'd, the while melodiously he said :
'How cam'st thou over the unfooted sea ?
'Or hath that antique mien and robed form
'Mov'd in these vales invisible till now ?
'Sure I have heard those vestments sweeping o'er

'The fallen leaves, when I have sat alone
'In cool mid-forest. Surely I have traced
'The rustle of those ample skirts about
'These grassy solitudes, and seen the flowers
'Lift up their heads, as still the whisper pass'd.
'Goddess ! I have beheld those eyes before,
'And their eternal calm, and all that face,
'Or I have dream'd.' — 'Yes,' said the supreme shape,
'Thou hast dream'd of me ; and awaking up
'Didst find a lyre all golden by thy side,
'Whose strings touch'd by thy fingers, all the vast
'Unwearied ear of the whole universe
'Listen'd in pain and pleasure at the birth
'Of such new tuneful wonder. Is 't not strange
'That thou shouldst weep, so gifted ? Tell me, youth,
'What sorrow thou canst feel ; for I am sad
'When thou dost shed a tear : explain thy griefs
'To one who in this lonely isle hath been
'The watcher of thy sleep and hours of life,
'From the young day when first thy infant hand
'Pluck'd witless the weak flowers, till thine arm
'Could bend that bow heroic to all times.
'Show thy heart's secret to an ancient Power
'Who hath forsaken old and sacred thrones
'For prophecies of thee, and for the sake
'Of loveliness new born.' — Apollo then,
With sudden scrutiny and gloomless eyes,
Thus answer'd, while his white melodious throat
Throbb'd with the syllables. — 'Mnemosyne !
'Thy name is on my tongue, I know not how ;
'Why should I tell thee what thou so well seest ?
'Why should I strive to show what from thy lips
'Would come no mystery ? For me, dark, dark,

'And painful vile oblivion seals my eyes :
'I strive to search wherefore I am so sad,
'Until a melancholy numbs my limbs ;
'And then upon the grass I sit, and moan,
'Like one who once had wings. — O why should I
'Feel curs'd and thwarted, when the liegeless air
'Yields to my step aspirant ? why should I
'Spurn the green turf as hateful to my feet ?
'Goddess benign, point forth some unknown thing :
'Are there not other regions than this isle ?
'What are the stars ? There is the sun, the sun !
'And the most patient brilliance of the moon !
'And stars by thousands ! Point me out the way
'To any one particular beauteous star,
'And I will flit into it with my lyre,
'And make its silvery splendour pant with bliss.
'I have heard the cloudy thunder : Where is power ?
'Whose hand, whose essence, what divinity
'Makes this alarum in the elements,
'While I here idle listen on the shores
'In fearless yet in aching ignorance ?
'O tell me, lonely Goddess, by thy harp,
'That waileth every morn and eventide,
'Tell me why thus I rave, about these groves !
'Mute thou remainest — mute ! yet I can read
'A wondrous lesson in thy silent face :
'Knowledge enormous makes a God of me.
'Names, deeds, grey legends, dire events, rebellions,
'Majesties, sovran voices, agonies,
'Creations and destroyings, all at once
'Pour into the wide hollows of my brain,
'And deify me, as if some blythe wine
'Or bright elixir peerless I had drunk,

'And so become immortal.' — Thus the God,
While his enkindled eyes, with level glance
Beneath his white soft temples, stedfast kept
Trembling with light upon Mnemosyne.
Soon wild commotions shook him, and made flush
All the immortal fairness of his limbs ;
Most like the struggle at the gate of death ;
Or liker still to one who should take leave
Of pale immortal death, and with a pang
As hot as death's is chill, with fierce convulse
Die into life : so young Apollo anguish'd :
His very hair, his golden tresses famed
Kept undulation round his eager neck.
During the pain Mnemosyne upheld
Her arms as one who prophesied. — At length
Apollo shriek'd ; — and lo ! from all his limbs
Celestial   *   *   *   *   *   *   *
        *   *   *   *   *   *   *   *

THE EVE OF ST. AGNES

Is a work of art made to be beautiful

contains no realism of the middle ages — is a romantic middle age

I

St. Agnes' Eve — Ah, bitter chill it was !
The owl, for all his feathers, was a-cold ;   *The poems is not sensual*
The hare limp'd trembling through the frozen grass, *but is sensitive*
And silent was the flock in woolly fold :
Numb were the Beadsman's fingers, while he told
His rosary, and while his frosted breath,
Like pious incense from a censer old,
Seem'd taking flight for heaven, without a death,
Past the sweet Virgin's picture, while his prayer he saith.

II

His prayer he saith, this patient, holy man ;
Then takes his lamp, and riseth from his knees,
And back returneth, meagre, barefoot, wan,
Along the chapel aisle by slow degrees :
The sculptur'd dead, on each side, seem to freeze,
Emprison'd in black, purgatorial rails :
Knights, ladies, praying in dumb orat'ries,
He passeth by ; and his weak spirit fails
To think how they may ache in icy hoods and mails.

suggests intensity

III

Northward he turneth through a little door,
And scarce three steps, ere Music's golden tongue
Flatter'd to tears this aged man and poor ;
But no — already had his deathbell rung :
The joys of all his life were said and sung :
His was harsh penance on St. Agnes' Eve :
Another way he went, and soon among
Rough ashes sat he for his soul's reprieve,
And all night kept awake, for sinners' sake to grieve.

Was going to die die night

IV

That ancient Beadsman heard the prelude soft ;
And so it chanc'd, for many a door was wide,
From hurry to and fro. Soon, up aloft,
The silver, snarling trumpets 'gan to chide :
The level chambers, ready with their pride,
Were glowing to receive a thousand guests :
The carved angels, ever eager-eyed,
Star'd, where upon their heads the cornice rests,

Uses these words for their sound — not eny, meaning

With hair blown back, and wings put cross-wise on their
    breasts.

V

  At length burst in the argent revelry,
  With plume, tiara, and all rich array,
  Numerous as shadows haunting faerily
  The brain, new stuff'd, in youth, with triumphs gay
  Of old romance. These let us wish away,
  And turn, sole-thoughted, to one Lady there,
  Whose heart had brooded, all that wintry day,
  On love, and wing'd St. Agnes' saintly care,
As she had heard old dames full many times declare.

VI

  They told her how, upon St. Agnes' Eve,
  Young virgins might have visions of delight.
  And soft adorings from their loves receive
  Upon the honey'd middle of the night,
  If ceremonies due they did aright ;
  As, supperless to bed they must retire,
  And couch supine their beauties, lilly white ;
  Nor look behind, nor sideways, but require
Of Heaven with upward eyes for all that they desire.

VII

  Full of this whim was thoughtful Madeline :
  The music, yearning like a God in pain,
  She scarcely heard : her maiden eyes divine,
  Fix'd on the floor, saw many a sweeping train
  Pass by — she heeded not at all : in vain
  Came many a tiptoe, amorous cavalier,

'And back retir'd ; not cool'd by high disdain,
But she saw not : her heart was otherwhere :
She sigh'd for Agnes' dreams, the sweetest of the year.

VIII

She danc'd along with vague, regardless eyes,
Anxious her lips, her breathing quick and short :
The hallow'd hour was near at hand : she sighs
Amid the timbrels, and the throng'd resort
Of whisperers in anger, or in sport ;
'Mid looks of love, defiance, hate, and scorn,
Hoodwink'd with faery fancy ; all amort,
Save to St. Agnes and her lambs unshorn,
And all the bliss to be before to-morrow morn.

IX

So, purposing each moment to retire,
She linger'd still. Meantime, across the moors,
Had come young Porphyro, with heart on fire
For Madeline. Beside the portal doors,
Buttress'd from moonlight, stands he, and implores
All saints to give him sight of Madeline,
But for one moment in the tedious hours,
That he might gaze and worship all unseen ;
Perchance speak, kneel, touch, kiss — in sooth such things
    have been.

X

He ventures in : let no buzz'd whisper tell :
All eyes be muffled, or a hundred swords
Will storm his heart, Love's fev'rous citadel :
For him, those chambers held barbarian hordes,

Hyena foemen, and hot-blooded lords,
Whose very dogs would execrations howl
Against his lineage : not one breast affords
Him any mercy, in that mansion foul,
Save one old beldame, weak in body and in soul.

XI

Ah, happy chance ! the aged creature came,
Shuffling along with ivory-headed wand,
To where he stood, hid from the torch's flame,
Behind a broad hall-pillar, far beyond
The sound of merriment and chorus bland :
He startled her ; but soon she knew his face,
And grasp'd his fingers in her palsied hand,
Saying, 'Mercy, Porphyro ! hie thee from this place :
'They are all here to-night, the whole blood-thirsty race !

XII

'Get hence ! get hence ! there 's dwarfish Hildebrand ;
'He had a fever late, and in the fit
'He cursed thee and thine, both house and land :
'Then there 's that old Lord Maurice, not a whit
'More tame for his gray hairs — Alas me ! flit !
'Flit like a ghost away.' — 'Ah, Gossip dear,
'We 're safe enough ; here in this arm-chair sit,
'And tell me how' — 'Good Saints ! not here, not here ;
'Follow me, child, or else these stones will be thy bier.'

XIII

He follow'd through a lowly arched way,
Brushing the cobwebs with his lofty plume,
And as she mutter'd 'Well-a — well-a-day !'

He found him in a little moonlight room,
Pale, lattic'd, chill, and silent as a tomb.
'Now tell me where is Madeline,' said he,
'O tell me, Angela, by the holy loom
'Which none but secret sisterhood may see,
'When they St. Agnes' wool are weaving piously.'

XIV

'St. Agnes ! Ah ! it is St. Agnes' Eve —
'Yet men will murder upon holy days :
'Thou must hold water in a witch's sieve,
'And be liege-lord of all the Elves and Fays,
'To venture so : it fills me with amaze
'To see thee, Porphyro ! — St. Agnes' Eve !
'God's help ! my lady fair the conjuror plays
'This very night : good angels her deceive !
'But let me laugh awhile, I 've mickle time to grieve.'

XV

Feebly she laugheth in the languid moon,
While Porphyro upon her face doth look,
Like puzzled urchin on an aged crone
Who keepeth clos'd a wond'rous riddle-book,
As spectacled she sits in chimney nook.
But soon his eyes grew brilliant, when she told
His lady's purpose ; and he scarce could brook
Tears, at the thought of those enchantments cold,
And Madeline asleep in lap of legends old.

XVI

Sudden a thought came like a full-blown rose,
Flushing his brow, and in his pained heart

Made purple riot : then doth he propose
A stratagem, that makes the beldame start :
'A cruel man and impious thou art :
'Sweet lady, let her pray, and sleep, and dream
'Alone with her good angels, far apart
'From wicked men like thee. Go, go ! — I deem
'Thou canst not surely be the same that thou didst seem.'

XVII

'I will not harm her, by all saints I swear,'
Quoth Porphyro : 'O may I ne'er find grace
'When my weak voice shall whisper its last prayer,
'If one of her soft ringlets I displace,
'Or look with ruffian passion in her face :
'Good Angela, believe me by these tears ;
'Or I will, even in a moment's space,
'Awake, with horrid shout, my foemen's ears,
'And beard them, though they be more fang'd than wolves
      and bears.'

XVIII

'Ah ! why wilt thou affright a feeble soul ?
'A poor, weak, palsy-stricken, churchyard thing,
'Whose passing-bell may ere the midnight toll ;
'Whose prayers for thee, each morn and evening,
'Were never miss'd.' — Thus plaining, doth she bring
A gentler speech from burning Porphyro ;
So woful, and of such deep sorrowing,
That Angela gives promise she will do
Whatever he shall wish, betide her weal or woe.

XIX

Which was, to lead him, in close secrecy,
Even to Madeline's chamber, and there hide
Him in a closet, of such privacy
That he might see her beauty unespied,
And win perhaps that night a peerless bride,
While legion'd faeries pac'd the coverlet,
And pale enchantment held her sleepy-eyed.
Never on such a night have lovers met,
Since Merlin paid his Demon all the monstrous debt.

XX

'It shall be as thou wishest,' said the Dame :
'All cates and dainties shall be stored there
'Quickly on this feast-night : by the tambour frame
'Her own lute thou wilt see : no time to spare,
'For I am slow and feeble, and scarce dare
'On such a catering trust my dizzy head.
'Wait here, my child, with patience ; kneel in prayer
'The while : Ah ! thou must needs the lady wed,
'Or may I never leave my grave among the dead.'

XXI

So saying, she hobbled off with busy fear.
The lover's endless minutes slowly pass'd ;
The dame return'd, and whisper'd in his ear
To follow her ; with aged eyes aghast
From fright of dim espial. Safe at last,
Through many a dusky gallery, they gain
The maiden's chamber, silken, hush'd, and chaste ;

Where Porphyro took covert, pleas'd amain.
His poor guide hurried back with agues in her brain.

XXII

Her falt'ring hand upon the balustrade,
Old Angela was feeling for the stair,
When Madeline, St. Agnes' charmed maid,
Rose, like a mission'd spirit, unaware :
With silver taper's light, and pious care,
She turn'd, and down the aged gossip led
To a safe level matting. Now prepare,
Young Porphyro, for gazing on that bed ;
She comes, she comes again, like ring-dove fray'd and fled.

XXIII

Out went the taper as she hurried in ;
Its little smoke, in pallid moonshine, died :
She clos'd the door, she panted, all akin
To spirits of the air, and visions wide :
No uttered syllable, or, woe betide !
But to her heart, her heart was voluble,
Paining with eloquence her balmy side ;
As though a tongueless nightingale should swell
Her throat in vain, and die, heart-stifled, in her dell.

XXIV

A casement high and triple-arch'd there was,
All garlanded with carven imag'ries
Of fruits, and flowers, and bunches of knot-grass,
And diamonded with panes of quaint device,
Innumerable of stains and splendid dyes,

As are the tiger-moth's deep-damask'd wings ;
And in the midst, 'mong thousand heraldries,
And twilight saints, and dim emblazonings,
A shielded scutcheon blush'd with blood of queens and kings.

XXV

Full on this casement shone the wintry moon,
And threw warm gules on Madeline's fair breast,
As down she knelt for heaven's grace and boon ;
Rose-bloom fell on her hands, together prest,
And on her silver cross soft amethyst,
And on her hair a glory, like a saint :
She seem'd a splendid angel, newly drest,
Save wings, for heaven : — Porphyro grew faint :
She knelt, so pure a thing, so free from mortal taint.

XXVI

Anon his heart revives : her vespers done,
Of all its wreathed pearls her hair she frees ;
Unclasps her warmed jewels one by one ;
Loosens her fragrant boddice ; by degrees
Her rich attire creeps rustling to her knees :
Half-hidden, like a mermaid in sea-weed,
Pensive awhile she dreams awake, and sees,
In fancy, fair St. Agnes in her bed,
But dares not look behind, or all the charm is fled.

XXVII

Soon, trembling in her soft and chilly nest,
In sort of wakeful swoon, perplex'd she lay,
Until the poppied warmth of sleep oppress'd
Her soothed limbs, and soul fatigued away ;

Flown, like a thought, until the morrow-day ;
Blissfully haven'd both from joy and pain ;
Clasp'd like a missal where swart Paynims pray ;
Blinded alike from sunshine and from rain,
As though a rose should shut, and be a bud again.

XXVIII

Stol'n to this paradise, and so entranced,
Porphyro gazed upon her empty dress,
And listen'd to her breathing, if it chanced
To wake into a slumberous tenderness ;
Which when he heard, that minute did he bless,
And breath'd himself : then from the closet crept,
Noiseless as fear in a wide wilderness.
And over the hush'd carpet, silent, stept,
And 'tween the curtains peep'd, where, lo ! — how fast she
      slept.

XXIX

Then by the bed-side, where the faded moon
Made a dim, silver twilight, soft he set
A table, and, half anguish'd, threw thereon
A cloth of woven crimson, gold, and jet : —
O for some drowsy Morphean amulet !
The boisterous, midnight, festive clarion,
The kettle-drum, and far-heard clarinet,
Affray his ears, though but in dying tone : —
The hall door shuts again, and all the noise is gone.

XXX

And still she slept an azure-lidded sleep,
In blanched linen, smooth, and lavender'd,

While he from forth the closet brought a heap
Of candied apple, quince, and plum, and gourd ;
With jellies soother than the creamy curd,
And lucent syrops, tinct with cinnamon ;
Manna and dates, in argosy transferr'd
From Fez ; and spiced dainties, every one,
From silken Samarcand to cedar'd Lebanon.

XXXI

These delicates he heap'd with glowing hand
On golden dishes and in baskets bright
Of wreathed silver : sumptuous they stand
In the retired quiet of the night,
Filling the chilly room with perfume light. —
'And now, my love, my seraph fair, awake !
'Thou art my heaven, and I thine eremite :
'Open thine eyes, for meek St. Agnes' sake,
'Or I shall drowse beside thee, so my soul doth ache.'

XXXII

Thus whispering, his warm, unnerved arm
Sank in her pillow. Shaded was her dream
By the dusk curtains : — 't was a midnight charm
Impossible to melt as iced stream :
The lustrous salvers in the moonlight gleam ;
Broad golden fringe upon the carpet lies :
It seem'd he never, never could redeem
From such a stedfast spell his lady's eyes ;
So mus'd awhile, entoil'd in woofed phantasies.

XXXIII

Awakening up, he took her hollow lute, —
Tumultuous, — and, in chords that tenderest be,

He play'd an ancient ditty, long since mute,
In Provence call'd, 'La belle dame sans mercy :'
Close to her ear touching the melody ; —
Wherewith disturb'd, she utter'd a soft moan :
He ceased — she panted quick — and suddenly
Her blue affrayed eyes wide open shone :
Upon his knees he sank, pale as smooth-sculptured stone.

XXXIV

Her eyes were open, but she still beheld,
Now wide awake, the vision of her sleep :
There was a painful change, that nigh expell'd
The blisses of her dream so pure and deep
At which fair Madeline began to weep,
And moan forth witless words with many a sigh ;
While still her gaze on Porphyro would keep ;
Who knelt, with joined hands and piteous eye,
Fearing to move or speak, she look'd so dreamingly.

XXXV

'Ah, Porphyro !' said she, 'but even now
'Thy voice was at sweet tremble in mine ear,
'Made tuneable with every sweetest vow ;
'And those sad eyes were spiritual and clear :
'How chang'd thou art ! how pallid, chill, and drear !
'Give me that voice again, my Porphyro,
'Those looks immortal, those complainings dear !
'Oh leave me not in this eternal woe,
'For if thou diest, my Love, I know not where to go.'

XXXVI

Beyond a mortal man impassion'd far
At these voluptuous accents, he arose,

Ethereal, flush'd, and like a throbbing star
Seen mid the sapphire heaven's deep repose ;
Into her dream he melted, as the rose
Blendeth its odour with the violet, —
Solution sweet : meantime the frost-wind blows
Like Love's alarum pattering the sharp sleet
Against the window-panes ; St. Agnes' moon hath set,

XXXVII

'Tis dark : quick pattereth the flaw-blown sleet :
'This is no dream, my bride, my Madeline !'
'Tis dark : the iced gusts still rave and beat :
'No dream, alas ! alas ! and woe is mine !
'Porphyro will leave me here to fade and pine. —
'Cruel ! what traitor could thee hither bring ?
'I curse not, for my heart is lost in thine,
'Though thou forsakest a deceived thing ; —
'A dove forlorn and lost with sick unpruned wing.'

XXXVIII

'My Madeline ! sweet dreamer ! lovely bride !
'Say, may I be for aye thy vassal blest ?
'Thy beauty's shield, heart-shap'd and vermeil dyed ?
'Ah, silver shrine, here will I take my rest
'After so many hours of toil and quest,
'A famish'd pilgrim, — sav'd by miracle.
'Though I have found, I will not rob thy nest
'Saving of thy sweet self ; if thou think'st well
'To trust, fair Madeline, to no rude infidel.

XXXIX

'Hark ! 'tis an elfin-storm from faery land,
'Of haggard seeming, but a boon indeed :

'Arise — arise ! the morning is at hand ; —
'The bloated wassaillers will never heed : —
'Let us away, my love, with happy speed ;
'There are no ears to hear, or eyes to see, —
'Drown'd all in Rhenish and the sleepy mead :
'Awake ! arise ! my love, and fearless be,
'For o'er the southern moors I have a home for thee.'

XL

She hurried at his words, beset with fears,
For there were sleeping dragons all around,
At glaring watch, perhaps, with ready spears —
Down the wide stairs a darkling way they found. —
In all the house was heard no human sound.
A chain-droop'd lamp was flickering by each door ;
The arras, rich with horseman, hawk, and hound,
Flutter'd in the besieging wind's uproar ;
And the long carpets rose along the gusty floor.

XLI

They glide, like phantoms, into the wide hall ;
Like phantoms, to the iron porch, they glide ;
Where lay the Porter, in uneasy sprawl,
With a huge empty flaggon by his side :
The wakeful bloodhound rose, and shook his hide,
But his sagacious eye an inmate owns :
By one, and one, the bolts full easy slide : —
The chains lie silent on the footworn stones ; —
The key turns, and the door upon its hinges groans.

XLII

And they are gone : aye, ages long ago
These lovers fled away into the storm.

That night the Baron dreamt of many a woe,
And all his warrior-guests, with shade and form
Of witch, and demon, and large coffin-worm,
Were long be-nightmar'd. Angela the old
Died palsy-twitch'd, with meagre face deform ;
The Beadsman, after thousand aves told,
For aye unsought for slept among his ashes cold.

"BRIGHT STAR! WOULD I WERE STEADFAST AS THOU ART"

Bright star ! would I were steadfast as thou art —
    Not in lone splendour hung aloft the night,
And watching, with eternal lids apart,
    Like Nature's patient, sleepless Eremite,
The moving waters at their priestlike task
    Of pure ablution round earth's human shores,
Or gazing on the new soft-fallen mask
    Of snow upon the mountains and the moors —
No — yet still steadfast, still unchangeable,
    Pillow'd upon my fair love's ripening breast,
To feel for ever its soft fall and swell,
    Awake for ever in a sweet unrest,
Still, still to hear her tender-taken breath,
And so live ever — or else swoon to death.

LA BELLE DAME SANS MERCI

I

Ah, what can ail thee, wretched wight,
    Alone and palely loitering ;

The sedge is wither'd from the lake,
    And no birds sing.

II

Ah, what can ail thee, wretched wight,
    So haggard and so woe-begone ?
The squirrel's granary is full,
    And the harvest 's done.

III

I see a lilly on thy brow,
    With anguish moist and fever dew ;
And on thy cheek a fading rose
    Fast withereth too.

IV

I met a lady in the meads
    Full beautiful, a faery's child ;
Her hair was long, her foot was light,
    And her eyes were wild.

V

I set her on my pacing steed,
    And nothing else saw all day long ;
For sideways would she lean, and sing
    A faery's song.

VI

I made a garland for her head,
    And bracelets too, and fragrant zone ;
She look'd at me as she did love,
    And made sweet moan.

VII

She found me roots of relish sweet,
　And honey wild, and manna dew ;
And sure in language strange she said,
　I love thee true.

VIII

She took me to her elfin grot,
　And there she gaz'd and sighed deep,
And there I shut her wild sad eyes —
　So kiss'd to sleep.

IX

And there we slumber'd on the moss,
　And there I dream'd, ah woe betide,
The latest dream I ever dream'd
　On the cold hill side.

X

I saw pale kings, and princes too,
　Pale warriors, death-pale were they all ;
Who cry'd — 'La belle Dame sans merci
　Hath thee in thrall !'

XI

I saw their starv'd lips in the gloam
　With horrid warning gaped wide,
And I awoke, and found me here
　On the cold hill side.

XII

And this is why I sojourn here
    Alone and palely loitering,
Though the sedge is wither'd from the lake,
    And no birds sing.

ODE TO PSYCHE

O Goddess ! hear these tuneless numbers, wrung
    By sweet enforcement and remembrance dear,
And pardon that thy secrets should be sung
    Even into thine own soft-conched ear :
Surely I dreamt to-day, or did I see
    The winged Psyche with awaken'd eyes ?
I wander'd in a forest thoughtlessly,
    And, on the sudden, fainting with surprise,
Saw two fair creatures, couched side by side
    In deepest grass, beneath the whisp'ring roof
    Of leaves and trembled blossoms, where there ran
        A brooklet, scarce espied :

'Mid hush'd, cool-rooted flowers, fragrant-eyed,
    Blue, silver-white, and budded Tyrian,
They lay calm-breathing on the bedded grass ;
    Their arms embraced, and their pinions too ;
    Their lips touch'd not, but had not bade adieu,
As if disjoined by soft-handed slumber,
And ready still past kisses to outnumber
    At tender eye-dawn of aurorean love :
        The winged boy I knew ;
    But who wast thou, O happy, happy dove ?
        His Psyche true !

O latest born and loveliest vision far
　　Of all Olympus' faded hierarchy!
Fairer than Phœbe's sapphire-region'd star,
　　Or Vesper, amorous glow-worm of the sky ;
Fairer than these, though temple thou hast none,
　　　　Nor altar heap'd with flowers ;
Nor virgin-choir to make delicious moan
　　　　Upon the midnight hours ;
No voice, no lute, no pipe, no incense sweet
　　From chain-swung censer teeming ;
No shrine, no grove, no oracle, no heat
　　Of pale-mouth'd prophet dreaming.

O brightest ! though too late for antique vows,
　　Too, too late for the fond believing lyre,
When holy were the haunted forest boughs,
　　Holy the air, the water, and the fire ;
Yet even in these days so far retir'd
　　From happy pieties, thy lucent fans,
　　Fluttering among the faint Olympians,
I see, and sing, by my own eyes inspir'd.
So let me be thy choir, and make a moan
　　　　Upon the midnight hours ;
Thy voice, thy lute, thy pipe, thy incense sweet
　　From swinged censer teeming ;
Thy shrine, thy grove, thy oracle, thy heat
　　Of pale-mouth'd prophet dreaming.

Yes, I will be thy priest, and build a fane
　　In some untrodden region of my mind,
Where branched thoughts, new grown with pleasant pain,
　　Instead of pines shall murmur in the wind :
Far, far around shall those dark-cluster'd trees

Fledge the wild-ridged mountains steep by steep ;
And there by zephyrs, streams, and birds, and bees,
    The moss-lain Dryads shall be lull'd to sleep ;
And in the midst of this wide quietness
A rosy sanctuary will I dress
With the wreath'd trellis of a working brain,
    With buds, and bells, and stars without a name,
With all the gardener Fancy e'er could feign,
    Who breeding flowers, will never breed the same :
And there shall be for thee all soft delight
    That shadowy thought can win,
A bright torch, and a casement ope at night,
    To let the warm Love in !

ODE ON INDOLENCE

"They toil not, neither do they spin."

I

One morn before me were three figures seen,
    With bowed necks, and joined hands, side-faced ;
And one behind the other stepp'd serene,
    In placid sandals, and in white robes graced ;
They pass'd, like figures on a marble urn,
    When shifted round to see the other side ;
        They came again ; as when the urn once more
Is shifted round, the first seen shades return ;
    And they were strange to me, as may betide
        With vases, to one deep in Phidian lore.

II

How is it, Shadows ! that I knew ye not ?
    How came ye muffled in so hush a mask ?

Was it a silent deep-disguised plot
  To steal away, and leave without a task
My idle days ? Ripe was the drowsy hour ;
  The blissful cloud of summer-indolence
    Benumb'd my eyes ; my pulse grew less and less ;
Pain had no sting, and pleasure's wreath no flower :
  O, why did ye not melt, and leave my sense
    Unhaunted quite of all but — nothingness ?

III

A third time pass'd they by, and, passing, turn'd
  Each one the face a moment whiles to me ;
Then faded, and to follow them I burn'd
  And ach'd for wings because I knew the three ;
The first was a fair Maid, and Love her name ;
  The second was Ambition, pale of cheek,
    And ever watchful with fatigued eye ;
The last, whom I love more, the more of blame
  Is heap'd upon her, maiden most unmeek, —
    I knew to be my demon Poesy.

IV

They faded, and, forsooth ! I wanted wings :
  O folly ! What is Love ! and where is it ?
And for that poor Ambition ! it springs
  From a man's little heart's short fever-fit ;
For Poesy ! — no, — she has not a joy, —
  At least for me, — so sweet as drowsy noons,
    And evenings steep'd in honied indolence ;
O, for an age so shelter'd from annoy,
  That I may never know how change the moons,
    Or hear the voice of busy common-sense !

V

And once more came they by ; — alas ! wherefore ?
  My sleep had been embroider'd with dim dreams ;
My soul had been a lawn besprinkled o'er
  With flowers, and stirring shades, and baffled beams :
The morn was clouded, but no shower fell,
    Tho' in her lids hung the sweet tears of May ;
      The open casement press'd a new-leav'd vine,
    Let in the budding warmth and throstle's lay ;
O Shadows ! 'twas a time to bid farewell !
    Upon your skirts had fallen no tears of mine.

VI

So, ye three Ghosts, adieu ! Ye cannot raise
  My head cool-bedded in the flowery grass ;
For I would not be dieted with praise,
  A pet-lamb in a sentimental farce !
Fade softly from my eyes, and be once more
  In masque-like figures on the dreamy urn ;
    Farewell ! I yet have visions for the night,
And for the day faint visions there is store ;
    Vanish, ye Phantoms ! from my idle spright,
Into the clouds, and never more return !

ODE TO A NIGHTINGALE

I

My heart aches, and a drowsy numbness pains
  My sense, as though of hemlock I had drunk,
Or emptied some dull opiate to the drains

One minute past, and Lethe-wards had sunk :
'Tis not through envy of thy happy lot,
But being too happy in thine happiness, —
That thou, light-winged Dryad of the trees,
In some melodious plot
Of beechen green, and shadows numberless,
Singest of summer in full-throated ease.

Stanza II
going farther into the
dream world

II

O, for a draught of <u>vintage</u> ! that hath been   *He's concious*
Cool'd a long age in the deep-delved earth, *he's dozing away*
Tasting of Flora and the country green, *falling into a trance*
Dance, and Provençal song, and sunburnt mirth !
O for a beaker full of the warm South,
Full of the true, the blushful Hippocrene,
With beaded bubbles winking at the brim,
And purple-stained mouth ;
That I might drink, and leave the world unseen,
And with thee fade away into the forest dim :

III

Fade far away, dissolve, and quite forget   *He's in his dream*
What thou among the leaves hast never known, *that he follows*
The weariness, the fever, and the fret *the nightingale — thi*
Here, where men sit and hear each other groan ; *stanza give*
Where palsy shakes a few, sad, last gray hairs, *his dream —*
Where youth grows pale, and spectre-thin, and dies ; *continue*
Where but to think is to be full of sorrow *through stanza V*
And leaden-eyed despairs,
Where Beauty cannot keep her lustrous eyes,
Or new Love pine at them beyond to-morrow.

Time makes his
dream possible

Stanza 3
The world Keats knew

IV

Away ! away ! for I will fly to thee,

   Not charioted by Bacchus and his pards,

But on the viewless wings of Poesy,

   Though the dull brain perplexes and retards :

Already with thee ! tender is the night,

   And haply the Queen-Moon is on her throne,

      Cluster'd around by all her starry Fays ;

         But here there is no light,

   Save what from heaven is with the breezes blown

      Through verdurous glooms and winding mossy ways.

V

I cannot see what flowers are at my feet,

   Nor what soft incense hangs upon the boughs,

But, in embalmed darkness, guess each sweet

   Wherewith the seasonable month endows

The grass, the thicket, and the fruit-tree wild ;

   White hawthorn, and the pastoral eglantine ;

      Fast fading violets cover'd up in leaves ;

         And mid-May's eldest child,

The coming musk-rose, full of dewy wine,

      The murmurous haunt of flies on summer eves.

VI

Darkling I listen ; and, for many a time

   I have been half in love with easeful Death,

Call'd him soft names in many a mused rhyme,

   To take into the air my quiet breath ;

Now more than ever seems it rich to die,

   To cease upon the midnight with no pain,

While thou art pouring forth thy soul abroad
  In such an ecstasy !
Still wouldst thou sing, and I have ears in vain —
  To thy high requiem become a sod.

The terms face in two directions / ambiguous   *This world isn't as glowing as we sometimes think it is.*

VII

Thou wast not born for death, immortal Bird !
  No hungry generations tread thee down ;
The voice I hear this passing night was heard
  In ancient days by emperor and clown :
Perhaps the self-same song that found a path
  Through the sad heart of Ruth, when, sick for home,
    She stood in tears amid the alien corn ;
      The same that oft-times hath
  Charm'd magic casements, opening on the foam
  Of perilous seas, in faery lands forlorn.

VIII

Helpless

Forlorn ! the very word is like a bell
  To toll me back from thee to my sole self !
Adieu ! the fancy cannot cheat so well
  As she is fam'd to do, deceiving elf.
Adieu ! adieu ! thy plaintive anthem fades
  Past the near meadows, over the still stream,
    Up the hill-side ; and now 'tis buried deep
      In the next valley-glades :
  Was it a vision, or a waking dream ?
    Fled is that music : — Do I wake or sleep ?

ODE ON A GRECIAN URN

I

Thou still unravish'd bride of quietness,
    Thou foster-child of silence and slow time,
Sylvan historian, who canst thus express
    A flowery tale more sweetly than our rhyme:
What leaf-fring'd legend haunts about thy shape
    Of deities or mortals, or of both,
        In Tempe or the dales of Arcady?
    What men or gods are these? What maidens loth?
What mad pursuit? What struggle to escape?
        What pipes and timbrels? What wild ecstasy?

II

Heard melodies are sweet, but those unheard
    Are sweeter; therefore, ye soft pipes, play on;
Not to the sensual ear, but, more endear'd,
    Pipe to the spirit ditties of no tone:
Fair youth, beneath the trees, thou canst not leave
    Thy song, nor ever can those trees be bare;
        Bold Lover, never, never canst thou kiss,
Though winning near the goal — yet, do not grieve;
        She cannot fade, though thou hast not thy bliss,
    For ever wilt thou love, and she be fair!

III

Ah, happy, happy boughs! that cannot shed
    Your leaves, nor ever bid the Spring adieu;
And, happy melodist, unwearied,

Contrasts — World of art and our world
the real world

Far above anything in the human world - more wonderful love

For ever piping songs for ever new ;
More happy love ! more happy, happy love !
    For ever warm and still to be enjoy'd,
        For ever panting, and for ever young ;
All breathing human passion far above,
    That leaves a heart high-sorrowful and cloy'd,
        A burning forehead, and a parching tongue.

IV

Best stanza - recovering one

Who are these coming to the sacrifice ?
    To what green altar, O mysterious priest, *mastery of words*
Lead'st thou that heifer lowing at the skies, *gives the*
    And all her silken flanks with garlands drest ? *effect of shelter*
What little town by river or sea shore,
    Or mountain-built with peaceful citadel,
        Is emptied of this folk, this pious morn ?
And, little town, thy streets for evermore
    Will silent be ; and not a soul to tell
        Why thou art desolate, can e'er return.

The town, residence is shelter from the world

V

Urn is being sum -up

O Attic shape ! Fair attitude ! with brede
    Of marble men and maidens overwrought,
With forest branches and the trodden weed ;
    Thou, silent form, dost tease us out of thought
As doth eternity : Cold Pastoral ! *summarising phase*
    When old age shall this generation waste,
        Thou shalt remain, in midst of other woe *The world will*
    Than ours, a friend to man, to whom thou say'st, *remain,*
"Beauty is truth, truth beauty," — that is all *we'll be gone*
        Ye know on earth, and all ye need to know.

The things are anything but cold

Contrast between the actual world and a world of beauty

The conclusion is troublesome
1. One of the poems flaws
    a. The last 3 or 4 lines are hard to understa

Trying to change depression into joy

ODE ON MELANCHOLY

Dramatized well
1. Do what makes a good poem:
Central theme:
Passing of things

I

forgetfulness of the past
No, no, go not to Lethe, neither twist
    Wolf's-bane, tight-rooted, for its poisonous wine ;
Nor suffer thy pale forehead to be kiss'd   *another type*
    By nightshade, ruby grape of Proserpine ; *of poisonous*
Make not your rosary of yew-berries,
    Nor let the beetle, nor the death-moth be   *symbols*
      Your mournful Psyche, nor the downy owl   *death*
A partner in your sorrow's mysteries ;
    For shade to shade will come too drowsily,   *If you take these*
      And drown the wakeful anguish of the soul. *poisons - you'll miss*

II

But when the melancholy fit shall fall
    Sudden from heaven like a weeping cloud,
That fosters the droop-headed flowers all,
    And hides the green hill in an April shroud :
Then glut thy sorrow on a morning rose,
    Or on the wealth *rainbow* of a salt sand-wave,
      Or on the wealth of globed peonies ;
Or if thy mistress some rich anger shows,
    Emprison her soft hand, and let her rave,
      And feed deep, deep upon her peerless eyes.

III

She dwells with Beauty — Beauty that must die ;
    And Joy, whose hand is ever at his lips
Bidding adieu ; and aching Pleasure nigh,

Turning to poison while the bee-mouth sips :
Ay, in the very temple of Delight
   Veiled Melancholy has her sovran shrine,
     Though seen of none save him whose strenuous tongue
Can burst Joy's grape against his palate fine ;
   His soul shall taste the sadness of her might,
     And be among her cloudy trophies hung.

Oct., 1819

TO AUTUMN *Descriptive: creates a female figure of autumn*

I

Season of mists and mellow fruitfulness,
   Close bosom-friend of the maturing sun ;
Conspiring with him how to load and bless
   With fruit the vines that round the thatch-eves run ;
To bend with apples the moss'd cottage-trees,
   And fill all fruit with ripeness to the core ;
     To swell the gourd, and plump the hazel shells
   With a sweet kernel ; to set budding more,
And still more, later flowers for the bees,
Until they think warm days will never cease,
     For Summer has o'er-brimm'd their clammy cells.

II

Who hath not seen thee oft amid thy store ?
   Sometimes whoever seeks abroad may find *in an old fashion house*
Thee sitting careless on a granary floor,
   Thy hair soft-lifted by the winnowing wind ;
Or on a half-reap'd furrow sound asleep,
   Drows'd with the fume of poppies, while thy hook
     Spares the next swath and all its twined flowers :

And sometimes like a gleaner thou dost keep
   Steady thy laden head across a brook ;
Or by a cyder-press, with patient look,
   Thou watchest the last oozings hours by hours.

III

Undramatic summarization of sights in autumn

Where are the songs of Spring ? Ay, where are they ?
   Think not of them, thou hast thy music too, —
While barred clouds bloom the soft-dying day,
   And touch the stubble-plains with rosy hue ;
Then in a wailful choir the small gnats mourn
   Among the river sallows, borne aloft
     Or sinking as the light wind lives or dies ;

No dramatic ending

And full-grown lambs loud bleat from hilly bourn ;
   Hedge-crickets sing ; and now with treble soft
The red-breast whistles from a garden-croft ;
   And gathering swallows twitter in the skies.

ALFRED, LORD TENNYSON

(1809–1892)

MARIANA

"Mariana in the moated grange"
Measure for Measure

With blackest moss the flower-plots
   Were thickly crusted, one and all ;
The rusted nails fell from the knots
   That held the pear to the gable-wall.
The broken sheds look'd sad and strange :

Unlifted was the clinking latch ;
Weeded and worn the ancient thatch
Upon the lonely moated grange.
    She only said, "My life is dreary,
      He cometh not," she said ;
    She said, "I am aweary, aweary,
      I would that I were dead !"

Her tears fell with the dews at even ;
    Her tears fell ere the dews were dried ;
She could not look on the sweet heaven,
    Either at morn or eventide.
After the flitting of the bats,
    When thickest dark did trance the sky,
    She drew her casement-curtain by,
And glanced athwart the glooming flats.
    She only said, "The night is dreary,
      He cometh not," she said ;
    She said, "I am aweary, aweary,
      I would that I were dead !"

Upon the middle of the night,
    Waking she heard the night-fowl crow ;
The cock sung out an hour ere light ;
    From the dark fen the oxen's low
Came to her ; without hope of change,
    In sleep she seem'd to walk forlorn,
    Till cold winds woke the gray-eyed morn
About the lonely moated grange.
    She only said, "The day is dreary,
      He cometh not," she said ;
    She said, "I am aweary, aweary,
      I would that I were dead !"

About a stone-cast from the wall
   A sluice with blacken'd waters slept,
And o'er it many, round and small,
   The cluster'd marish-mosses crept.
Hard by a poplar shook alway,
   All silver-green with gnarled bark :
   For leagues no other tree did mark
The level waste, the rounding gray.
      She only said, "The night is dreary,
        He cometh not," she said ;
      She said, "I am aweary, aweary,
        I would that I were dead."

And ever when the moon was low,
   And the shrill winds were up and away,
In the white curtain, to and fro,
   She saw the gusty shadow sway.
But when the moon was very low,
   And wild winds bound within their cell,
   The shadow of the poplar fell
Upon her bed, across her brow.
      She only said, "My life is dreary,
        He cometh not," she said ;
      She said, "I am aweary, aweary,
        I would that I were dead !"

All day within the dreamy house,
   The doors upon their hinges creak'd ;
The blue fly sung in the pane ; the mouse
   Behind the mouldering wainscot shriek'd,
Or from the crevice peer'd about.
   Old faces glimmer'd thro' the doors,
   Old footsteps trod the upper floors,

Old voices called her from without.
She only said, "My life is dreary,
    He cometh not," she said ;
She said, "I am aweary, aweary,
    I would that I were dead !"

The sparrow's chirrup on the roof,
    The slow clock ticking, and the sound
Which to the wooing wind aloof
    The poplar made, did all confound
Her sense ; but most she loathed the hour
    When the thick-moted sunbeam lay
Athwart the chambers, and the day
Was sloping toward his western bower.
    Then, she said, "I am very dreary,
        He will not come," she said ;
    She wept, "I am aweary, aweary,
        O God, that I were dead !"

THE LOTOS-EATERS

"Courage !" he said, and pointed toward the land,
"This mounting wave will roll us shoreward soon."
In the afternoon they came unto a land
In which it seemed always afternoon.
All round the coast the languid air did swoon,
Breathing like one that hath a weary dream.
Full-faced above the valley stood the moon ;
And like a downward smoke, the slender stream
Along the cliff to fall and pause and fall did seem.

A land of streams ! some, like a downward smoke,
Slow-dropping veils of thinnest lawn, did go ;
And some thro' wavering lights and shadows broke,
Rolling a slumbrous sheet of foam below.
They saw the gleaming river seaward flow
From the inner land ; far off, three mountain-tops,
Three silent pinnacles of aged snow,
Stood sunset-flush'd ; and, dew'd with showery drops,
Up-clomb the shadowy pine above the woven copse.

The charmed sunset linger'd low adown
In the red West ; thro' mountain clefts the dale
Was seen far inland, and the yellow down
Border'd with palm, and many a winding vale
And meadow, set with slender galingale ;
A land where all things always seem'd the same !
And round about the keel with faces pale,
Dark faces pale against that rosy flame,
The mild-eyed melancholy Lotos-eaters came.

Branches they bore of that enchanted stem,
Laden with flower and fruit, whereof they gave
To each, but whoso did receive of them,
And taste, to him the gushing of the wave
Far far away did seem to mourn and rave
On alien shores ; and if his fellow spake,
His voice was thin, as voices from the grave ;
And deep-asleep he seem'd, yet all awake,
And music in his ears his beating heart did make.

They sat them down upon the yellow sand,
Between the sun and moon upon the shore ;

And sweet it was to dream of Fatherland,
Of child and wife, and slave ; but evermore
Most weary seem'd the sea, weary the oar,
Weary the wandering fields of barren foam.
Then some one said, "We will return no more ;"
And all at once they sang, "Our island home
Is far beyond the wave ; we will no longer roam."

CHORIC SONG

I

There is sweet music here that softer falls
Than petals from blown roses on the grass,
Or night-dews on still waters between walls
Of shadowy granite, in a gleaming pass ;
Music that gentlier on the spirit lies,
Than tir'd eyelids upon tir'd eyes ;
Music that brings sweet sleep down from the blissful skies.
Here are cool mosses deep,
And thro' the moss the ivies creep,
And in the stream the long-leaved flowers weep,
And from the craggy ledge the poppy hangs in sleep.

II

Why are we weigh'd upon with heaviness,
And utterly consumed with sharp distress,
While all things else have rest from weariness ?
All things have rest : why should we toil alone,
We only toil, who are the first of things,
And make perpetual moan,
Still from one sorrow to another thrown ;
Nor ever fold our wings,

And cease from wanderings,
Nor steep our brows in slumber's holy balm ;
Nor hearken what the inner spirit sings,
"There is no joy but calm !"
Why should we only toil, the roof and crown of things ?

III

Lo ! in the middle of the wood,
The folded leaf is woo'd from out the bud
With winds upon the branch, and there
Grows green and broad, and takes no care,
Sun-steep'd at noon, and in the moon
Nightly dew-fed ; and turning yellow
Falls, and floats adown the air.
Lo ! sweeten'd with the summer light,
The full-juiced apple, waxing over-mellow,
Drops in a silent autumn night.
All its allotted length of days,
The flower ripens in its place,
Ripens and fades, and falls, and hath no toil,
Fast-rooted in the fruitful soil.

IV

Hateful is the dark-blue sky,
Vaulted o'er the dark-blue sea.
Death is the end of life ; ah, why
Should life all labour be ?
Let us alone. Time driveth onward fast,
And in a little while our lips are dumb.
Let us alone. What is it that will last ?
All things are taken from us, and become
Portions and parcels of the dreadful Past.

Let us alone. What pleasure can we have
To war with evil ? Is there any peace
In ever climbing up the climbing wave ?
All things have rest, and ripen toward the grave
In silence ; ripen, fall and cease :
Give us long rest or death, dark death, or dreamful ease.

V

How sweet it were, hearing the downward stream,
With half-shut eyes ever to seem
Falling asleep in a half-dream !
To dream and dream, like yonder amber light,
Which will not leave the myrrh-bush on the height ;
To hear each other's whisper'd speech ;
Eating the Lotos day by day,
To watch the crisping ripples on the beach,
And tender curving lines of creamy spray ;
To lend our hearts and spirit wholly
To the influence of mild-minded melancholy ;
To muse and brood and live again in memory,
With those old faces of our infancy
Heap'd over with a mound of grass,
Two handfuls of white dust, shut in an urn of brass !

VI

Dear is the memory of our wedded lives,
And dear the last embraces of our wives
And their warm tears ; but all hath suffer'd change ;
For surely now our household hearths are cold,
Our sons inherit us, our looks are strange,
And we should come like ghosts to trouble joy.
Or else the island princes over-bold

Have eat our substance, and the minstrel sings,
Before them of the ten years' war in Troy,
And our great deeds, as half-forgotten things.
Is there confusion in the little isle ?
Let what is broken so remain.
The Gods are hard to reconcile ;
'Tis hard to settle order once again.
There *is* confusion worse than death,
Trouble on trouble, pain on pain,
Long labour unto aged breath,
Sore task to hearts worn out by many wars
And eyes grown dim with gazing on the pilot-stars.

VII

But, propt on beds of amaranth and moly,
How sweet (while warm airs lull us, blowing lowly)
With half-dropt eyelid still,
Beneath a heaven dark and holy,
To watch the long bright river drawing slowly
His waters from the purple hill —
To hear the dewy echoes calling
From cave to cave thro' the thick-twined vine —
To watch the emerald-colour'd water falling
Thro' many a wov'n acanthus-wreath divine !
Only to hear and see the far-off sparkling brine,
Only to hear were sweet, stretch'd out beneath the pine.

VIII

The Lotos blooms below the barren peak,
The Lotos blows by every-winding creek ;
All day the wind breathes low with mellower tone ;
Thro' every hollow cave and alley lone

Round and round the spicy downs the yellow Lotos-dust is
  blown.
We have had enough of action, and of motion we,
Roll'd to starboard, roll'd to larboard, when the surge was
  seething free,
Where the wallowing monster spouted his foam-fountains in
  the sea.
Let us swear an oath, and keep it with an equal mind,
In the hollow Lotos-land to live and lie reclined
On the hills like Gods together, careless of mankind.
For they lie beside their nectar, and the bolts are hurl'd
Far below them in the valleys, and the clouds are lightly curl'd
Round their golden houses, girdled with the gleaming world ;
Where they smile in secret, looking over wasted lands,
Blight and famine, plague and earthquake, roaring deeps and
  fiery sands,
Clanging fights, and flaming towns, and sinking ships, and
  praying hands.
But they smile, they find a music centred in a doleful song
Steaming up, a lamentation and an ancient tale of wrong,
Like a tale of little meaning tho' the words are strong ;
Chanted from an ill-used race of men that cleave the soil,
Sow the seed, and reap the harvest with enduring toil,
Storing yearly little dues of wheat, and wine and oil ;
Till they perish and they suffer — some, 't is whisper'd —
  down in hell
Suffer endless anguish, others in Elysian valleys dwell,
Resting weary limbs at last on beds of asphodel.
Surely, surely, slumber is more sweet than toil, the shore
Than labour in the deep mid-ocean, wind and wave and oar ;
O rest ye, brother mariners, we will not wander more.

ULYSSES

It little profits that an idle king,
By this still hearth, among these barren crags,
Match'd with an aged wife, I mete and dole
Unequal laws into a savage race,
That hoard, and sleep, and feed, and know not me.
I cannot rest from travel : I will drink
Life to the lees. All times I have enjoy'd
Greatly, have suffer'd greatly, both with those
That loved me, and alone ; on shore, and when
Thro' scudding drifts the rainy Hyades
Vext the dim sea. I am become a name ;
For always roaming with a hungry heart
Much have I seen and known, — cities of men
And manners, climates, councils, governments,
Myself not least, but honour'd of them all, —
And drunk delight of battle with my peers,
Far on the ringing plains of windy Troy.
I am a part of all that I have met ;
Yet all experience is an arch wherethro'
Gleams that untravell'd world, whose margin fades
For ever and for ever when I move.
How dull it is to pause, to make an end,
To rust unburnish'd, not to shine in use !
As tho' to breathe were life ! Life piled on life
Were all too little, and of one to me
Little remains : but every hour is saved
From that eternal silence, something more,
A bringer of new things ; and vile it were
For some three suns to store and hoard myself,
And this gray spirit yearning in desire

To follow knowledge like a sinking star,
Beyond the utmost bound of human thought.
   This is my son, mine own Telemachus,
To whom I leave the sceptre and the isle —
Well-loved of me, discerning to fulfil
This labour, by slow prudence to make mild
A rugged people, and thro' soft degrees
Subdue them to the useful and the good.
Most blameless is he, centred in the sphere
Of common duties, decent not to fail
In offices of tenderness, and pay
Meet adoration to my household gods,
When I am gone. He works his work, I mine.
   There lies the port ; the vessel puffs her sail ;
There gloom the dark, broad seas. My mariners,
Souls that have toil'd, and wrought, and thought with me —
That ever with a frolic welcome took
The thunder and the sunshine, and opposed
Free hearts, free foreheads — you and I are old ;
Old age hath yet his honour and his toil ;
Death closes all ; but something ere the end,
Some work of noble note, may yet be done,
Not unbecoming men that strove with Gods.
The lights begin to twinkle from the rocks ;
The long day wanes ; the slow moon climbs ; the deep
Moans round with many voices. Come, my friends,
'T is not too late to seek a newer world.
Push off, and sitting well in order smite
The sounding furrows ; for my purpose holds
To sail beyond the sunset, and the baths
Of all the western stars, until I die.
It may be that the gulfs will wash us down ;
It may be we shall touch the Happy Isles,

And see the great Achilles, whom we knew.
Tho' much is taken, much abides ; and tho'
We are not now that strength which in old days
Moved earth and heaven, that which we are, we are, —
One equal temper of heroic hearts,
Made weak by time and fate, but strong in will
To strive, to seek, to find, and not to yield.

"BREAK, BREAK, BREAK"

Break, break, break,
    On thy cold gray stones, O Sea !
And I would that my tongue could utter
    The thoughts that arise in me.

O, well for the fisherman's boy,
    That he shouts with his sister at play !
O, well for the sailor lad,
    That he sings in his boat on the bay !

And the stately ships go on
    To their haven under the hill ;
But O for the touch of a vanish'd hand,
    And the sound of a voice that is still !

Break, break, break,
    At the foot of thy crags, O Sea !
But the tender grace of a day that is dead
    Will never come back to me.

"TEARS, IDLE TEARS, I KNOW NOT WHAT THEY MEAN"

Tears, idle tears, I know not what they mean,
Tears from the depth of some divine despair
Rise in the heart and gather to the eyes,
In looking on the happy Autumn-fields,
And thinking of the days that are no more.

Fresh as the first beam glittering on a sail,
That brings our friends up from the underworld,
Sad as the last which reddens over one
That sinks with all we love below the verge ;
So sad, so fresh, the days that are no more.

Ah, sad and strange, as in dark summer dawns
The earliest pipe of half-awaken'd birds
To dying ears, when unto dying eyes
The casement slowly grows a glimmering square ;
So sad, so strange, the days that are no more.

Dear as remember'd kisses after death,
And sweet as those by hopeless fancy feign'd
On lips that are for others ; deep as love,
Deep as first love, and wild with all regret ;
O Death in Life, the days that are no more !

from
IN MEMORIAM

VII

"DARK HOUSE, BY WHICH ONCE MORE I STAND"

Dark house, by which once more I stand
   Here in the long unlovely street,
   Doors, where my heart was used to beat
So quickly, waiting for a hand,

A hand that can be clasp'd no more —
   Behold me, for I cannot sleep,
   And like a guilty thing I creep
At earliest morning to the door.

He is not here ; but far away
   The noise of life begins again,
   And ghastly thro' the drizzling rain
On the bald street breaks the blank day.

CROSSING THE BAR

Sunset and evening star,
   And one clear call for me !
And may there be no moaning of the bar,
   When I put out to sea,

But such a tide as moving seems asleep,
   Too full for sound and foam,

When that which drew from out the boundless deep
   Turns again home.

Twilight and evening bell,
   And after that the dark !
And may there be no sadness of farewell,
   When I embark ;

For tho' from out our bourne of Time and Place
   The flood may bear me far,
I hope to see my Pilot face to face
   When I have crost the bar.

ROBERT BROWNING

(1812–1889)

MY LAST DUCHESS

FERRARA

That 's my last Duchess painted on the wall,
Looking as if she were alive ; I call
That piece a wonder, now : Frà Pandolf's hands
Worked busily a day, and there she stands.
Will 't please you sit and look at her ? I said
'Frà Pandolf' by design, for never read
Strangers like you that pictured countenance,
The depth and passion of its earnest glance,
But to myself they turned (since none puts by
The curtain I have drawn for you, but I)
And seemed as they would ask me, if they durst,
How such a glance came there ; so, not the first

Are you to turn and ask thus. Sir, 't was not
Her husband's presence only, called that spot
Of joy into the Duchess' cheek : perhaps
Frà Pandolf chanced to say 'Her mantle laps
Over my Lady's wrist too much,' or 'Paint
Must never hope to reproduce the faint
Half-flush that dies along her throat ;' such stuff
Was courtesy, she thought, and cause enough
For calling up that spot of joy. She had
A heart . . . how shall I say ? . . . too soon made glad,
Too easily impressed ; she liked whate'er
She looked on, and her looks went everywhere.
Sir, 't was all one ! My favour at her breast,
The dropping of the daylight in the West,
The bough of cherries some officious fool
Broke in the orchard for her, the white mule
She rode with round the terrace — all and each
Would draw from her alike the approving speech,
Or blush, at least. She thanked men, — good ; but thanked
Somehow . . . I know not how . . . as if she ranked
My gift of a nine-hundred-years-old name
With anybody's gift. Who 'd stoop to blame
This sort of trifling ? Even had you skill
In speech — (which I have not) — to make your will
Quite clear to such an one, and say 'Just this
Or that in you disgusts me ; here you miss,
Or there exceed the mark' — and if she let
Herself be lessoned so, nor plainly set
Her wits to yours, forsooth, and made excuse,
— E'en then would be some stooping, and I chuse
Never to stoop. Oh, Sir, she smiled, no doubt,
Whene'er I passed her ; but who passed without
Much the same smile ? This grew ; I gave commands ;

Then all smiles stopped together. There she stands
As if alive. Will 't please you rise ? We 'll meet
The company below, then. I repeat,
The Count your Master's known munificence
Is ample warrant that no just pretence
Of mine for dowry will be disallowed ;
Though his fair daughter's self, as I avowed
At starting, is my object. Nay, we 'll go
Together down, Sir ! Notice Neptune, though,
Taming a sea-horse, thought a rarity,
Which Claus of Innsbruck cast in bronze for me.

PORPHYRIA'S LOVER

The rain set early in to-night,
  The sullen wind was soon awake,
It tore the elm-tops down for spite,
  And did its worst to vex the lake,
I listened with heart fit to break.
When glided in Porphyria ; straight
  She shut the cold out and the storm,
And kneeled and made the cheerless grate
  Blaze up, and all the cottage warm ;
Which done, she rose, and from her form
Withdrew the dripping cloak and shawl,
  And laid her soiled gloves by, untied
Her hat and let the damp hair fall,
  And, last, she sat down by my side
And called me. When no voice replied,
She put my arm about her waist,
  And made her smooth white shoulder bare,
And all her yellow hair displaced,

And, stooping, made my cheek lie there,
And spread o'er all her yellow hair,
Murmuring how she loved me — she
 Too weak, for all her heart's endeavour,
To set its struggling passion free
 From pride, and vainer ties dissever,
And give herself to me for ever.
But passion sometimes would prevail,
 Nor could to-night's gay feast restrain
A sudden thought of one so pale
 For love of her, and all in vain ;
So, she was come through wind and rain.
Be sure I looked up at her eyes
 Happy and proud ; at last I knew
Porphyria worshipped me ; surprise
 Made my heart swell, and still it grew
While I debated what to do.
That moment she was mine, mine, fair,
 Perfectly pure and good : I found
A thing to do, and all her hair
 In one long yellow string I wound
Three times her little throat around,
And strangled her. No pain felt she ;
 I am quite sure she felt no pain.
As a shut bud that holds a bee,
 I warily oped her lids ; again
Laughed the blue eyes without a stain.
And I untightened next the tress
 About her neck ; her cheek once more
Blushed bright beneath my burning kiss :
 I propped her head up as before,
Only, this time *my* shoulder bore
Her head, which droops upon it still :

The smiling rosy little head,
So glad it has its utmost will,
    That all it scorned at once is fled,
And I, its love, am gained instead !
Porphyria's love : she guessed not how
    Her darling one wish would be heard.
And thus we sit together now,
    And all night long we have not stirred,
And yet God has not said a word !

MATTHEW ARNOLD

(1822–1888)

MEMORIAL VERSES

APRIL, 1850

Goethe in Weimar sleeps, and Greece,
Long since, saw Byron's struggle cease.
But one such death remain'd to come ;
The last poetic voice is dumb —
We stand to-day by Wordsworth's tomb.
When Byron's eyes were shut in death,
We bow'd our head and held our breath.
He taught us little ; but our soul
Had *felt* him like the thunder's roll.
With shivering heart the strife we saw
Of passion with eternal law ;
And yet with reverential awe
We watch'd the fount of fiery life
Which served for that Titanic strife.

When Goethe's death was told, we said :
Sunk, then, is Europe's sagest head.
Physician of the iron age,
Goethe has done his pilgrimage.
He took the suffering human race,
He read each wound, each weakness clear ;
And struck his finger on the place,
And said : *Thou ailest here, and here !*
He look'd on Europe's dying hour
Of fitful dream and feverish power ;
His eye plunged down the weltering strife,
The turmoil of expiring life —
He said : *The end is everywhere,*
Art still has truth, take refuge there !
And he was happy, if to know
Causes of things, and far below
His feet to see the lurid flow
Of terror, and insane distress,
And headlong fate, be happiness.

And Wordsworth ! — Ah, pale ghosts, rejoice !
For never has such soothing voice
Been to your shadowy world convey'd,
Since erst, at morn, some wandering shade
Heard the clear song of Orpheus come
Through Hades, and the mournful gloom.
Wordsworth has gone from us — and ye,
Ah, may ye feel his voice as we !
He too upon a wintry clime
Had fallen — on this iron time
Of doubts, disputes, distractions, fears.
He found us when the age had bound
Our souls in its benumbing round ;

false expression

He spoke, and loosed our heart in tears.
He laid us as we lay at birth
On the cool flowery lap of earth,
Smiles broke from us and we had ease ;
The hills were round us, and the breeze
Went o'er the sun-lit fields again ;
Our foreheads felt the wind and rain.
Our youth returned ; for there was shed
On spirits that had long been dead,
Spirits dried up and closely furl'd,
The freshness of the early world.

Ah ! since dark days still bring to light
Man's prudence and man's fiery might,
Time may restore us in his course
Goethe's sage mind and Byron's force ;
But where will Europe's latter hour
Again find Wordsworth's healing power ?
Others will teach us how to dare,
And against fear our breast to steel ;
Others will strengthen us to bear —
But who, ah ! who, will make us feel ?
The cloud of mortal destiny,
Others will front it fearlessly —
But who, like him, will put it by ?
Keep fresh the grass upon his grave
O Rotha, with thy living wave !
Sing him thy best ! for few or none
Hears thy voice right, now he is gone.

DOVER BEACH

The sea is calm to-night,
The tide is full, the moon lies fair
Upon the straits ; — on the French coast the light
Gleams and is gone ; the cliffs of England stand,
Glimmering and vast, out in the tranquil bay.
Come to the window, sweet is the night-air !

Only, from the long line of spray
Where the sea meets the moon-blanch'd land,
Listen ! you hear the grating roar
Of pebbles which the waves draw back, and fling,
At their return, up the high strand,
Begin, and cease, and then again begin,
With tremulous cadence slow, and bring
The eternal note of sadness in.

Sophocles long ago
Heard it on the Ægæan, and it brought
Into his mind the turbid ebb and flow
Of human misery ; we
Find also in the sound a thought,
Hearing it by this distant northern sea.

The Sea of Faith
Was once, too, at the full, and round earth's shore
Lay like the folds of a bright girdle furl'd.
But now I only hear
Its melancholy, long, withdrawing roar,
Retreating, to the breath

Of the night-wind, down the vast edges drear
And naked shingles of the world.
        Ah, love, let us be true
To one another ! for the world, which seems
To lie before us like a land of dreams,
So various, so beautiful, so new,
Hath really neither joy, nor love, nor light,

Nor certitude, nor peace, nor help for pain ;
And we are here as on a darkling plain
Swept with confused alarms of struggle and flight,
Where ignorant armies clash by night.

DANTE GABRIEL ROSSETTI

(1828–1882)

from
THE HOUSE OF LIFE

SONNET XIX

SILENT NOON

Your hands lie open in the long fresh grass, —
    The finger-points look through like rosy blooms :
    Your eyes smile peace. The pasture gleams and glooms
'Neath billowing skies that scatter and amass.
All round our nest, far as the eye can pass,
    Are golden kingcup-fields with silver edge
    Where the cow-parsley skirts the hawthorn-hedge.
'Tis visible silence, still as the hour-glass.

Deep in the sun-searched growths the dragon-fly
Hangs like a blue thread loosened from the sky : —
   So this wing'd hour is dropt to us from above.
Oh ! clasp we to our hearts, for deathless dower,
This close-companioned inarticulate hour
   When twofold silence was the song of love.

SUDDEN LIGHT

   I have been here before,
      But when or how I cannot tell :
   I know the grass beyond the door,
      The sweet, keen smell,
The sighing sound, the lights around the shore.

   You have been mine before, —
      How long ago I may not know :
   But just when at that swallow's soar
      Your neck turned so,
Some veil did fall, — I knew it all of yore.

   Has this been thus before ?
      And shall not thus time's eddying flight
   Still with our lives our love restore
      In death's despite,
And day and night yield one delight once more ?

ALGERNON CHARLES SWINBURNE

(1837–1909)

THE GARDEN OF PROSERPINE

Here, where the world is quiet,
   Here, where all trouble seems
Dead winds' and spent waves' riot
   In doubtful dreams of dreams ;
I watch the green field growing
For reaping folk and sowing,
For harvest time and mowing,
   A sleepy world of streams.

I am tired of tears and laughter,
   And men that laugh and weep ;
Of what may come hereafter
   For men that sow to reap :
I am weary of days and hours,
Blown buds of barren flowers,
Desires and dreams and powers
   And everything but sleep.

Here life has death for neighbor,
   And far from eye or ear
Wan waves and wet winds labor,
   Weak ships and spirits steer ;
They drive adrift, and whither
They wot not who make thither ;
But no such winds blow hither,
   And no such things grow here.

No growth of moor or coppice,
    No heather-flower or vine,
But bloomless buds of poppies,
    Green grapes of Proserpine,
Pale beds of blowing rushes
Where no leaf blooms or blushes,
Save this whereout she crushes
    For dead men deadly wine.

Pale, without name or number,
    In fruitless fields of corn,
They bow themselves and slumber
    All night till light is born ;
And like a soul belated,
In hell and heaven unmated,
By cloud and mist abated
    Comes out of darkness morn.

Though one were strong as seven,
    He too with death shall dwell,
Nor wake with wings in heaven,
    Nor weep for pains in hell ;
Though one were fair as roses,
His beauty clouds and closes ;
And well though love reposes,
    In the end it is not well.

Pale, beyond porch and portal,
    Crowned with calm leaves, she stands
Who gathers all things mortal
    With cold immortal hands ;
Her languid lips are sweeter
Than love's who fears to greet her

        To men that mix and meet her
        From many times and lands.

    She waits for each and other,
        She waits for all men born ;
    Forgets the earth her mother,
        The life of fruits and corn ;
    And spring and seed and swallow
    Take wing for her and follow
    Where summer song rings hollow,
        And flowers are put to scorn.

    There go the loves that wither,
        The old loves with wearier wings ;
    And all dead years draw thither,
        And all disastrous things ;
    Dead dreams of days forsaken,
    Blind buds that snows have shaken,
    Wild leaves that winds have taken,
        Red strays of ruined springs.

    We are not sure of sorrow,
        And joy was never sure ;
    To-day will die to-morrow ;
        Time stoops to no man's lure ;
    And love, grown faint and fretful,
    With lips but half regretful
    Sighs, and with eyes forgetful
        Weeps that no loves endure.

    From too much love of living,
    From hope and fear set free,
    We thank with brief thanksgiving

Whatever gods may be
That no life lives for ever ;
That dead men rise up never ;
That even the weariest river
  Winds somewhere safe to sea.

Then star nor sun shall waken,
  Nor any change of light :
Nor sound of waters shaken,
  Nor any sound or sight :
Nor wintry leaves nor vernal,
Nor days nor things diurnal ;
Only the sleep eternal
  In an eternal night.

THOMAS HARDY
(1840–1928)

Shows he wants to enjoy the world — but he can't see how

THE DARKLING THRUSH

I leaned upon a coppice gate
  When Frost was specter-gray,
And Winter's dregs made desolate
  The weakening eye of day.
The tangled bine-stems scored the sky
  Like strings of broken lyres,
And all mankind that haunted nigh
  Had sought their household fires.

The land's sharp features seemed to be
  The Century's corpse outleant ;

His crypt the cloudy canopy,
   The wind his death-lament.
The ancient pulse of germ and birth
   Was shrunken hard and dry,
And every spirit upon earth
   Seemed fervorless as I.

At once a voice burst forth among
   The bleak twigs overhead
In a full-hearted evensong
   Of joy illimited ;
An aged thrush, frail, gaunt and small,
   In blast-beruffled plume,
Had chosen thus to fling his soul
   Upon the growing gloom.

So little cause for carollings
   Of such ecstatic sound
Was written on terrestrial things
   Afar or nigh around,
That I could think there trembled through
   His happy good-night air
Some blessed Hope, whereof he knew
   And I was unaware.

BEENY CLIFF

MARCH 1870–MARCH 1913

I

O the opal and the sapphire of that wandering western sea,
And the woman riding high above with bright hair flapping
   free —
The woman whom I loved so, and who loyally loved me.

[handwritten annotations: "Means we can't change things. that's that." and "a very good station & a fine poem"]

II

The pale mews plained below us, and the waves seemed far
    away
In a nether sky, engrossed in saying their ceaseless babbling
    say,
As we laughed light-heartedly aloft on that clear-sunned
    March day.

III

A little cloud then cloaked us, and there flew an irised rain,
And the Atlantic dyed its levels with a dull misfeatured stain,
And then the sun burst out again, and purples prinked the
    main.

IV

— Still in all its chasmal beauty bulks old Beeny to the sky,
And shall she and I not go there once again now March is
    nigh,
And the sweet things said in that March say anew there by
    and by?

V

What if still in chasmal beauty looms that wild weird western
    shore,
The woman now is — elsewhere — whom the ambling pony
    bore,
And nor knows nor cares for Beeny, and will laugh there
    nevermore.

Shows his wish to enjoy the world

THE OXEN

Christmas Eve and twelve of the clock.
  "Now they are all on their knees,"
An elder said as we sat in a flock
  By the embers in hearthside ease.

We pictured the meek mild creatures where
  They dwelt in their strawy pen,
Nor did it occur to one of us there
  To doubt they were kneeling then.

So fair a fancy few would weave
  In these years ! Yet, I feel,
If some one said on Christmas Eve
  "Come ; see the oxen kneel

"In the lonely barton by yonder coomb
  Our childhood used to know,"
I should go with him in the gloom,
  Hoping it might be so.

Saying the cattle are kneeling at the Christ childrens feet.
1. Its not so says Hardy
*   a. But I wish it were*

A. E. HOUSMAN

(1859–1936)

from

A SHROPSHIRE LAD

II

"LOVELIEST OF TREES, THE CHERRY NOW"

Loveliest of trees, the cherry now
Is hung with bloom along the bough,
And stands about the woodland ride
Wearing white for Eastertide.

Now, of my threescore years and ten,
Twenty will not come again,
And take from seventy springs a score,
It only leaves me fifty more.

And since to look at things in bloom
Fifty springs are little room,
About the woodlands I will go
To see the cherry hung with snow.

Few trick statement
man is in love — but can't
marry yet — has to
go out & earn some
capital.

but will lead him back
seems straight,
to his love

XXXVI

"WHITE IN THE MOON
— THE LONG ROAD LIES"

White in the moon the long road lies,
  The moon stands blank above ;
White in the moon the long road lies
  That leads me from my love.

Still hangs the hedge without a gust,
  Still, still the shadows stay :
My feet upon the moonlit dust
  Pursue the ceaseless way.

The world is round, so travellers tell,
  And straight though reach the track,
Trudge on, trudge on, 'twill all be well,
  The way will guide one back.

But ere the circle homeward hies
  Far, far must it remove :
White in the moon the long road lies
  That leads me from my love.

LII

"FAR IN A WESTERN BROOKLAND"

Homesickness

Far in a western brookland
  That bred me long ago
The poplars stand and tremble
  By pools I used to know.

There, in the windless night-time,
   The wanderer, marvelling why,
Halts on the bridge to hearken
   How soft the poplars sigh.

He hears : no more remembered
   In fields where I was known,
Here I lie down in London
   And turn to rest alone.

There, by the starlit fences,
   The wanderer halts and hears
My soul that lingers sighing
   About the glimmering weirs.

THE TWENTIETH CENTURY

Hopkins to Spender

extremely complicated

GERARD MANLEY HOPKINS

(1844–1889)

His best poem

THE WINDHOVER:

To Christ our Lord

Inscape – gives the energy on the inside of things

religious beauty

I caught this morning morning's minion, kingdom of day-
    light's dauphin, dapple-dawn-drawn Falcon, in his
    riding
  Of the rolling level underneath him steady air, and striding
High there, how he rung upon the rein of a wimpling wing
In his ecstasy ! then off, off forth on swing,
  As a skate's heel sweeps smooth on a bow-bend : the hurl
    and gliding
  Rebuffed the big wind. My heart in hiding
Stirred for a bird, — the achieve of, the mastery of the thing !

you get the feel of the bird

empathy

Brute beauty and valour and act, oh, air, pride, plume, here
— Buckle ! AND the fire that breaks from thee then, a billion
Times told lovelier, more dangerous, O my chevalier !

a night

Tragic is more beautiful than pleasure

  No wonder of it : shéer plód makes plough down sillion
Shine, and blue-bleak embers, ah my dear,
  Fall, gall themselves, and gash gold-vermilion.

PIED BEAUTY

  Glory be to God for dappled things —
    For skies of couple-colour as a brinded cow ;

307

loves to make up strange words

> For rose-moles all in stipple upon trout that swim ;
> Fresh-firecoal chestnut-falls ; finches' wings ;
> Landscape plotted and pieced — fold, fallow, and
> plough ;
> And áll trádes, their gear and tackle and trim. *Picture*
> *of countryside*
>
> All things counter, original, spare, strange ;
> Whatever is fickle, freckled (who knows how ?)
> With swift, slow ; sweet, sour ; adazzle, dim ; *The rest has*
> He fathers-forth whose beauty is past change : *been working*
> Praise him. *up to this*

Not religious   **SPRING AND FALL :** *Best of his poems*

to a young child *addressed to a young child*
1. why is she moved
at the sight of fall
leaves

> Márgarét, are you gríeving
> Over Goldengrove unleaving ?
> Leáves, líke the things of man, you
> With your fresh thoughts care for, can you ?
> Áh ! ás the heart grows older
> It will come to such sights colder
> By and by, nor spare a sigh   *our worries*
you weep > Though worlds of wanwood leafmeal lie ; *concern ourselves*
subject — > And yet you wíll weep and know why.   *as we grow*
me to know > Now no matter, child, the name :   *older*
why > Sórrow's spríngs áre the same.
> Nor mouth had, no nor mind, expressed
> What heart heard of, ghost guessed :
> It ís the blight man was born for,
> It is Margaret you mourn for.

Autumn suggests death of nature
Death of nature suggests death of man

Strange language is effective

Great with child — self expression by poets

"I WAKE AND FEEL THE FELL *fell* OF DARK, NOT DAY"

I wake and feel the fell of dark, not day.
What hours, O what black hoùrs we have spent
This night ! what sights you, heart, saw ; ways you went !
And more must, in yet longer light's delay.
    With witness I speak this. But where I say
Hours I mean years, mean life. And my lament
Is cries countless, cries like dead letters sent
To dearest him that lives alas ! away.

irritated
I am gall, I am heartburn. God's most deep decree
Bitter would have me taste : my taste was me ;
Bones built in me, flesh filled, blood brimmed the curse. *original sin*
Selfyeast of spirit a dull dough sours. I see
The lost are like this, and their scourge to be
As I am mine, their sweating selves ; but worse. *means he's not lost*

WILLIAM BUTLER YEATS

(1865–1939)

THE MAGI *— great historical events* *are the people who sense*

Now as at all times I can see in the mind's eye,
In their stiff, painted clothes, the pale unsatisfied ones
Appear and disappear in the blue depth of the sky
With all their ancient faces like rain-beaten stones,
And all their helms of silver hovering side by side,
And all their eyes still fixed, hoping to find once more,

Coming to the end of 2,000 yrs. of Christianity

Being by Calvary's turbulence unsatisfied,
The uncontrollable mystery on the bestial floor.

THE DOLLS *

[handwritten: Darling dolls / Raging child]

A doll in the doll-maker's house
Looks at the cradle and bawls :
'That is an insult to us.'
But the oldest of all the dolls,
Who had seen, being kept for show,
Generations of his sort,
Out-screams the whole shelf : 'Although
There 's not a man can report
Evil of this place,
The man and the woman bring
Hither, to our disgrace,
A noisy and filthy thing.'
Hearing him groan and stretch
The doll-maker's wife is aware
Her husband has heard the wretch,
And crouched by the arm of his chair,
She murmurs into his ear,
Head upon shoulder leant :
'My dear, my dear, O dear,
It was an accident.'

[handwritten: child was / an accident]

* Author's note: "The fable for this poem came into my head while I was
giving some lectures in Dublin. I had noticed once again how all thought
among us is frozen into 'something other than human life.' After I had made
the poem, I looked up one day into the blue of the sky, and suddenly im-
agined, as if lost in the blue of the sky, stiff figures in procession. I remem-
bered that they were the habitual image suggested by blue sky, and looking for
a second fable called them 'The Magi' . . . complementary forms of those
enraged dolls. — 1914."

THE WILD SWANS AT COOLE

The trees are in their autumn beauty,
The woodland paths are dry,
Under the October twilight the water
Mirrors a still sky ;
Upon the brimming water among the stones
Are nine-and-fifty swans.

The nineteenth autumn has come upon me
Since I first made my count ;
I saw, before I had well finished,
All suddenly mount
And scatter wheeling in great broken rings
Upon their clamorous wings.

I have looked upon those brilliant creatures,
And now my heart is sore.
All 's changed since I, hearing at twilight,
The first time on this shore,
The bell-beat of their wings above my head,
Trod with a lighter tread.

Unwearied still, lover by lover,
They paddle in the cold
Companionable streams or climb the air ;
Their hearts have not grown old ;
Passion or conquest, wander where they will,
Attend upon them still.

But now they drift on the still water
Mysterious, beautiful ;

Among what rushes will they build,
By what lake's edge or pool
Delight men's eyes when I awake some day
To find they have flown away?

W.W., Shelly + Keats — have ideas in common around 1802

THE SECOND COMING

Turning and turning in the widening gyre
The falcon cannot hear the falconer;
Things fall apart; the centre cannot hold;
Mere anarchy is loosed upon the world,
The blood-dimmed tide is loosed, and everywhere
The ceremony of innocence is drowned;
The best lack all conviction, while the worst
Are full of passionate intensity.

things are falling apart of our time

Has lost belief

Surely some revelation is at hand;
Surely the Second Coming is at hand.
The Second Coming! Hardly are those words out
When a vast image out of *Spiritus Mundi*
Troubles my sight: somewhere in sands of the desert
A shape with lion body and the head of a man,
A gaze blank and pitiless as the sun,
Is moving its slow thighs, while all about it
Reel shadows of the indignant desert birds.
The darkness drops again; but now I know
That twenty centuries of stony sleep
Were vexed to nightmare by a rocking cradle,
And what rough beast, its hour come round at last,
Slouches towards Bethlehem to be born?

SAILING TO BYZANTIUM

I

That is no country for old men. The young
In one another's arms, birds in the trees,
— Those dying generations — at their song,
The salmon-falls, the mackerel-crowded seas,
Fish, flesh, or fowl, commend all summer long
Whatever is begotten, born, and dies.
Caught in that sensual music all neglect
Monuments of unageing intellect.

II

An aged man is but a paltry thing,
A tattered coat upon a stick, unless
Soul clap its hands and sing, and louder sing
For every tatter in its mortal dress,
Nor is there singing school but studying
Monuments of its own magnificence ;
And therefore I have sailed the seas and come
To the holy city of Byzantium.

III

O sages standing in God's holy fire
As in the gold mosaic of a wall,
Come from the holy fire, perne in a gyre,
And be the singing-masters of my soul.
Consume my heart away ; sick with desire
And fastened to a dying animal
It knows not what it is ; and gather me
Into the artifice of eternity.

IV

Once out of nature I shall never take
My bodily form from any natural thing,
But such a form as Grecian goldsmiths make
Of hammered gold and gold enamelling
To keep a drowsy Emperor awake ;
Or set upon a golden bough to sing
To lords and ladies of Byzantium
Of what is past, or passing, or to come.

LEDA AND THE SWAN

A sudden blow : the great wings beating still
Above the staggering girl, her thighs caressed
By the dark webs, her nape caught in his bill,
He holds her helpless breast upon his breast.

How can those terrified vague fingers push
The feathered glory from her loosening thighs ?
And how can body, laid in that white rush,
But feel the strange heart beating where it lies ?

A shudder in the loins engenders there
The broken wall, the burning roof and tower
And Agamemnon dead.
                    Being so caught up,
So mastered by the brute blood of the air,
Did she put on his knowledge with his power
Before the indifferent beak could let her drop ?

AMONG SCHOOL CHILDREN

I

I walk through the long schoolroom questioning ;
A kind old nun in a white hood replies ;
The children learn to cipher and to sing,
To study reading-books and history,
To cut and sew, be neat in everything
In the best modern way — the children's eyes
In momentary wonder stare upon
A sixty-year-old smiling public man.

II

I dream of a Ledaean body, bent
Above a sinking fire, a tale that she
Told of a harsh reproof, or trivial event
That changed some childish day to tragedy —
Told, and it seemed that our two natures blent
Into a sphere from youthful sympathy,
Or else, to alter Plato's parable,
Into the yolk and white of the one shell.

III

And thinking of that fit of grief or rage
I look upon one child or t' other there
And wonder if she stood so at that age —
For even daughters of the swan can share
Something of every paddler's heritage —
And had that colour upon cheek or hair,

And thereupon my heart is driven wild :
She stands before me as a living child.

IV

Her present image floats into the mind —
Did Quattrocento finger fashion it
Hollow of cheek as though it drank the wind
And took a mess of shadows for its meat ?
And I though never of Ledaean kind
Had pretty plumage once — enough of that,
Better to smile on all that smile, and show
There is a comfortable kind of old scarecrow.

V

What youthful mother, a shape upon her lap
Honey of generation had betrayed,
And that must sleep, shriek, struggle to escape
As recollection or the drug decide,
Would think her son, did she but see that shape
With sixty or more winters on its head,
A compensation for the pang of his birth,
Or the uncertainty of his setting forth ?

VI

Plato thought nature but a spume that plays
Upon a ghostly paradigm of things ;
Soldier Aristotle played the taws
Upon the bottom of a king of kings ;
World-famous golden-thighed Pythagoras
Fingered upon a fiddle-stick or strings
What a star sang and careless Muses heard :
Old clothes upon old sticks to scare a bird.

VII

Both nuns and mothers worship images,
But those the candles light are not as those
That animate a mother's reveries,
But keep a marble or a bronze repose.
And yet they too break hearts — O Presences
That passion, piety or affection knows,
And that all heavenly glory symbolise —
O self-born mockers of man's enterprise ;

VIII

Labour is blossoming or dancing where
The body is not bruised to pleasure soul,
Nor beauty born out of its own despair,
Nor blear-eyed wisdom out of midnight oil.
O chestnut tree, great rooted blossomer,
Are you the leaf, the blossom or the bole ?
O body swayed to music, O brightening glance,
How can we know the dancer from the dance ?

BLOOD AND THE MOON

I

Blessed be this place,
More blessed still this tower ;
A bloody, arrogant power
Rose out of the race
Uttering, mastering it,
Rose like these walls from these
Storm-beaten cottages —

In mockery I have set
A powerful emblem up,
And sing it rhyme upon rhyme
In mockery of a time
Half dead at the top.

II

Alexandria's was a beacon tower, and Babylon's
An image of the moving heavens, a log-book of the sun's jour-
     ney and the moon's ;
And Shelley had his towers, thought's crowned powers he
     called them once.

I declare this tower is my symbol ; I declare
This winding, gyring, spiring treadmill of a stair is my an-
     cestral stair ;
That Goldsmith and the Dean, Berkeley and Burke have
     travelled there.

Swift beating on his breast in sibylline frenzy blind
Because the heart in his blood-sodden breast had dragged
     him down into mankind,
Goldsmith deliberately sipping at the honey-pot of his mind,

And haughtier-headed Burke that proved the State a tree,
That this unconquerable labyrinth of the birds, century after
     century,
Cast but dead leaves to mathematical equality ;

And God-appointed Berkeley that proved all things a dream,
That this pragmatical, preposterous pig of a world, its farrow
     that so solid seem,

Must vanish on the instant if the mind but change its
    theme ;

Saeva Indignatio and the labourer's hire,
The strength that gives our blood and state magnanimity of
    its own desire ;
Everything that is not God consumed with intellectual fire.

III

The purity of the unclouded moon
Has flung its arrowy shaft upon the floor.
Seven centuries have passed and it is pure,
The blood of innocence has left no stain.
There, on blood-satured ground, have stood
Soldier, assassin, executioner,
Whether for daily pittance or in blind fear
Or out of abstract hatred, and shed blood,
But could not cast a single jet thereon.
Odour of blood on the ancestral stair !
And we that have shed none must gather there
And clamour in drunken frenzy for the moon.

IV

Upon the dusty, glittering windows cling,
And seem to cling upon the moonlit skies,
Tortoiseshell butterflies, peacock butterflies,
A couple of night-moths are on the wing.
Is every modern nation like the tower,
Half dead at the top ? No matter what I said,
For wisdom is the property of the dead,
A something incompatible with life ; and power,
Like everything that has the stain of blood,

A property of the living ; but no stain
Can come upon the visage of the moon
When it has looked in glory from a cloud.

BYZANTIUM

The unpurged images of day recede ;
The Emperor's drunken soldiery are abed ;
Night resonance recedes, night-walkers' song
After great cathedral gong ;
A starlit or a moonlit dome disdains
All that man is,
All mere complexities,
The fury and the mire of human veins.

Before me floats an image, man or shade,
Shade more than man, more image than a shade ;
For Hades' bobbin bound in mummy-cloth
May unwind the winding path ;
A mouth that has no moisture and no breath
Breathless mouths may summon ;
I hail the superhuman ;
I call it death-in-life and life-in-death.

Miracle, bird or golden handiwork,
More miracle than bird or handiwork,
Planted on the star-lit golden bough,
Can like the cocks of Hades crow,
Or, by the moon embittered, scorn aloud
In glory of changeless metal
Common bird or petal
And all complexities of mire or blood.

At midnight on the Emperor's pavement flit
Flames that no faggot feeds, nor steel has lit,
Nor storm disturbs, flames begotten of flame,
Where blood-begotten spirits come
And all complexities of fury leave,
Dying into a dance,
An agony of trance,
An agony of flame that cannot singe a sleeve.

Astraddle on the dolphin's mire and blood,
Spirit after spirit ! The smithies break the flood,
The golden smithies of the Emperor !
Marbles of the dancing floor
Break bitter furies of complexity,
Those images that yet
Fresh images beget,
That dolphin-torn, that gong-tormented sea.

THE MAN AND THE ECHO

MAN

In a cleft that 's christened Alt
Under broken stone I halt
At the bottom of a pit
That broad noon has never lit,
And shout a secret to the stone.
All that I have said and done,
Now that I am old and ill,
Turns into a question till
I lie awake night after night
And never get the answers right.

Did that play of mine send out
Certain men the English shot?
Did words of mine put too great strain
On that woman's reeling brain?
Could my spoken words have checked
That whereby a house lay wrecked?
And all seems evil until I
Sleepless would lie down and die.

ECHO

Lie down and die.

MAN

That were to shirk
The spiritual intellect's great work,
And shirk it in vain. There is no release
In a bodkin or disease,
Nor can there be work so great
As that which cleans man's dirty slate.
While man can still his body keep
Wine or love drug him to sleep,
Waking he thanks the Lord that he
Has body and its stupidity,
But body gone he sleeps no more,
And till his intellect grows sure
That all 's arranged in one clear view,
Pursues the thoughts that I pursue,
Then stands in judgment on his soul,
And, all work done, dismisses all
Out of intellect and sight
And sinks at last into the night.

ECHO

Into the night.

MAN

O Rocky Voice,
Shall we in that great night rejoice ?
What do we know but that we face
One another in this place ?
But hush, for I have lost the theme,
Its joy or night seem but a dream ;
Up there some hawk or owl has struck,
Dropping out of sky or rock,
A stricken rabbit is crying out,
And its cry distracts my thought.

T. S. ELIOT

(1888 ——)

PORTRAIT OF A LADY

Thou hast committed —
Fornication : but that was in another country,
And besides, the wench is dead.
                              The Jew of Malta.

I

Among the smoke and fog of a December afternoon
You have the scene arrange itself — as it will seem to do —
With "I have saved this afternoon for you" ;
And four wax candles in the darkened room,
Four rings of light upon the ceiling overhead,

An atmosphere of Juliet's tomb
Prepared for all the things to be said, or left unsaid.
We have been, let us say, to hear the latest Pole
Transmit the Preludes, through his hair and fingertips.
"So intimate, this Chopin, that I think his soul
Should be resurrected only among friends
Some two or three, who will not touch the bloom
That is rubbed and questioned in the concert room."
— And so the conversation slips
Among velleities and carefully caught regrets
Through attenuated tones of violins
Mingled with remote cornets
And begins.
"You do not know how much they mean to me, my friends,
And how, how rare and strange it is, to find
In a life composed so much, so much of odds and ends,
(For indeed I do not love it . . . you knew? you are not
        blind!
How keen you are!)
To find a friend who has these qualities,
Who has, and gives
Those qualities upon which friendship lives.
How much it means that I say this to you —
Without these friendships — life, what *cauchemar!*"
Among the windings of the violins
And the ariettes
Of cracked cornets
Inside my brain a dull tom-tom begins
Absurdly hammering a prelude of its own,
Capricious monotone
That is at least one definite "false note."
— Let us take the air, in a tobacco trance,
Admire the monuments,

Discuss the late events,
Correct our watches by the public clocks.
Then sit for half an hour and drink our bocks.

II

Now that lilacs are in bloom
She has a bowl of lilacs in her room
And twists one in her fingers while she talks.
"Ah, my friend, you do not know, you do not know
What life is, you should hold it in your hands" ;
(Slowly twisting the lilac stalks)
"You let it flow from you, you let it flow,
And youth is cruel, and has no remorse
And smiles at situations which it cannot see."
I smile, of course,
And go on drinking tea.
"Yet with these April sunsets, that somehow recall
My buried life, and Paris in the Spring,
I feel immeasurably at peace, and find the world
To be wonderful and youthful, after all."

The voice returns like the insistent out-of-tune
Of a broken violin on an August afternoon :
"I am always sure that you understand
My feelings, always sure that you feel,
Sure that across the gulf you reach your hand.

You are invulnerable, you have no Achilles' heel.
You will go on, and when you have prevailed
You can say : at this point many a one has failed.
But what have I, but what have I, my friend,

To give you, what can you receive from me ?
Only the friendship and the sympathy
Of one about to reach her journey's end.

I shall sit here, serving tea to friends. . . ."

I take my hat : how can I make a cowardly amends
For what she has said to me ?
You will see me any morning in the park
Reading the comics and the sporting page.
Particularly I remark
An English countess goes upon the stage.
A Greek was murdered at a Polish dance,
Another bank defaulter has confessed.
I keep my countenance,
I remain self-possessed
Except when a street piano, mechanical and tired
Reiterates some worn-out common song
With the smell of hyacinths across the garden
Recalling things that other people have desired.
Are these ideas right or wrong ?

III

The October night comes down ; returning as before
Except for a slight sensation of being ill at ease
I mount the stairs and turn the handle of the door
And feel as if I had mounted on my hands and knees.
"And so you are going abroad ; and when do you return ?
But that 's a useless question.
You hardly know when you are coming back,
You will find so much to learn."
My smile falls heavily among the bric-à-brac.

"Perhaps you can write to me."
My self-possession flares up for a second ;
This is as I had reckoned.

"I have been wondering frequently of late
(But our beginnings never know our ends !)
Why we have not developed into friends."
I feel like one who smiles, and turning shall remark
Suddenly, his expression in a glass.
My self-possession gutters ; we are really in the dark.

"For everybody said so, all our friends,
They all were sure our feelings would relate
So closely ! I myself can hardly understand.
We must leave it now to fate.
You will write, at any rate.
Perhaps it is not too late.
I shall sit here, serving tea to friends."

And I must borrow every changing shape
To find expression . . . dance, dance
Like a dancing bear,
Cry like a parrot, chatter like an ape.
Let us take the air, in a tobacco trance —
Well ! and what if she should die some afternoon,
Afternoon grey and smoky, evening yellow and rose ;
Should die and leave me sitting pen in hand
With the smoke coming down above the housetops ;
Doubtful, for a while
Not knowing what to feel or if I understand
Or whether wise or foolish, tardy or too soon . . .
Would she not have the advantage, after all ?
This music is successful with a "dying fall"

Now that we talk of dying —
And should I have the right to smile ?

not a love poem
a drama is taking place

SWEENEY
AMONG THE NIGHTINGALES

ὤμοι, πέπληγμαι καιρίαν πληγὴν ἔσω.

looks like an ape.
smells like an ape

Will make
I amusing

Apeneck Sweeney spreads his knees
Letting his arms hang down to laugh,
The zebra stripes along his jaw
Swelling to maculate giraffe.

stinking

The circles of the stormy moon
Slide westward toward the River Plate, *S. A.*
Death and the Raven drift above
And Sweeney guards the horned gate.

motion

Gloomy Orion and the Dog
Are veiled ; and hushed the shrunken seas ;
The person in the Spanish cape
Tries to sit on Sweeney's knees

Sweeney a victim
is a circumstances
between women

Slips and pulls the table cloth
Overturns a coffee-cup,
Reorganised upon the floor
She yawns and draws a stocking up ;

a gun man

The silent man in mocha brown
Sprawls at the window-sill and gapes ;
The waiter brings in oranges
Bananas figs and hothouse grapes ;

The silent vertebrate in brown
Contracts and concentrates, withdraws ;
Rachel *née* Rabinovitch
Tears at the grapes with murderous paws ;

She and the lady in the cape
Are suspect, thought to be in league ;
Therefore the man with heavy eyes
Declines the gambit, shows fatigue,

Leaves the room and reappears
Outside the window, leaning in,
Branches of wistaria
Circumscribe a golden grin ;

The host with someone indistinct
Converses at the door apart,
The nightingales are singing near
The Convent of the Sacred Heart,

And sang within the bloody wood
When Agamemnon cried aloud,
And let their liquid siftings fall
To stain the stiff dishonoured shroud.

THE HOLLOW MEN

A penny for the Old Guy

symbol —

I

We are the hollow men
We are the stuffed men
Leaning together
Headpiece filled with straw. Alas !
Our dried voices, when
We whisper together
Are quiet and meaningless
As wind in dry grass
Or rats' feet over broken glass
In our dry cellar

everything is meaningless

Shape without form, shade without colour,
Paralysed force, gesture without motion ;

all four mean meaningless

Those who have crossed
With direct eyes, to death's other Kingdom
Remember us — if at all — not as lost
Violent souls, but only
As the hollow men
The stuffed men.

this world

Damn people who are in hell because they believe in nothing

II

directness

Eyes I dare not meet in dreams
In death's dream kingdom
These do not appear :
There, the eyes are

Sunlight on a broken column
There, is a tree swinging
And voices are
In the wind's singing
More distant and more solemn
Than a fading star.

Let me be no nearer
In death's dream kingdom
Let me also wear
Such deliberate disguises
Rat's skin, crowskin, crossed staves
In a field
Behaving as the wind behaves
No nearer —

Not that final meeting
In the twilight kingdom

III

This is the dead land
This is cactus land
Here the stone images
Are raised, here they receive
The supplication of a dead man's hand
Under the twinkle of a fading star.

Is it like this
In death's other kingdom
Waking alone
At the hour when we are
Trembling with tenderness

Lips that would kiss
Form prayers to broken stone.

IV

The eyes are not here
There are no eyes here
In this valley of dying stars
In this hollow valley
This broken jaw of our lost kingdoms.

In this last of meeting places
We grope together
And avoid speech
Gathered on this beach of the tumid river.

[handwritten: We're lost, unless we can find the organizing principle]

Sightless, unless
The eyes reappear
As the perpetual star
Multifoliate rose *[handwritten: roses in an Cathedral]*
Of death's twilight kingdom
The hope only
Of empty men.

[handwritten left margin: — timeless]

V

Here we go round the prickly pear
Prickly pear prickly pear
Here we go round the prickly pear
At five o'clock in the morning.

[handwritten left margin: mature people act more like honest children]

Between the idea
And the reality
Between the motion

And the act
Falls the Shadow
For Thine is the Kingdom

Between the conception
And the creation
Between the emotion
And the response
Falls the Shadow
Life is very long

Between the desire
And the spasm
Between the potency
And the existence
Between the essence
And the descent
Falls the Shadow
For Thine is the Kingdom

For Thine is
Life is
For Thine is the

This is the way the world ends
This is the way the world ends
This is the way the world ends
Not with a bang but a whimper.

physical, spiritual, exhaustion

Sums up the world during the 1920's

I

Because I do not hope to turn again
Because I do not hope
Because I do not hope to turn
Desiring this man's gift and that man's scope
I no longer strive to strive towards such things
(Why should the agèd eagle stretch its wings ?)
Why should I mourn
The vanished power of the usual reign ?

Because I do not hope to know again
The infirm glory of the positive hour
Because I do not think
Because I know I shall not know
The one veritable transitory power
Because I cannot drink
There, where trees flower, and springs flow, for there is noth-
    ing again

Because I know that time is always time
And place is always and only place
And what is actual is actual only for one time
And only for one place
I rejoice that things are as they are and
I renounce the blessèd face
And renounce the voice
Because I cannot hope to turn again

Consequently I rejoice, having to construct something
Upon which to rejoice

And pray to God to have mercy upon us
And I pray that I may forget
These matters that with myself I too much discuss
Too much explain
Because I do not hope to turn again
Let these words answer
For what is done, not to be done again
May the judgement not be too heavy upon us

Because these wings are no longer wings to fly
But merely vans to beat the air
The air which is now thoroughly small and dry
Smaller and dryer than the will
Teach us to care and not to care
Teach us to sit still.

Pray for us sinners now and at the hour of our death
Pray for us now and at the hour of our death.

JOURNEY OF THE MAGI

'A cold coming we had of it,
Just the worst time of the year
For a journey, and such a long journey:
The ways deep and the weather sharp,
The very dead of winter.'
And the camels galled, sore-footed, refractory,
Lying down in the melting snow.
There were times we regretted
The summer palaces on slopes, the terraces,

And the silken girls bringing sherbet.
Then the camel men cursing and grumbling
And running away, and wanting their liquor and women,
And the night-fires going out, and the lack of shelters,
And the cities hostile and the towns unfriendly
And the villages dirty and charging high prices :
A hard time we had of it.
At the end we preferred to travel all night,
Sleeping in snatches,
With the voices singing in our ears, saying
That this was all folly.

Then at dawn we came down to a temperate valley,
Wet, below the snow line, smelling of vegetation ;
With a running stream and a water-mill beating the darkness,
And three trees on the low sky,
And an old white horse galloped away in the meadow.
Then we came to a tavern with vine-leaves over the lintel,
Six hands at an open door dicing for pieces of silver,
And feet kicking the empty wine-skins.
But there was no information, and so we continued
And arrived at evening, not a moment too soon
Finding the place ; it was (you may say) satisfactory.

All this was a long time ago, I remember,
And I would do it again, but set down
This set down
This : were we led all that way for
Birth or Death ? There was a Birth, certainly,
We had evidence and no doubt. I had seen birth and death,
But had thought they were different ; this Birth was - Christo
Hard and bitter agony for us, like Death, our death. Birth
We returned to our places, these Kingdoms,

But no longer at ease here, in the old dispensation,
With an alien people clutching their gods.
I should be glad of another death.

from
FOUR QUARTETS

BURNT NORTON

τοῦ λόγου δ'ἐόντος ξυνοῦ ζώουσιν οἱ πολλοί
ὡς ἰδίαν ἔχοντες φρόνησιν.

I. p. 77. Fr. 2.

ὁδὸς ἄνω κάτω μία καὶ ωὐτή.

I. p. 89. Fr. 60.

Diels : *Die Fragmente der Vorsokratiker* (Herakleitos).

I

Time present and time past
Are both perhaps present in time future,
And time future contained in time past.
If all time is eternally present
All time is unredeemable.
What might have been is an abstraction
Remaining a perpetual possibility
Only in a world of speculation.
What might have been and what has been
Point to one end, which is always present.
Footfalls echo in the memory
Down the passage which we did not take
Towards the door we never opened
Into the rose-garden. My words echo
Thus, in your mind.

                  But to what purpose
Disturbing the dust on a bowl of rose-leaves
I do not know.
                Other echoes
Inhabit the garden. Shall we follow?
Quick, said the bird, find them, find them,
Round the corner. Through the first gate,
Into our first world, shall we follow
The deception of the thrush? Into our first world.
There they were, dignified, invisible,
Moving without pressure, over the dead leaves,
In the autumn heat, through the vibrant air,
And the bird called, in response to
The unheard music hidden in the shrubbery,
And the unseen eyebeam crossed, for the roses
Had the look of flowers that are looked at.
There they were as our guests, accepted and accepting.
So we moved, and they, in a formal pattern,
Along the empty alley, into the box circle,
To look down into the drained pool.
Dry the pool, dry concrete, brown edged,
And the pool was filled with water out of sunlight,
And the lotos rose, quietly, quietly,
The surface glittered out of heart of light,
And they were behind us, reflected in the pool.
Then a cloud passed, and the pool was empty.
Go, said the bird, for the leaves were full of children,
Hidden excitedly, containing laughter.
Go, go, go, said the bird : human kind
Cannot bear very much reality.
Time past and time future
What might have been and what has been
Point to one end, which is always present.

II

Garlic and sapphires in the mud
Clot the bedded axle-tree.
The trilling wire in the blood
Sings below inveterate scars
And reconciles forgotten wars.
The dance along the artery
The circulation of the lymph
Are figured in the drift of stars
Ascend to summer in the tree
We move above the moving tree
In light upon the figured leaf
And hear upon the sodden floor
Below, the boarhound and the boar
Pursue their pattern as before
But reconciled among the stars.

At the still point of the turning world. Neither flesh nor flesh-
   less ;
Neither from nor towards ; at the still point, there the
   dance is,
But neither arrest nor movement. And do not call it fixity,
Where past and future are gathered. Neither movement from
   nor towards,
Neither ascent nor decline. Except for the point, the still
   point,
There would be no dance, and there is only the dance.
I can only say, *there* we have been : but I cannot say where.
And I cannot say, how long, for that is to place it in time.

The inner freedom from the practical desire,
The release from action and suffering, release from the inner

And the outer compulsion, yet surrounded
By a grace of sense, a white light still and moving,
Erhebung without motion, concentration
Without elimination, both a new world
And the old made explicit, understood
In the completion of its partial ecstasy,
The resolution of its partial horror.
Yet the enchainment of past and future
Woven in the weakness of the changing body,
Protects mankind from heaven and damnation
Which flesh cannot endure.
                    Time past and time future
Allow but a little consciousness.
To be conscious is not to be in time
But only in time can the moment in the rose-garden,
The moment in the arbour where the rain beat,
The moment in the draughty church at smokefall
Be remembered ; involved with past and future.
Only through time time is conquered.

                              III

Here is a place of disaffection
Time before and time after
In a dim light : neither daylight
Investing form with lucid stillness
Turning shadow into transient beauty
With slow rotation suggesting permanence
Nor darkness to purify the soul
Emptying the sensual with deprivation
Cleansing affection from the temporal.
Neither plenitude nor vacancy. Only a flicker
Over the strained time-ridden faces

Distracted from distraction by distraction
Filled with fancies and empty of meaning
Tumid apathy with no concentration
Men and bits of paper, whirled by the cold wind
That blows before and after time,
Wind in and out of unwholesome lungs
Time before and time after.
Eructation of unhealthy souls
Into the faded air, the torpid
Driven on the wind that sweeps the gloomy hills of London,
Hampstead and Clerkenwell, Campden and Putney,
Highgate, Primrose and Ludgate. Not here
Not here the darkness, in this twittering world.

Descend lower, descend only
Into the world of perpetual solitude,
World not world, but that which is not world,
Internal darkness, deprivation
And destitution of all property,
Desiccation of the world of sense,
Evacuation of the world of fancy,
Inoperancy of the world of spirit ;
This is the one way, and the other
Is the same, not in movement
But abstention from movement ; while the world moves
In appetency, on its metalled ways
Of time past and time future.

IV

Time and the bell have buried the day,
The black cloud carries the sun away.
Will the sunflower turn to us, will the clematis
Stray down, bend to us ; tendril and spray

Clutch and cling ?
Chill
Fingers of yew be curled
Down on us ? After the kingfisher's wing
Has answered light to light, and is silent, the light is still
At the still point of the turning world.

V

Words move, music moves
Only in time ; but that which is only living
Can only die. Words, after speech, reach
Into the silence. Only by the form, the pattern,
Can words or music reach
The stillness, as a Chinese jar still
Moves perpetually in its stillness.
Not the stillness of the violin, while the note lasts,
Not that only, but the co-existence,
Or say that the end precedes the beginning,
And the end and the beginning were always there
Before the beginning and after the end.
And all is always now. Words strain,
Crack and sometimes break, under the burden,
Under the tension, slip, slide, perish,
Decay with imprecision, will not stay in place,
Will not stay still. Shrieking voices
Scolding, mocking, or merely chattering,
Always assail them. The Word in the desert
Is most attacked by voices of temptation,
The crying shadow in the funeral dance,
The loud lament of the disconsolate chimera.

The detail of the pattern is movement,
As in the figure of the ten stairs.

Desire itself is movement
Not in itself desirable ;
Love is itself unmoving,
Only the cause and end of movement,
Timeless, and undesiring
Except in the aspect of time
Caught in the form of limitation
Between un-being and being.
Sudden in a shaft of sunlight
Even while the dust moves
There rises the hidden laughter
Of children in the foliage
Quick now, here, now, always —
Ridiculous the waste sad time
Stretching before and after.

ROBERT FROST

(1875–   )

Deep tragic background
Gives inter-feeling

THE DEATH OF THE HIRED MAN

Mary sat musing on the lamp-flame at the table
Waiting for Warren. When she heard his step,
She ran on tip-toe down the darkened passage
To meet him in the doorway with the news
And put him on his guard. 'Silas is back.'
She pushed him outward with her through the door
And shut it after her. 'Be kind,' she said.
She took the market things from Warren's arms
And set them on the porch, then drew him down
To sit beside her on the wooden steps.

'When was I ever anything but kind to him?
But I 'll not have the fellow back,' he said.
'I told him so last haying, didn't I?
"If he left then," I said, "that ended it."
What good is he? Who else will harbour him
At his age for the little he can do?
What help he is there 's no depending on.
Off he goes always when I need him most.
"He thinks he ought to earn a little pay,
Enough at least to buy tobacco with,
So he won't have to beg and be beholden."
"All right," I say, "I can't afford to pay
Any fixed wages, though I wish I could."
"Someone else can." "Then someone else will have to."
I shouldn't mind his bettering himself
If that was what it was. You can be certain,
When he begins like that, there 's someone at him
Trying to coax him off with pocket-money, —
In haying time, when any help is scarce.
In winter he comes back to us. I 'm done.'

'Sh! not so loud: he 'll hear you,' Mary said.

'I want him to: he 'll have to soon or late.'

'He 's worn out. He 's asleep beside the stove.
When I came up from Rowe's I found him here,
Huddled against the barn-door fast asleep,
A miserable sight, and frightening, too —
You needn't smile — I didn't recognise him —
I wasn't looking for him — and he 's changed.
Wait till you see.'

                    'Where did you say he 'd been?'

'He didn't say. I dragged him to the house,
And gave him tea and tried to make him smoke.
I tried to make him talk about his travels.
Nothing would do : he just kept nodding off.'

'What did he say ? Did he say anything ?'

'But little.'

          'Anything ? Mary, confess
He said he 'd come to ditch the meadow for me.'

'Warren !'

          'But did he ? I just want to know.'

'Of course he did. What would you have him say ?
Surely you wouldn't grudge the poor old man
Some humble way to save his self-respect.
He added, if you really care to know,
He meant to clear the upper pasture, too.
That sounds like something you have heard before ?
Warren, I wish you could have heard the way
He jumbled everything. I stopped to look
Two or three times — he made me feel so queer —
To see if he was talking in his sleep.
He ran on Harold Wilson — you remember —
The boy you had in haying four years since.
He 's finished school, and teaching in his college.
Silas declares you 'll have to get him back.
He says they two will make a team for work :
Between them they will lay this farm as smooth !

The way he mixed that in with other things.
He thinks young Wilson a likely lad, though daft
On education — you know how they fought
All through July under the blazing sun,
Silas up on the cart to build the load,
Harold along beside to pitch it on.'

'Yes, I took care to keep well out of earshot.'

'Well, those days trouble Silas like a dream.
You wouldn't think they would. How some things linger !
Harold's young college boy's assurance piqued him.
After so many years he still keeps finding
Good arguments he sees he might have used.
I sympathise. I know just how it feels
To think of the right thing to say too late.
Harold 's associated in his mind with Latin.
He asked me what I thought of Harold's saying
He studied Latin like the violin
Because he liked it — that an argument !
He said he couldn't make the boy believe
He could find water with a hazel prong —
Which showed how much good school had ever done him.
He wanted to go over that. But most of all
He thinks if he could have another chance
To teach him how to build a load of hay — '

'I know, that 's Silas' one accomplishment.
He bundles every forkful in its place,
And tags and numbers it for future reference,
So he can find and easily dislodge it
In the unloading. Silas does that well.
He takes it out in bunches like big birds' nests.

You never see him standing on the hay
He's trying to lift, straining to lift himself.'

'He thinks if he could teach him that, he'd be
Some good perhaps to someone in the world.
He hates to see a boy the fool of books.
Poor Silas, so concerned for other folk,
And nothing to look backward to with pride,
And nothing to look forward to with hope,
So now and never any different.'

Part of a moon was falling down the west,
Dragging the whole sky with it to the hills.
Its light poured softly in her lap. She saw it
And spread her apron to it. She put out her hand
Among the harp-like morning-glory strings,
Taut with the dew from garden bed to eaves,
As if she played unheard some tenderness
That wrought on him beside her in the night.
'Warren,' she said, 'he has come home to die :
You needn't be afraid he'll leave you this time.'

'Home,' he mocked gently.

                              'Yes, what else but home ?
It all depends on what you mean by home.
Of course he's nothing to us, any more
Than was the hound that came a stranger to us
Out of the woods, worn out upon the trail.'

'Home is the place where, when you have to go there,
They have to take you in.'

                                      'I should have called it
Something you somehow haven't to deserve.'

Warren leaned out and took a step or two,
Picked up a little stick, and brought it back
And broke it in his hand and tossed it by.
'Silas has better claim on us you think
Than on his brother ? Thirteen little miles
As the road winds would bring him to his door.
Silas has walked that far no doubt to-day.
Why didn't he go there ? His brother 's rich,
A somebody — director in the bank.'

'He never told us that.'

                        'We know it though.'

'I think his brother ought to help, of course.
I 'll see to that if there is need. He ought of right
To take him in, and might be willing to —
He may be better than appearances.
But have some pity on Silas. Do you think
If he had any pride in claiming kin
Or anything he looked for from his brother,
He 'd keep so still about him all this time ?'

'I wonder what 's between them.'

                              'I can tell you.
Silas is what he is — we wouldn't mind him —
But just the kind that kinsfolk can't abide.
He never did a thing so very bad.
He don't know why he isn't quite as good

As anybody. Worthless though he is,
He won't be made ashamed to please his brother.'

'*I* can't think Si ever hurt anyone.'

'No, but he hurt my heart the way he lay
And rolled his old head on that sharp-edged chair-back
He wouldn't let me put him on the lounge.
You must go in and see what you can do.
I made the bed up for him there to-night.
You 'll be surprised at him — how much he 's broken.
His working days are done ; I 'm sure of it.'

'I 'd not be in a hurry to say that.'

'I haven't been. Go, look, see for yourself.
But, Warren, please remember how it is :
He 's come to help you ditch the meadow.
He has a plan. You mustn't laugh at him.
He may not speak of it, and then he may.
I 'll sit and see if that small sailing cloud
Will hit or miss the moon.'

                It hit the moon.
Then there were three there, making a dim row,
The moon, the little silver cloud, and she.

Warren returned — too soon, it seemed to her,
Slipped to her side, caught up her hand and waited.

'Warren ?' she questioned.

                'Dead,' was all he answered.

NOTHING GOLD CAN STAY

Nature's first green is gold,
Her hardest hue to hold.
Her early leaf's a flower ;
But only so an hour.
Then leaf subsides to leaf.
So Eden sank to grief,
So dawn goes down to day.
Nothing gold can stay.

TREE AT MY WINDOW

Tree at my window, window tree,
My sash is lowered when night comes on ;
But let there never be curtain drawn
Between you and me.

Vague dream-head lifted out of the ground,
And thing next most diffuse to cloud,
Not all your light tongues talking aloud
Could be profound.

But tree, I have seen you taken and tossed,
And if you have seen me when I slept,
You have seen me when I was taken and swept
And all but lost.

That day she put our heads together,
Fate had her imagination about her,

Your head so much concerned with outer,
Mine with inner, weather.

TO A THINKER

The last step taken found your heft
Decidedly upon the left.
One more would throw you on the right.
Another still — you see your plight.
You call this thinking, but it 's walking.
Not even that, it 's only rocking,
Or weaving like a stabled horse :
From force to matter and back to force,
From form to content and back to form,
From norm to crazy and back to norm,
From bound to free and back to bound,
From sound to sense and back to sound.
So back and forth. It almost scares
A man the way things come in pairs.
Just now you 're off democracy
(With a polite regret to be),
And leaning on dictatorship ;
But if you will accept the tip,
In less than no time, tongue and pen,
You 'll be a democrat again.
A reasoner and good as such,
Don't let it bother you too much
If it makes you look helpless please
And a temptation to the tease.
Suppose you 've no direction in you,
I don't see but you must continue
To use the gift you do possess,

And sway with reason more or less.
I own I never really warmed
To the reformer or reformed.
And yet conversion has its place
Not half way down the scale of grace.
So if you find you must repent
From side to side in argument,
At least don't use your mind too hard,
But trust my instinct — I 'm a bard.

ARCHIBALD MACLEISH

(1892–   )

THE SEAFARER

And learn O voyager to walk
The roll of earth, the pitch and fall
That swings across these trees those stars :
That swings the sunlight up the wall.

And learn upon these narrow beds
To sleep in spite of sea, in spite
Of sound the rushing planet makes :
And learn to sleep against the ground.

THE TOO-LATE BORN

We too, we too, descending once again
The hills of our own land, we too have heard
Far off — Ah, que ce cor a longue haleine —

The horn of Roland in the passages of Spain,
The first, the second blast, the failing third,
And with the third turned back and climbed once more
The steep road southward, and heard faint the sound
Of swords, of horses, the disastrous war,
And crossed the dark defile at last, and found
At Roncevaux upon the darkening plain
The dead against the dead and on the silent ground
The silent slain —

THE NIGHT DREAM

To R.L.

Neither her voice, her name,
Eyes, quietness neither,
That moved through the light, that came
Cold stalk in her teeth
Bitten of some blue flower
Knew I before nor saw.
This was a dream. Ah,
This was a dream. There was sun
Laid on the cloths of a table.
We drank together. Her mouth
Was a lion's mouth out of jade
Cold with a fable of water.
Faces I could not see
Watched me with gentleness. Grace
Folded my body with wings.
I cannot love you she said.
My head she laid on her breast.
As stillness with ringing of bees
I was filled with a singing of praise.

Knowledge filled me and peace.
We were silent and not ashamed.

Ah we were glad that day.
They asked me but it was one
Dead they meant and not I.
She was beside me she said.
We rode in a desert place.
We were always happy. Her sleeves
Jangled with earrings of gold.
They told me the wind from the south
Was the cold wind to be feared.
We were galloping under the leaves —

This was a dream, Ah
This was a dream.
                    And her mouth
Was not your mouth nor her eyes,
But the rivers were four and I knew
As a secret between us, the way
Hands touch, it was you.

"NOT MARBLE NOR THE GILDED MONUMENTS"

The praisers of women in their proud and beautiful poems
Naming the grave mouth and the hair and the eyes
Boasted those they loved should be forever remembered
These were lies

The words sound but the face in the Istrian sun is forgotten
The poet speaks but to her dead ears no more

The sleek throat is gone — and the breast that was troubled
    to listen
Shadow from door

Therefore I will not praise your knees nor your fine walking
Telling you men shall remember your name as long
As lips move or breath is spent or the iron of English
Rings from a tongue

I shall say you were young and your arms straight and your
    mouth scarlet
I shall say you will die and none will remember you
Your arms change and none remember the swish of your
    garments
Nor the click of your shoe

Not with my hand's strength not with difficult labor
Springing the obstinate words to the bones of your breast
And the stubborn line to your young stride and the breath to
    your breathing
And the beat to your haste
Shall I prevail on the hearts of unborn men to remember

(What is a dead girl but a shadowy ghost
Or a dead man's voice but a distant and vain affirmation
Like dream words most)

Therefore I will not speak of the undying glory of women
I will say you were young and straight and your skin fair
And you stood in the door and the sun was a shadow of leaves
    on your shoulders
And a leaf on your hair

I will not speak of the famous beauty of dead women
I will say the shape of a leaf lay once on your hair
Till the world ends and the eyes are out and the mouths
    broken
Look ! It is there !

YOU, ANDREW MARVELL

And here face down beneath the sun
And here upon earth's noonward height
To feel the always coming on
The always rising of the night

To feel creep up the curving east
The earthy chill of dusk and slow
Upon those under lands the vast
And ever climbing shadow grow

And strange at Ecbatan the trees
Take leaf by leaf the evening strange
The flooding dark about their knees
The mountains over Persia change

And now at Kermanshah the gate
Dark empty and the withered grass
And through the twilight now the late
Few travelers in the westward pass

And Baghdad darken and the bridge
Across the silent river gone
And through Arabia the edge
Of evening widen and steal on

And deepen on Palmyra's street
The wheel rut in the ruined stone
And Lebanon fade out and Crete
High through the clouds and overblown

And over Sicily the air
Still flashing with the landward gulls
And loom and slowly disappear
The sails above the shadowy hulls

And Spain go under and the shore
Of Africa the gilded sand
And evening vanish and no more
The low pale light across that land

Nor now the long light on the sea

And here face downward in the sun
To feel how swift how secretly
The shadow of the night comes on . . .

THE END OF THE WORLD

Quite unexpectedly as Vasserot
The armless ambidextrian was lighting
A match between his great and second toe
And Ralph the lion was engaged in biting
The neck of Madame Sossman while the drum
Pointed, and Teeny was about to cough
In waltz-time swinging Jocko by the thumb —
Quite unexpectedly the top blew off :

And there, there overhead, there, there, hung over
Those thousands of white faces, those dazed eyes,
There in the starless dark the poise, the hover,
There with vast wings across the canceled skies,
There in the sudden blackness the black pall
Of nothing, nothing, nothing — nothing at all.

ARS POETICA

A poem should be palpable and mute
As a globed fruit

Dumb
As old medallions to the thumb

Silent as the sleeve-worn stone
Of casement ledges where the moss has grown —

A poem should be wordless
As the flight of birds

                    *   *   *

A poem should be motionless in time
As the moon climbs

Leaving, as the moon releases
Twig by twig the night-entangled trees,

Leaving, as the moon behind the winter leaves,
Memory by memory the mind —

A poem should be motionless in time
As the moon climbs

                    *   *   *

A poem should be equal to :
Not true

For all the history of grief
An empty doorway and a maple leaf

For love
The leaning grasses and two lights above the sea —

A poem should not mean
But be

*First trip to this land,
going there only for the
Memorial Rain*

MEMORIAL RAIN

Ambassador Puser the ambassador
Reminds himself in French, felicitous tongue,
What these (young men no longer) lie here for
In rows that once, and somewhere else, were young —

All night in Brussels the wind had tugged at my door :
I had heard the wind at my door and the trees strung
Taut, and to me who had never been before
In that country it was a strange wind blowing
Steadily, stiffening the walls, the floor,
The roof of my room. I had not slept for knowing
He too, dead, was a stranger in that land
And felt beneath the earth in the wind's flowing
A tightening of roots and would not understand,
Remembering lake winds in Illinois,
That strange wind. I had felt his bones in the sand
Listening.

         — Reflects that these enjoy
Their country's gratitude, that deep repose,
That peace no pain can break, no hurt destroy,
That rest, that sleep —

         At Ghent the wind rose.
There was a smell of rain and a heavy drag
Of wind in the hedges but not as the wind blows
Over fresh water when the waves lag
Foaming and the willows huddle and it will rain :
I felt him waiting.

         — Indicates the flag
Which (may he say) enisles in Flanders' plain
This little field these happy, happy dead
Have made America —

         In the ripe grain
The wind coiled glistening, darted, fled,
Dragging its heavy body : at Waereghem
The wind coiled in the grass above his head :
Waiting — listening —

         — Dedicates to them
This earth their bones have hallowed, this last gift
A grateful country —

         Under the dry grass stem
The words are blurred, are thickened, the words sift
Confused by the rasp of the wind, by the thin grating
Of ants under the grass, the minute shift
And tumble of dusty sand separating

From dusty sand. The roots of the grass strain,
Tighten, the earth is rigid, waits — he is waiting —

And suddenly, and all at once, the rain !

The living scatter, they run into houses, the wind
Is trampled under the rain, shakes free, is again
Trampled. The rain gathers, running in thinned
Spurts of water that ravel in the dry sand
Seeping in the sand under the grass roots, seeping
Between cracked boards to the bones of a clenched hand :
The earth relaxes, loosens ; he is sleeping,
He rests, he is quiet, he sleeps in a strange land.

from
FRESCOES FOR MR. ROCKEFELLER'S CITY

6

BACKGROUND WITH REVOLUTIONARIES

And the corn singing Millennium !
Lenin ! Millennium ! Lennium !

When they 're shunting the cars on the Katy a mile off
When they 're shunting the cars when they 're shunting the
cars on the Katy
You can hear the clank of the couplings riding away

Also Comrade Devine who writes of America
Most instructively having in 'Seventy-four
Crossed to the Hoboken side on the Barclay Street Ferry

She sits on a settle in the State of North Dakota
O she sits on a settle in the State of North Dakota
She can hear the engines whistle over Iowa and Idaho

Also Comrade Edward Remington Ridge
Who has prayed God since the April of 'Seventeen
To replace in his life his lost (M.E.) religion

And The New York Daily Worker *goes a'blowing over Ar-*
kansas
The New York Daily Worker *goes a'blowing over Arkansas*
The grasses let it go along the Ozarks over Arkansas

Even Comrade Grenadine Grilt who has tried since
August tenth for something to feel about strongly in
Verses — his personal passions having tired

I can tell my land by the jays in the apple-trees
Tell my land by the jays in the apple-trees
I can tell my people by the blue-jays in the apple-trees

Aindt you read in d' books you are all brudders?
D' glassic historic objective broves you are brudders!
You and d' Wops and d' Chinks you are all brudders!
Havend't you got it d' same ideology? Havend't you?

When it's yesterday in Oregon it's one A M in Maine
And she slides : and the day slides : and it runs : runs over us :
And the bells strike twelve strike twelve strike twelve
In Marblehead in Buffalo in Cheyenne in Cherokee
Yesterday runs on the states like a crow's shadow

For Marx has said to us Workers what do you need ?
And Stalin has said to us Starvers what do you need ?
You need the Dialectical Materialism !

She 's a tough land under the corn mister :
She has changed the bone in the cheeks of many races :
She has winced the eyes of the soft Slavs with her sun on
*   them :*
She has tried the fat from the round rumps of Italians :
Even the voice of the English has gone dry
And hard on the tongue and alive in the throat speaking :

She 's a tough land under the oak-trees mister :
It may be she can change the word in the book
As she changes the bone of a man's head in his children :
It may be that the earth and the men remain. . .

There is too much sun on the lids of my eyes to be listening

W. H. AUDEN

(1907–   )

MUSÉE DES BEAUX ARTS

About suffering they were never wrong,
The Old Masters : how well they understood
Its human position ; how it takes place
While someone else is eating or opening a window or just
    walking dully along ;
How, when the aged are reverently, passionately waiting

For the miraculous birth, there always must be
Children who did not specially want it to happen, skating
On a pond at the edge of the wood :
They never forgot
That even the dreadful martyrdom must run its course
Anyhow in a corner, some untidy spot
Where the dogs go on with their doggy life and the torturer's
    horse
Scratches its innocent behind on a tree.

In Brueghel's *Icarus,* for instance : how everything turns away
Quite leisurely from the disaster ; the ploughman may
Have heard the splash, the forsaken cry,
But for him it was not an important failure ; the sun shone
As it had to on the white legs disappearing into the green
Water ; and the expensive delicate ship that must have seen
Something amazing, a boy falling out of the sky,
Had somewhere to get to and sailed calmly on.

IN WAR TIME

(For Caroline Newton)

Abruptly mounting her ramshackle wheel,
Fortune has pedalled furiously away ;
The sobbing mess is on our hands today.

Those accidental terrors, Famine, Flood,
Were never trained to diagnose or heal
Nightmares that are intentional and real.

Nor lust nor gravity can preach an aim
To minds disordered by a lucid dread
Of seeking peace by going off one's head.

Nor will the living waters whistle ; though
Diviners cut their throats to prove their claim,
The desert remains arid all the same.

If augurs take up flying to fulfill
The doom they prophesy, it must be so ;
The herons have no modern sign for No.

If nothing can upset but total war
The massive fancy of the heathen will
That solitude is something you can kill,

If we are right to choose our suffering
And be tormented by an Either-Or,
The right to fail that is worth dying for,

If so, the sweets of victory are rum :
A pride of earthly cities premising
The Inner Life as socially the thing,

Where, even to the lawyers, Law is what,
For better or for worse, our vows become
When no one whom we need is looking, Home

A sort of honour, not a building site,
Wherever we are, when, if we chose, we might
Be somewhere else, yet trust that we have chosen right.

THE CULTURAL PRESUPPOSITION

Happy the hare at morning, for she cannot read
The Hunter's waking thoughts, lucky the leaf
Unable to predict the fall, lucky indeed
The rampant suffering suffocating jelly
Burgeoning in pools, lapping the grits of the desert,
But what shall man do, who can whistle tunes by heart,
Knows to the bar when death shall cut him short like the cry
    of the shearwater,
What can he do but defend himself from his knowledge ?

How comely are his places of refuge and the tabernacles of his
    peace,
The new books upon the morning table, the lawns and the
    afternoon terraces !
Here are the playing-fields where he may forget his ignorance
To operate within a gentleman's agreement : twenty-two sins
    have here a certain licence.
Here are the thickets where accosted lovers combatant
May warm each other with their wicked hands,
Here are the avenues for incantation and workshops for the
    cunning engravers.
The galleries are full of music, the pianist is storming the keys,
    the great cellist is crucified over his instrument,
That none may hear the ejaculations of the sentinels
Nor the sigh of the most numerous and the most poor ; the
    thud of their falling bodies
Who with their lives have banished hence the serpent and the
    faceless insect.

IN MEMORY OF W. B. YEATS

(d. Jan. 1939)

1

He disappeared in the dead of winter :
The brooks were frozen, the airports almost deserted,
And snow disfigured the public statues ;
The mercury sank in the mouth of the dying day.
O all the instruments agree
The day of his death was a dark cold day.

Far from his illness
The wolves ran on through the evergreen forests,
The peasant river was untempted by the fashionable quays ;
By mourning tongues
The death of the poet was kept from his poems.

But for him it was his last afternoon as himself,
An afternoon of nurses and rumours ;
The provinces of his body revolted,
The squares of his mind were empty,
Silence invaded the suburbs,
The current of his feeling failed : he became his admirers.

Now he is scattered among a hundred cities
And wholly given over to unfamiliar affections ;
To find his happiness in another kind of wood
And be punished under a foreign code of conscience.
The words of a dead man
Are modified in the guts of the living.

But in the importance and noise of tomorrow
When the brokers are roaring like beasts on the floor of the
   Bourse,
And the poor have the sufferings to which they are fairly
   accustomed,
And each in the cell of himself is almost convinced of his
   freedom ;
A few thousand will think of this day
As one thinks of a day when one did something slightly un-
   usual.
O all the instruments agree
The day of his death was a dark cold day.

2

You were silly like us : your gift survived it all ;
The parish of rich women, physical decay,
Yourself ; mad Ireland hurt you into poetry.
Now Ireland has her madness and her weather still,
For poetry makes nothing happen : it survives
In the valley of its saying where executives
Would never want to tamper ; it flows south
From ranches of isolation and the busy griefs,
Raw towns that we believe and die in ; it survives,
A way of happening, a mouth.

3

Earth, receive an honoured guest ;
William Yeats is laid to rest :
Let the Irish vessel lie
Emptied of its poetry.

Time that is intolerant
Of the brave and innocent,
And indifferent in a week
To a beautiful physique,

Worships language and forgives
Everyone by whom it lives ;
Pardons cowardice, conceit,
Lays its honours at their feet.

Time that with this strange excuse
Pardoned Kipling and his views,
And will pardon Paul Claudel,
Pardons him for writing well.

In the nightmare of the dark
All the dogs of Europe bark,
And the living nations wait,
Each sequestered in its hate ;

Intellectual disgrace
Stares from every human face,
And the seas of pity lie
Locked and frozen in each eye.

Follow, poet, follow right
To the bottom of the night,
With your unconstraining voice
Still persuade us to rejoice ;

With the farming of a verse
Make a vineyard of the curse,
Sing of human unsuccess
In a rapture of distress ;

In the deserts of the heart
Let the healing fountain start,
In the prison of his days
Teach the free man how to praise.

SEPTEMBER 1, 1939

Written in this country as well as war II was coming language of our modern world

I sit in one of the dives
On Fifty-second Street
Uncertain and afraid   *Invasion of Poland*
As the clever hopes expire
Of a low dishonest decade :
Waves of anger and fear
Circulate over the bright
And darkened lands of the earth,
Obsessing our private lives ;
The unmentionable odour of death
Offends the September night.

What difference is the history of you.

Accurate scholarship can
Unearth the whole offence
From Luther until now   *This had*
That has driven a culture mad,   *been building*
Find what occurred at Linz,   *up in our*
What huge imago made   *civilization*
A psychopathic god :
I and the public know
What all schoolchildren learn,
Those to whom evil is done
Do evil in return. *To those who won the wars in the past*

Exiled Thucydides knew
All that a speech can say

About Democracy,
And what dictators do,
The elderly rubbish they talk
To an apathetic grave ;
Analysed all in his book,
The enlightenment driven away,
The habit-forming pain,
Mismanagement and grief :
We must suffer them all again.

Into this neutral air
Where blind skyscrapers use
Their full height to proclaim
The strength of Collective Man,
Each language pours its vain
Competitive excuse :
But who can live for long
In an euphoric dream ;
Out of the mirror they stare,
Imperialism's face
And the international wrong.

Faces along the bar
Cling to their average day :
The lights must never go out,
The music must always play,
All the conventions conspire
To make this fort assume
The furniture of home ;
Lest we should see where we are,
Lost in a haunted wood,
Children afraid of the night
Who have never been happy or good.

The windiest militant trash
Important Persons shout
Is not so crude as our wish :
What mad Nijinsky wrote
About Diaghilev
Is true of the normal heart ;
For the error bred in the bone
Of each woman and each man
Craves what it cannot have,
Not universal love
But to be loved alone.

[handwritten margin note: Great dancer who went mad]

[handwritten margin note: still climax]

From the conservative dark
Into the ethical life
The dense commuters come,
Repeating their morning vow ;
"I *will* be true to the wife,
I 'll concentrate more on my work,"
And helpless governors wake
To resume their compulsory game :
Who can release them now,
Who can reach the deaf,
Who can speak for the dumb ?

Defenceless under the night
Our world in stupor lies ;
Yet, dotted everywhere,
Ironic points of light
Flash out wherever the Just
Exchange their messages :
May I, composed like them
Of Eros and of dust,

Beleaguered by the same
Negation and despair,
Show an affirming flame.

PETITION

Modern sonnet

Sir, no man's enemy, forgiving all
But will its negative inversion, be prodigal :
Send to us power and light, a sovereign touch
Curing the intolerable neural itch,
The exhaustion of weaning, the liar's quinsy,
And the distortions of ingrown virginity.
Prohibit sharply the rehearsed response
And gradually correct the coward's stance ;
Cover in time with beams those in retreat
That, spotted, they turn though the reverse were great ;
Publish each healer that in city lives
Or country houses at the end of drives ;
Harrow the house of the dead ; look shining at
New styles of architecture, a change of heart.

HAPPY ENDING

The silly fool, the silly fool
Was sillier in school
But beat the bully as a rule.

The youngest son, the youngest son
Was certainly no wise one
Yet could surprise one.

Or rather, or rather
To be posh, we gather,
One should have no father.

Simple to prove
That deeds indeed
In life succeed
But love in love
And tales in tales
Where no one fails.

PUR

This lunar beauty
Has no history,
Is complete and early ;
If beauty later
Bear any feature,
It had a lover
And is another.

This like a dream
Keeps other time,
And daytime is
The loss of this ;
For time is inches
And the heart's changes,
Where ghost has haunted,
Lost and wanted.

But this was never
A ghost's endeavour

Nor, finished this,
Was ghost at ease ;
And till it pass
Love shall not near
The sweetness here,
Nor sorrow take
His endless look.

from

THE SEA AND THE MIRROR

"SING, ARIEL, SING"

Spirit presides over our thought

Sing, Ariel, sing,
Sweetly, dangerously
Out of the sour
And shiftless water,
Lucidly out
Of the dozing tree,
Entrancing, rebuking
The raging heart
With a smoother song
Than this rough world,
Unfeeling god.

O brilliantly, lightly,
Of separation,
Of bodies and death,
Unanxious one, sing
To man, meaning me,
As now, meaning always,
In love or out,

                    Whatever that mean,
                    Trembling he takes
                    The silent passage
                    Into discomfort.

                    LOUIS   MACNEICE

                       (1907–   )

                AN ECLOGUE FOR CHRISTMAS

A. I meet you in an evil time.
B.   The evil bells
    Put out of our heads, I think, the thought of everything
        else.
A. The jaded calendar revolves,
    Its nuts need oil, carbon chokes the valves,
    The excess sugar of a diabetic culture
    Rotting the nerve of life and literature ;
    Therefore when we bring out the old tinsel and frills
    To announce that Christ is born among the barbarous
        hills
    I turn to you whom a morose routine
    Saves from the mad vertigo of being what has been.
B. Analogue of me, you are wrong to turn to me,
    My country will not yield you any sanctuary,
    There is no pinpoint in any of the ordnance maps
    To save you when your towns and town-bred thoughts col-
        lapse,
    It is better to die *in situ* as I shall,
    One place is as bad as another. Go back where your in-
        stincts call

And listen to the crying of the town-cats and the taxis
    again,
Or wind your gramophone and eavesdrop on great men.

A. Jazz-weary of years of drums and Hawaiian guitar,
Pivoting on the parquet I seem to have moved far
From bombs and mud and gas, have stuttered on my feet
Clinched to the streamlined and butter-smooth trulls of
    the élite,
The lights irritating and gyrating and rotating in gauze —
Pomade-dazzle, a slick beauty of gewgaws —
I who was Harlequin in the childhood of the century,
Posed by Picasso beside an endless opaque sea,
Have seen myself sifted and splintered in broken facets,
Tentative pencillings, endless liabilities, no assets,
Abstractions scalpelled with a palette-knife
Without reference to this particular life.
And so it has gone on ; I have not been allowed to be
Myself in flesh or face, but abstracting and dissecting me
They have made of me pure form, a symbol or a pastiche,
Stylised profile, anything but soul and flesh :
And that is why I turn this jaded music on
To forswear thought and become an automaton.

B. There are in the country also of whom I am afraid —
Men who put beer into a belly that is dead,
Women in the forties with terrier and setter who whistle
    and swank
Over down and plough and Roman road and daisied
    bank,
Half-conscious that these barriers over which they stride
Are nothing to the barbed wire that has grown round
    their pride.

A. And two there are, as I drive in the city, who suddenly
    perturb —

The one sirening me to draw up by the curb

The other, as I lean back, my right leg stretched creating
speed,

Making me catch and stamp, the brakes shrieking, pull up
dead :

She wears silk stockings taunting the winter wind,

He carries a white stick to mark that he is blind.

B. In the country they are still hunting, in the heavy shires

Greyness is on the fields and sunset like a line of pyres

Of barbarous heroes smoulders through the ancient air

Hazed with factory dust and, orange opposite, the moon's
glare,

Goggling yokel-stubborn through the iron trees,

Jeers at the end of us, our bland ancestral ease ;

We shall go down like palaeolithic man

Before some new Ice Age or Genghiz Khan.

A. It is time for some new coinage, people have got so old.

Hacked and handled and shiny from pocketing they have
made bold

To think that each is himself through these accidents, be-
ing blind

To the fact that they are merely the counters of an un-
known Mind.

B. A Mind that does not think, if such a thing can be,

Mechanical Reason, capricious Identity.

That I could be able to face this domination nor flinch —

A. The tin toys of the hawker move on the pavement inch by
inch

Not knowing that they are wound up ; it is better to be so

Than to be, like us, wound up and while running down
to know —

B. But everywhere the pretence of individuality recurs —

A. Old faces frosted with powder and choked in furs.

B. The jutlipped farmer gazing over the humpbacked wall.
A. The commercial traveller joking in the urinal —
B. I think things draw to an end, the soil is stale.
A. And over-elaboration will nothing now avail,
   The street is up again, gas, electricity or drains,
   Ever-changing conveniences, nothing comfortable remains,
   Un-improved, as flagging Rome improved villa and sewer
   (A sound-proof library and a stable temperature).
   Our street is up, red lights sullenly mark
   The long trench of pipes, iron guts in the dark,
   And not till the Goths again come swarming down the hill
   Will cease the clangour of the pneumatic drill.
   But yet there is beauty narcotic and deciduous
   In this vast organism grown out of us :
   On all the traffic-islands stand white globes like moons,
   The city's haze is clouded amber that purrs and croons,
   And tilting by the noble curve bus after tall bus comes
   With an osculation of yellow light, with a glory like chrysanthemums.
B. The country gentry cannot change, they will die in their shoes
   From angry circumstance and moral self-abuse,
   Dying with a paltry fizzle they will prove their lives to be
   An ever-diluted drug, a spiritual tautology.
   They cannot live once their idols are turned out,
   None of them can endure, for how could they, possibly, without
   The flotsam of private property, pekingese and polyanthus,
   The good things which in the end turn to poison and pus,
   Without the bandy chairs and the sugar in the silver tongs
   And the inter-ripple and resonance of years of dinner-gongs ?

Or if they could find no more that cumulative proof
In the rain dripping off the conservatory roof ?
What will happen when the only sanction the country-
    dweller has —
A. What will happen to us, planked and panelled with jazz ?
Who go to the theatre where a black man dances like an
    eel,
Where pink thighs flash like the spokes of a wheel, where
    we feel
That we know in advance all the jogtrot and the cakewalk
    jokes
All the bumfun and the gags of the comedians in boaters
    and toques,
All the tricks of the virtuosos who invert the usual —
B. What will happen to us when the State takes down the
    manor wall,
When there is no more private shooting or fishing, when
    the trees are all cut down,
When faces are all dials and cannot smile or frown —
A. What will happen when the sniggering machine-guns in
    the hands of the young men
Are trained on every flat and club and beauty parlour and
    Father's den ?
What will happen when our civilisation like a long pent
    balloon —
B. What will happen will happen ; the whore and the buffoon
Will come off best ; no dreamers, they cannot lose their
    dream
And are at least likely to be reinstated in the new régime.
But one thing is not likely —
A.   Do not gloat over yourself
Do not be your own vulture ; high on some mountain shelf
Huddle the pitiless abstractions bald about the neck

Who will descend when you crumple in the plains a wreck.
Over the randy of the theatre and cinema I hear songs
Unlike anything —

B.   The lady of the house poises the silver tongs
And picks a lump of sugar, 'ne plus ultra' she says
'I cannot do otherwise, even to prolong my days' —

A. I cannot do otherwise either, tonight I will book my
seat —

B. I will walk about the farm-yard which is replete
As with the smell of dung so with memories —

A. I will gorge myself to satiety with the oddities
Of every artiste, official or amateur,
Who has pleased me in my rôle of hero-worshipper
Who has pleased me in my rôle of individual man —

B. Let us lie once more, say 'What we think, we can'
The old idealist lie —

A.   And for me before I die
Let me go the round of the garish glare —

B.   And on the bare and high
Places of England, the Wiltshire Downs and the Long
Mynd
Let the balls of my feet bounce on the turf, my face burn
in the wind
My eyelashes stinging in the wind, and the sheep like grey
stones
Humble my human pretensions —

A.   Let the saxophones and the xylophones
And the cult of every technical excellence, the miles of
canvas in the galleries
And the canvas of the rich man's yacht snapping and tack-
ing on the seas
And the perfection of a grilled steak —

B.   Let all these so ephemeral things

Be somehow permanent like the swallow's tangent wings :
Goodbye to you, this day remember is Christmas, this
  morn
They say, interpret it your own way, Christ is born.

THE SUNLIGHT ON THE GARDEN

The sunlight on the garden
Hardens and grows cold,
We cannot cage the minute
Within its nets of gold,
When all is told
We cannot beg for pardon.

Our freedom as free lances
Advances towards its end ;
The earth compels, upon it
Sonnets and birds descend ;
And soon, my friend,
We shall have no time for dances.

The sky was good for flying
Defying the church bells
And every evil iron
Siren and what it tells :
The earth compels,
We are dying, Egypt, dying

And not expecting pardon,
Hardened in heart anew,
But glad to have sat under

Thunder and rain with you,
And grateful too
For sunlight on the garden.

REFUGEES

With prune-dark eyes, thick lips, jostling each other
These, disinterred from Europe, throng the deck
To watch their hope heave up in steel and concrete
Powerful but delicate as a swan's neck,

Thinking, each of them, the worst is over
And we do not want any more to be prominent or rich,
Only to be ourselves, to be unmolested
And make ends meet — an ideal surely which

Here if anywhere is feasible. Their glances
Like wavering antennae feel
Around the sliding limber towers of Wall Street
And count the numbered docks and gingerly steal

Into the hinterland of their own future
Behind this excessive annunciation of towers,
Tracking their future selves through a continent of strange-
    ness.
The liner moves to the magnet ; the quay flowers

With faces of people's friends. But these are mostly
Friendless and all they look to meet
Is a secretary who holds his levée among ledgers
Tells them to take a chair and wait . . .

And meanwhile the city will go on, regardless
Of any new arrival, trains like prayers
Radiating from stations haughty as cathedrals,
Tableaux of spring in milliners' windows, great affairs

Being endorsed on a vulcanite table, lines of washing
Feebly garish among grimy brick and dour
Iron fire-escapes ; barrows of cement are rumbling
Up airy planks ; a florist adds a flower

To a bouquet that is bound for somebody's beloved
Or for someone ill ; in a sombre board-room great
Problems wait to be solved or shelved. The city
Goes on but you, you will probably find, must wait

Till something or other turns up. Something-or-Other
Becomes an expected angel from the sky
But do not trust the sky, the blue that looks so candid
Is non-committal, frigid as a harlot's eye.

Gangways — the handclasp of the land. The resurrected,
The brisk or resigned Lazaruses, who want
Another chance, go trooping ashore. But chances
Are dubious. Fate is stingy, recalcitrant

And officialdom greets them blankly as they fumble
Their foreign-looking baggage ; they still feel
The movement of the ship while through their imagination
Seen and unheard-of constellations wheel.

STEPHEN SPENDER

(1909–   )

"*I THINK CONTINUALLY OF THOSE WHO WERE TRULY GREAT*"

I think continually of those who were truly great.
Who, from the womb, remembered the soul's history
Through corridors of light where the hours are suns
Endless and singing. Whose lovely ambition
Was that their lips, still touched with fire,
Should tell of the Spirit clothed from head to foot in song.
And who hoarded from the Spring branches
The desires falling across their bodies like blossoms.

What is precious is never to forget
The essential delight of the blood drawn from ageless springs
Breaking through rocks in worlds before our earth.
Never to deny its pleasure in the morning simple light
Nor its grave evening demand for love.
Never to allow gradually the traffic to smother
With noise and fog the flowering of the spirit.

Near the snow, near the sun, in the highest fields
See how these names are fêted by the waving grass
And by the streamers of white cloud
And whispers of wind in the listening sky.
The names of those who in their lives fought for life
Who wore at their hearts the fire's centre.
Born of the sun they travelled a short while towards the sun,
And left the vivid air signed with their honour.

THE FATES

I

In the theatre,
The actors act the ritual of their parts,
Clowns, killers, lovers, captains,
At the end falling on the sword
Which opens out a window through their hearts
And through the darkness to the gleaming eyes
Of the watching masks slightly bored,

Of the audience
Acting the part of their indifference,
Pretending the thrusting pistons of the passions,
Contorted masks of tears and mockery,
Do not penetrate the surface fashions
Covering their own naked skins.

"We are not green fools nor black-eyed tragedians,
Though perhaps, long ago, we were the killers.
Still, still we have our moments of romance
Under the moon, when we are the lovers.
But the rules of fate do not apply to us.
The howling consequences can be bribed away
Discreetly, without fuss.
When we have left the play
The furies of atonement will not follow after
Our feet, into the street
Where the traffic is controlled all day."

Sitting in stalls or pit, they pray
That the externalized disaster

Gesticulating puppets display
Will not, with finger of catastrophe
Revolve on them its hissing frontal limelight :
Not lift the curtains of their windows,
Not rape their daughters in the coarse embrace
Of the promiscuous newspapers
Running with them in headlines through the streets.
In their lives, they have cut few capers
So death, they hope, will be discreet,
Raising a silk hat,
Dressed in black, with a smile for each tear, polite.

Oh which are the actors, which the audience ?
Those who sit back with a tear, a smile, a sigh,
Where they deny deny deny ?
Or those on the stage who rip open their ribs
Lift the lids from their skulls, tear the skin from their arms,
Revealing the secret corridors of dreams,
The salt savour of the passions,
The crushed hyacinths of corruption,
The opera-singing sexual organs :
And within all, as in a high room,
Filled with a vacuum containing infinite space,
The soul playing at being a gull by a lake,
Turning somersaults, immensely bored,
Whistling to itself, writing memoirs of God,
Forgetting
What time and the undertakers undertake ?

Oh which are the actors, which the audience ?
The actors, who simulate ?
Or those who are, who watch the actors
Prove to them there is no fate ?

Where then is the real performance
Which finally sweeps actors and audience
Into a black box at the end of the play?

Both, both, vowing the real is the unreal,
Are stared at by the silent stars
Of the comprehensive universe
Staging its play of passions in their hearts.
It carries them off at the end in a hearse.

II

O brave, powdered mask of weeded motherhood
For twenty years denying that the real
Was ever anything but the exceptional,
You were an excellent stage manager,
For your dear son's sake, of your theatre,
Family life, not sombre, but light :
"This is the play where nothing happens that can matter
Except that we are sensible healthy and bright."

Your problem was no easy one,
Somehow to spare your only son
From the gloomy brooding blue of his father's eyes,
After the War, for twenty years
Pacing the lawn between two wars,
His sombre way of staring at the table.
You were courageous and capable
Gaily you called these things his "moods".
Just "moods," "moods," like anything else,
A chair, the empty clanging of alarm bells.

You rebuilt the Georgian house with the old lawn,
And the kitchen garden surrounded by a wall,

And the servants in the servants' hall
Tidying the rooms downstairs at dawn ;
And you bought a fishing rod, a pony and a gun
And gave these serious playthings to your son.

The fresh air and the scenery did the rest.
He ripened and his laughter floated on the lake,
A foretaste of the memories that now suggest
His photograph with the shirt open at the neck.
He came downstairs to dinner, "dressed."
Then your triumphant happiness bound cords
Around his silken glance into one bow.
Catching your husband's eye, your face spoke words
"This is the world, we've left the past below."

If a guest came, and in the course
Of conversation, spoke of "so-and-so's divorce,"
Or else, "Poor Lady X, she died of cancer,"
You had your fine frank answer,
Questioning him with vivid curiosity,
Poverty, adultery, disease, what strange monstrosity !
You smiled, perhaps, at your guest's eccentricity
Dragging such specimens out on your floor.

Your son grew up, and thought it all quite real.
Hunting, the family, the business man's ideal.
The poor and the unhappy had his sympathy.
They were exceptions made to prove his rule.
And yet he had his moments of uneasiness
When in the dazzling garden of his family
With the green sunlight tilted on your dress,
His body suddenly seemed an indecency,
A changeling smuggled to the wrong address.

Still, he got married. *She* was dull, of course.
But everything had turned out quite all right.
The bride sailed on the picture page in white
Arm linked in his, face squinting in the light.
Your son wore uniform. You, the mother-in-law
Who 'd brought him up into a world at war,
At last felt tired. You wondered what he knew of life,
Whether enough to satisfy his wife.
Perhaps he 'd learned from nature, or his horse.

III

Oh, but in vain
Do men bar themselves behind their doors
Within the well-appointed house
Painting, in designed acts, life as they would see it,
By the fireside, in the garden, round the table.

The storm rises,
The thunderbolt falls, and how feeble
Is the long tradition strengthened with reverence
Made sacred to respect by all appearance,
Or the most up-to-date steel-and-concrete
To withstand fate.

The walls fall, tearing down
The fragile life of the interior.
The cherishing fire in its grate
Consumes the house, grown to a monster,
As though the cat had turned into a tiger
Leaping out of a world become a jungle
To destroy its master.

The parents fall
Clutching with weak hands beams snapped like straw,
And the handsome only son,
Tanned leader of his village team,
Is shaken out of the soft folds
Of silk, spoiled life, as from a curtain.

He is thrown out onto a field abroad.
A whip of lead
Strikes a stain of blood from his pure forehead.
Into the dust he falls,
The virginal face carved from a mother's kisses
As though from sensitive ivory,
Staring up at the sun, the eyes at last made open.

IN A GARDEN

Had I pen ink and paper,
I think that they could carry
The weight of all these roses,
These rocks and massive trees.

The hills weigh peacefully on my mind,
The grottoed skull encloses
Shifting lights and shade.
Soft on the flesh all the green scene reposes

But that the singing of those birds
Pressed to the hot wall of the sky,
Tears through the listening writing of the eye
To a space beyond words.

INTO LIFE

Aiming from clocks and space,
   O Man of Flesh, I hew
      Your features, blow on blow.
I cut away each surface
      To lay bare what I know —
Universe within you.

Shut close in your mind,
   You never quite will learn
      To see your life as whole.
Your mirrors are too blind ;
   They have no eyes that turn
      From each age on your soul.

Your sense flies to each facet
   Striking from each hour ;
      Now all heat, now all brain,
   All sex, sickness, power ;
That severe line, when I place it,
      Seems nothing but pain.

Yet all experience, like stars
   (In distances of night,
      Their brilliant separate incidents
Divided by light-years)
   Hangs in your eyes the lights
      Of sustained co-existence.

What you were, you are,
   And what you will be, you are, too.

Born, you 're dead ; loving, are sad.
The years add, star by star,
    The whole of life consuming you
    In fires of good and bad.

2 $\frac{50}{5}$